AMAZON

AMAZON

DENNISON BERWICK

HUTCHINSON

London Sydney Auckland Johannesburg

Copyright © Dennison Berwick 1990

All rights reserved

This edition first published in 1990 by
Hutchinson

Century Hutchinson Ltd,
20 Vauxhall Bridge Road, London SW1V 2SA

Century Hutchinson Australia (Pty) Ltd
20 Alfred Street, Milsons Point, Sydney NSW 2061, Australia

Century Hutchinson New Zealand Limited
PO Box 40–086, Glenfield, Auckland 10, New Zealand

Century Hutchinson South Africa (Pty) Ltd
PO Box 337, Bergvlei, 2012 South Africa

British Library Cataloguing in Publication Data
Berwick, Dennison, *1956–*
  Amazon.
  1. South America. Amazon River Basin. Description & travel
  I. Title
  918.1'10463

ISBN 0 09 173490 8

Typeset by Speedset Ltd, Ellesmere Port
Printed and bound in Great Britain
by Butler and Tanner Ltd, Frome, Somerset

'How do people imagine the landscape they find themselves in? How does the land shape the imaginations of the people who dwell in it? How does desire itself, the desire to comprehend, shape knowledge? These questions seemed to me to go deeper than the topical issues, to underlie any consideration of them.'

Barry Lopez, *Arctic Dreams*.

In memory of
John Ruthven Berwick 1918–1989

Contents

List of Maps

Acknowledgments

The traveller depends heavily on the help of many people both abroad and at home. I mention as many as possible in appreciation of them all. Most of all I acknowledge the encouragement and help of my parents, despite their private misgivings. They shared their sense of wonder at the world and a very practical perseverance. Sadly, my father died shortly after this book was completed.

In Belém, my thanks and admiration to Joacelli Contente Tavares who for three months taught me as much Portuguese as I could absorb and who thereby opened to me the Amazon and the Portuguese world. I am especially indebted to Altair and Alberto Carvalhães and all their family who were wonderful hosts for many weeks: and to Robin Burnett, the Hon. British Consul, and his wife Sara, who looked after heaps of notebooks, provided the best Christmas dinner I have ever enjoyed on a journey, a home for three months, and to their staff, Raímunda, Cely, Milton and Marcos. Raímundo do Carmo Costa, Peter and Helen Nibblett and Aliete Costa de Souza were generous with their hospitality. My thanks for the help of Elaine Elizabetsky, Dan Nepstad, João Rego and Beth-Ann Smith, and Anthony Anderson and Bill Overal at the Museu Goeldi.

In Manaus, my thanks to Armando Ribeiro da Costa, owner of the Riomar Hotel where I stayed very happily many times and a generous friend who put a roof over my head during many difficulties; Francisco Arlos (Chicinho), his parents Dona Izabel and Senhor Oscar and the whole Viana family; Nesto Sgarioni and his family of the Iguacu Hotel (also to be recommended), who were always helpful and friendly; George Clarke, Hon. British Consul in Manaus; Richard Clayton, Felipe Lettersten, Joaquim Marinho, Anísio Mello, Mario Y. Monteiro, Mario Porto Severiano, Eldizia Martins da Silva, Roland Stevenson, Emidio Viana, builder of my three canoes, and Oliver Sam Walkey. My thanks at the National

Amazon Research Institute (INPA) to Dr Lessi, assistant director, and to Philip Fearnside, Albertina Pimental Lima, Renato Cintra Soares, and the library staff; Mariam Wong of the Worldwide Fund for Nature. My thanks and regrets to Ernesto de Carvalho and his wife Luzimar who made me welcome at their lodge on Lago Janauacá before wrecking our friendship, and to the families I met on the lake.

On the Rio Negro, my thanks to Darcy, Fernando, Dona Freida, Grandão, Helcio, Fr. Norbeto Hohenscherer, Senhor João, Juaré, Dona Maria, Antonio Moraes and his son Marido, Senhor Raimundo, Carlos da Silva and his wife, Dona Maria, Senhor Felipe and Senhor Marcelino.

I am deeply grateful to the Yanomami Indians of Irapachate, on the Marauiá river, who collectively took the risk of having me to stay.

In Peru, my thanks especially to Julio Cesar Osorio Bardales who, despite what eventually happened, taught me to feel comfortable in the forest, and all his family; Betsy Wagenhauser, co-president of the South American Explorers' Club which all travellers to that continent should join.

On the Tamshiyacu river thanks to Adriano, Dom Felix and Dona Lucia, Gustavo, Dom Julio and Dona Tereze, Luciano, Juan and his wife.

On the Tambopata river, thanks to guides Dom Gerardo and Victor Hugo, Rachel Byers, Dom Juan and his wife Dona Adriana, Pisango and Willy Withers.

At the source of the Amazon, thanks to Ascencio Saico Hincho, Huayna Flores, Ignacia, Jesus, Juan, Mario Mamami and his wife, and Victor Raul. Special thanks to Boris Ehret in Cuzco and his girlfriend Beatrice in Lima who bought a map of the source of the Amazon in Lima and couriered it to me in Cuzco to replace mine that was stolen.

In Canada, I am especially indebted to Joanne Lavkulich who with amazing energy and patience handled my affairs during the first year in the Amazon and to her husband Bruce Elniski; and to Simone Marler and her husband Blaine who handled my affairs during the second year with equal diligence and generosity of spirit.

I must also thank friends and family in Canada and England who have watched me come and go on many journeys and who have always been enthusiastic and patient: Jack Bales, Marcel and Bev Deschene, Terry Holliss, Peter Holt, Marye Smith, Graeme and Aly

Thompson, Marian and Robin White, and my sister Sarah, her husband Stan Konschuh, and nephews Ryan, Grant and Mark.

My additional thanks to Sir John Ure, former British Ambassador to Brazil, and to Wilfred Thesiger; Dr W. Csokanay and the staff of the Travel Clinic in Calgary, Mike Farmworth, John Gardner, Chester Gabriel, John 'Jungle Boy' Lewis, Caese Levo, Dr Dorval Magalhães, Nancy Lee Nash, Fr. Ray O'Toole, Robert Schoene, and Brian Keating and Paula Rice of the Calgary Zoo who helped me to overcome a loathing of snakes. Special thanks to Kodak Canada Inc. who generously provided films.

Introduction

THIS IS THE STORY OF A QUEST. It begins in an insignificant place on a tributary one thousand miles up the River Amazon, and ends with the embrace of a Yanomami chief in a rackety, stinking city of a million people. Between the fears with which my journey started and the new, saddened understanding of my return to civilisation lies an experience of wilderness that was for me both exhilarating and unsettling. I went there because I wanted to examine people's relationship with and thoughts about the natural world, and I chose the Amazon because, in spite of many recent changes, it still remains the greatest single expression of untamed nature on this planet.

The vast area has inspired dreams and nightmares ever since reports of the river and forest reached Europe in 1500. Even the name men gave it was mysterious, based on highly speculative early reports of female warriors similar to the Amazons of Greek mythology. But soon even this mighty rain forest will be broken up into mere patches of wilderness, disciplined between roads and fields, towns and plantations, and I wanted to see it while it was still outside man's control.

My father had had a similar wish, though he remained an armchair traveller only. When he was nine years old an aunt gave him a gook: *On the Banks of the Amazon; or a Boy's Journal of his Adventure in the Tropical Wilds of South America*. My father read it often and kept it with him all his life. Four 'pirates' with cutlasses were pictured on its cover, and the book described their adventures among the animals and savages of the forest. Written by W. H. Kingston, it was published in 1901.

'You can't know how much this book fired my imagination when I was a lad,' my father told me. He gave me the book shortly before he died: 'I never thought I'd have a son who would actually go there. Here – you must take this book now.'

My own interest in tropical rain forests began with a book called *The Forest Doctor*, describing the life of Albert Schweitzer in the Congo. It was the contrast between the man, a sophisticated doctor of medicine, divinity and music, and the wild surroundings in which he worked that delighted my juvenile imagination.

Despite this fascination, I kept away from the Amazon for many years – partly, I think, because it was made up largely of deep apprehensions about the dark forest and the creatures within it. Eventually, when I overcame these forebodings and arrived in the Amazon, they were quickly transformed into humility and respect.

So much is being said these days about the destruction of the Amazon forest and the need for conservation there that in this book I largely avoid adding my own voice to the argument. The fact remains, however, that approximately eight per cent of the forest has already been cleared (the Brazilian government admits to only four per cent), the percentage disturbed by European-style hunting and logging is much higher, and the speed of the despoilation is increasing. But my own search in the Amazon was for the reasons – other than the obvious and purely commercial – that lie behind such actions.

Indians have lived in the Amazon rain forest for about ten thousand years and have never felt the need to clear away the forest and make other use of the land. The need to replace wilderness with cultivation comes from the white man. The forces of technology and economics –much invoked today as making change 'inevitable' – come into action only as the result of an initial mind-set. The purpose of my journey was to explore the ideas and attitudes that bring about this mind-set. I have therefore tried to let the land and its people speak for themselves.

By now, sadly, if the traveller wants to visit forest that is relatively undisturbed, he must already get well away from the main channel of the Amazon river. My itinerary, therefore, was somewhat random: basically I went wherever there was an opportunity to travel off the beaten track: starting on the Rio Negro, one thousand miles up the Amazon, I switched to rivers in Peru, visited the Amazon's source in the Andes, and returned eventually to the Rio Negro in Brazil.

My finances for the journey turned out to be inadequate, largely due to theft, both minor and major. I took six thousand American dollars, planning to spend a hundred dollars a week for a year, and to keep the surplus as a contingency fund. But after my year in the

Amazon I had only fifteen dollars left, and I had to go home to earn and save money to pay for the few more months' travelling I felt I needed.

Lastly, I must repeat Evelyn Waugh's apology, given after his travels in Guinea and Brazil in his book *Ninety-two Days*, for including so much about the difficulties of getting from place to place. 'It seems to me to be unavoidable,' he wrote, 'for it is the preoccupation of two-thirds of the traveller's waking hours and the matter of all his nightmares.'

1

Rio Negro: 'Do You Eat Alligator?'

'The Amazon is not kind to poets and dreamers but she respects and helps those who are not afraid to roll up their sleeves and work. Who says this land is not good?'

Isaac Sabba, Manaus industrialist.

WHEN I WOKE our small boat was already moving up the Rio Negro. Pink light in the eastern sky showed a new day was beginning, but the forest had not yet emerged from darkness and the river was black to the horizon. We eight passengers could doze a little longer in our hammocks in the hold before breakfast.

'Do you eat alligator?' the master of the boat had asked the night before when deciding whether or not to take me as a passenger.

'Of course,' I lied. 'I have often eaten alligator. Delicious, and turtle too.'

The master smiled. 'Have you much luggage?'

'No.'

'Are you going to travel with us, then?'

'Without doubt.'

I collected my few belongings from the hotel at the other end of Barcelos and walked back down the main street, called Avenida Ajuricaba after the Manau Indian chief who had fought the Portuguese invaders in the 17th century. The small town was founded as a base for punitive raids against his tribe, and also as a missionary station. I had chosen it as my own starting point perhaps for similar reasons: the Rio Negro is a gentle river to travellers and Barcelos is the first of only three towns along one thousand miles of its length. It is generally calm, and its black, slightly acid water breeds few mosquitoes. And a plus for me was that, unlike the main Amazon, the Rio Negro still has forests standing close along its banks – they haven't yet been cleared for cattle ranching.

Barcelos is situated 268 miles upstream of the state capital

Manaus, which lies at the junction of the Rio Negro and the Amazon river flowing from Peru. There is no regular passenger boat up beyond the town, and getting farther up river depends therefore on hitching a ride on a privately-owned trading boat. Luckily for me a *balsa* (a boat pushing a flat-topped barge) had arrived on its way upstream to São Gabriel, 279 miles away, after I'd waited only one day.

As I passed a small bar with my grey backpack strapped to my shoulders a youth had called after me, 'Look at the turtle.'

'Down below', the master of the boat said when I presented myself on the deck. I hadn't seen that there was a lower deck. I climbed down into the darkness trying not to be smeared on the greasy steering chains hanging from the wheelhouse above. I expected to slip in oily bilge water but instead stood amid dark hammocks hung across the narrow boat. There seemed to be no more room for an extra passenger but I squeezed my hammock between the steering chains and a dark form lying in another hammock. We were so close when I lay down that I could feel the person's body heat. A man peered over the edge and watched while I tried to get comfortable.

By the light of dawn, the passengers' accommodation seemed not so unpleasant. Light entered through the gap between the sides and the open deck above. The master and his family of eight lived there, while the mate and two deckhands slept in hammocks over the engine. Silver and blue light filled the sky and the palest grey clouds appeared where stars had been. Parrots flew over the water now silver in colour. As yet, the day had no sound, except the thumping of our engine. Perhaps I should pinch myself to be sure the sight was not a dream, I thought, lying in my hammock watching yellow light strike tangled vines and trees on the river bank. But although to be in the Amazon was a wish fulfilled, this did not slacken the grip of apprehension in my stomach.

This is the barrier the traveller must break. I was very afraid of snakes and piranhas, and of being diminished and lost in that wilderness, yet it could never be enough simply to peer at the forest from a passing boat, nor to venture inside for only a few days. I wanted to be *with* the forest – comfortably and calmly, as if it were a garden. Then, perhaps I might understand those unconscious fears and delights which underlie conscious ideas of landscapes and nature and which, I believe, fuel man's wish to destroy the Amazon forest and to civilise the Indians.

My initial challenge had been learning Portuguese, which I had

more or less accomplished after three months of intensive tutoring.
Now I wanted to travel far up the Rio Negro away from civilisation,
and to find a guide who would take me into the forest to begin my
education. First, however, the outsider in the Amazon must learn to
relax; let time drift and enjoy the present moment instead of future
expectations; watch the new sun rising on this first day behind
clouds that thickened until the sky was grey. All can be accomplished eventually; and if not, then at least enjoy the journey.

Breakfast was served on the upper open deck with the master's
family; sweet, black coffee, crisp crackers and boiled *pupunhas*, the
fruit of the peach palm. The fruit looks like a spinning top and after
cooking in salty water tastes of dry sweet potato. We sat on benches
along the sides of the deck while the *balsa* pushed its way across two
miles of calm open water, between forested islands.

'The two banks of the river can never be seen at once, they are
probably ten to twenty-five miles apart. Some of the islands are of
great size,' wrote the English naturalist Alfred Russel Wallace when
he sailed up the Rio Negro in 1850 to collect thousands of insects and
animals.

Wallace was a passenger on a boat carrying cloths, knives,

mirrors, gunpowder and shot, beads and fish hooks to trade with the
'semi-civilised and savage inhabitants' in exchange for forest
products. Civilisation has spread in the intervening century, but the
goods he carried are still to be found on store shelves throughout the
Amazon, along with batteries for radios, soap powder, tinned milk
and bottled beer.

Our cargo, on the flat-topped barge joined to the boat with steel
ropes, included drums of aviation fuel, bags of cement, bricks,
wheelbarrows, steel rods, well pipes, crates of Coca Cola and
Antarctica beer and a chest of packaged foods for the stores in São
Gabriel da Cachoeira, far up the Rio Negro, near the border with
Colombia.

I sat on the deck beside the wheelhouse for much of the morning,
observing my neighbour from the hammock earn his passage by
steering the *balsa* and watching for pink or grey dolphins cutting
through the black surface of the river. There is a belief, widespread
in the Amazon, that these creatures turn themselves into men or
women and bewitch people at parties in order to make love to them.
It is not uncommon for children born out of wedlock to be called
'child of the dolphins' and such children are accepted by married
couples as their own offspring.

The level of the Amazon river was already rising to the south,
with melting snow from the Andes. The Rio Negro, fed only by rain
water over forests in the north, was falling however, exposing huge
beaches and sandbanks. The pilot looked far ahead over the open
water to the waves and the breakers watching for clues to the
location and depth of the sands. Once during the morning the
master dropped a hammer tied on to a piece of wire over the side as a
depth-gauge. The river was only twelve feet deep, even though we
were far out in its centre.

The morning passed quickly and we were soon eating the area's
staple foods; fish, rice, beans, *farinha* (manioc flour) and drinking
cool river water. There was nothing to do after lunch except snooze
in the hammock, but we were woken after an hour. The *balsa* was
stuck in the middle of a mile of water. The master called all the men
to help and the two deckhands, José and Julio, were already in the
water. I hesitated, then jumped over the side. The water came up
only to my waist. I could feel the pull of the current and held onto the
barge. We dug a two-foot trough in the bed of the river along one
side of the barge with our feet and with the jet of an outboard motor
on the master's speedboat, but the barge didn't move. We dug with

paddles and pulled and pushed with the boat on the steel ropes. The barge still did not move, but settled steadily into the sandbank, in the middle of a river now as grey as the sky.

We disconnected the boat and attached ropes from its stern to the bow of the barge. Grey smoke spewed from the exhaust pipes. Eventually the barge came free of the suction of the sandbank and floated clear.

Heavy drizzle was falling by the time we had reconnected boat and barge with their double cables. We tightened these by standing on them over the water, inserting a wooden board between the wires, and turning it. Once, without warning, the wet wood slipped in our hands and, spinning like a propeller, missed my head so narrowly that we all stopped, suddenly frozen, and stared at each other in our fright.

We were quickly underway again, moving up the middle of the wide river, deafened once more by the steady roar of the engine. I changed into dry shorts, dried my hair, and retired to my hammock until little cups of sweet black coffee were served about an hour later. By then the drizzle had stopped. The sun was shining again, making the faces of the master's several small daughters glow with a soft clear brown as they played on the deck – complicated games with their blonde, blue-eyed dolls, a yellow plastic dog, a pink sheep, two spectacle cases, a stainless steel watch strap and an empty nail varnish bottle.

The low sun turned the black river to gold and, when we sailed close to the north shore it seemed that every leaf of the forest had been freshly painted by the rain. We passed a community of three thatched houses and a small blue chapel with a cross, built in the middle of a field with goalposts and surrounded by the forest. Too soon the sun set behind clouds and the girls laid their dolls to sleep in hammocks of hand towels and covered them with blankets of denim cloth. Light faded and the sky shone with planets and stars.

The engine room bell clanged twice, the boat slowed and we approached the downstream end of an island between sandbanks. Using the boat's searchlight, we nudged into overhanging vegetation, black and formless. José and Julio went forward with a rope to tie us up for the night. It was dangerous to travel after dark when the river was low. The engine stopped but the generator motor continued its clattering roar, the cabin lights robbing us of night's stillness. We watched for the yellow eyes of caymans – alligators – but saw none and settled down to eat a supper of fried fish, rice, *farofa*, hot green peppers and water with the tint of brown from the river. Then it was bedtime.

I began each morning by pouring tepid water over myself from a bucket and scrubbing with soap. I didn't shave every day because, without a mirror, I usually forgot. We were always underway by dawn and usually having breakfast before sunrise, eating doughy crackers softened by the humidity.

After breakfast on the third day, José climbed into the motorboat with a kitchen knife, to inspect the three caymans that he and the captain had killed the previous night. The smallest, about two feet long, was thrown overboard as food for piranhas. The other caymans were four and five feet long from snout to tail. José cut off the heads, slit open the white bellies and threw away the entrails. He washed each body in the river and cut them into pieces. Working with a skill that made me feel clumsy and added to my feeling of basic inadequacy. I was still hopeful of soon being able to get away into the forest and cope on my own, however, and it was only occasionally, when I thought seriously of the coming challenges, that they appalled me.

'How do you kill a cayman?' I asked the captain, disappointed to have missed going hunting in the night.

'With a harpoon or a shotgun.'

The reptiles have good vision in darkness, but they are blinded by a flashlight, and if they don't dive small caymans can be caught by grabbing them behind the neck with a strong hand. Cooked in a little water, the white meat tastes something like lobster, with the texture of chicken.

Hours passed every day sitting in silence outside the wheelhouse. Twice the captain went off in the motorboat as we travelled to collect certain types of leaves to make a tea to help his children sleep.

The *balsa* zig-zagged up the river, avoiding beaches and sand-banks, making the forest grow from a fringe on the horizon to a green wall reaching eight feet above our heads. I counted a dozen colours of vegetation, from bright lime to almost black, but my eyes could not yet distinguish the bush, tree or vine to which the patches of colour belonged. Only the Brazil nut tree, taller than the surrounding forest and full of beige flowers, was easy to recognise. Each was a friendly beacon in this new green world.

The colours disappeared when the sky turned black behind us. We steered into the shore and stopped beside bushes in the water to await the storm. Wind rushed over the river, blowing spray off the waves, battering tarpaulins on the sides of the boat and bending the trunks of palm trees on the shore like plant stems. The rain came in thick grey mist, bouncing off the waves and clattering on the tin roof over our heads. But it did not last long. The water calmed again and the air filled with buzzing insects.

At teatime, we passed a dozen granite boulders lying on the north shore. This was the first *cachoeira*, meaning rapids or cataract. The level of the river was still high enough for us to pass without difficulty, but the rocks marked the beginning of a slower passage.

The roof of a white tower appeared above the trees on the shore. Half a dozen naked children watched from the beach. A chapel was being built behind, in the centre of a community of wooden houses and others made of palm leaves. We passed a herd of cattle, the first we had seen since Manaus, in a large meadow cleared from the forest.

'How beautiful!' exclaimed Maria, the captain's wife, reflecting the enthusiasm of all Brazilians when they see their forest put to good, civilised use.

It was on my second journey up the Rio Negro, a year later, that I learned the history of the tower. It and a magnificent villa had been built there in the forest during the Amazon rubber boom at the end of the 19th century, by one Joaquim Gonçalves de Aguiar from Portugal. Their walls were thick and strong, built of brick, with cement imported in barrels from France and transported four hundred miles up the Rio Negro from Manaus in steam launches. Small trees now engulf the ruins of the villa, one side of the tower has collapsed, and the interior stairs, up past graceful Romanesque windows, have rotted and fallen.

The surrounding community today is called Santomé, and I asked them why Joaquim had built there, and in such a fine manner. None of them could tell me.

. . . Look on my works, ye Mighty, and despair!
Nothing beside remains. Round the decay
of that colossal wreck, boundless and bare,
The lone and level sands stretch far away.

I remembered Shelley's poem, and thought about the tropical forest, the sand and the vegetation, the wastelands of the desert and the wilderness of the Amazon: all the places that city dwellers fear. Is it the indifference of nature that distresses them, the knowledge that all record of humanity may be erased like a Brazil nut tree rotting in the forest? Is this why civilised man prefers to look on countrysides made and remade by his ancestors down the centuries, so that nature grows meekly to his design?

Pink light after sunset shone on thunderclouds towering into the sky, and when the light faded the clouds were left as grey mountains floating over the forest. By then, we were above Santomé, travelling between small islands looking for a place to stop for the night. The *balsa* pulled towards the steep bank of a white beach.

José and Julio disappeared into the bushes on the island to gather dry wood and, with a splash of gasoline and a match, there was soon a lively fire. Two Y-shaped sticks were stuck in the sand and a grill of straight, green sticks assembled against the beach. The orange light beyond the clouds had faded and the first stars were appearing in the blue-black sky. Our fire glowed in the dark and the sizzle of fish on the grill quickened our appetites.

We ate supper on deck, picking out the bones with our fingers and helping ourselves to rice and *farinha* from bowls. Insects buzzed round the lights but the air was mercifully free of mosquitoes. And after supper, you could lie in the blackness on the front deck, staring at the Milky Way, watching galaxies and shooting stars before going to sleep.

Despite the cramped space and the perils of the greasy steering chains, I had learned to get comfortable now, sleeping diagonally across my hammock. It was pleasant to rock gently . . . until suddenly I felt the hammock slipping beneath me and tumbled in the dark onto loose boards and the motor of a chain saw on the floor. People laughed. I retied the knot, tested both ends and lay down again; happy that two other people had fallen out of their hammocks before me!

It rained hard during the night. The sky at dawn was cream in colour when I knelt on one side of the barge to wet my face to shave. The sun rose, minutes later, with such intense orange spilling over the sky, sparkling on the river, that I stopped shaving to enjoy the exquisite light.

The pool of colour from which the sun had risen was fading when Luís, the motor man, came onto the barge carrying a large turtle and a machete. The turtle had appeared without explanation in the toilet compartment after one of the captain's excursions in the motorboat to gather plants. Luís climbed onto the clear deck area where I was standing and put down the turtle on its back, its long neck turning from side to side.

The creature was decapitated with two blows of the machete. The first strike was followed by the dire sound of air being sucked into the lungs. The second strike severed the neck, but even after the underside of the shell had been cracked on both sides and cut away, the turtle's legs and the stump of its neck still wriggled with such life-like movements that I had to look at the severed head to remind myself the creature was dead.

We went through another rapid after breakfast, unhurriedly avoiding a large submerged rock twenty feet to our right. I was beginning to feel restless after days with no physical exercise. I never tired of gazing at the colours and shapes of the trees when we were close to the bank but I grew bored quickly in the middle of the calm river with the forest far away.

Grey boulders lined the river bank at the third *cachoeira* and beyond the grass bank stood a row of small painted houses, street lights and power poles leading to the two-storey white Salesian Mission with long rows of windows and a large church. This was Santa Isabel, 155 miles upstream from Barcelos, reached at midday after a four-day journey. The captain's children jumped into the water holding hands as soon as we stopped and their mother jumped in fully clothed after them, still wearing her gold necklaces and earrings that I had noticed were different every day.

A man came to spray the boat with insecticide later in the afternoon, so I went for a walk up the street. Passing the gasoline pumps, noisy diesel engines of the electricity generating station, clothing and grocery stores and a cascade of bourgainvillea outside one of the houses of painted rough boards, I came to other houses, beyond the top of the hill, which were built of wood frames filled with orange mud where the street ended before the television satellite dish on the edge of the town.

One disadvantage of spraying a boat with insecticide was that the bugs left their hiding places. Big cockroaches and beetle-like creatures ran everywhere, but we accepted them because they didn't bite. The mosquitoes were worse, breeding in the pools and puddles in the town. The wind faded completely that evening and sitting on the deck was like sweating in an insect-ridden sauna. By morning, I was itching with bites. Scrubbing with soap and diving into the river at dawn lessened the irritation but I didn't like swimming in dark water, where snakes and stingrays might be waiting.

Everyone, it seemed, had had a bad night; woken three times by
the roar of the bilge pump motor because the boat had sprung a
slight leak, and once by the sounds of José and an Indian girl making
love on the floor beneath our hammocks.

We did not leave on the Saturday morning because ascending the
rapids to São Gabriel needed a pilot, and he was drunk. The man
arrived, smiling, next morning after a late breakfast and we set out
serenely on the wide river beyond islands of rocks and trees. In fact
the rapids were not difficult until later in the year, the pilot told me,
when the river would be even lower and the rocks more exposed.

Within an hour of leaving Santa Isabel, the *balsa* was caught
midway through a set of rapids, unable to move against the current.
The pilot swung the *balsa* from side to side between massive flat
rocks feeling for a weakness in the flow of the water, keeping the
engine screaming at full power, shaking the deck and pouring smoke
from the exhaust to stop us being washed onto the rocks behind us.

Whatever demon inhabits the rapids, it lost its chance to destroy
us when the master went down into his motorboat, started up the
outboard motor, and revved it at full power.

This small engine added just enough to pull the *balsa* forward and,
twenty minutes later we emerged into slack water beyond the
rapids, grateful to have been spared.

Our difficulties were small, however, compared to those of
ascending these rapids by paddling and pulling on a tow-rope.
Wallace describes how, to reach a rock upstream, a naked Indian,
'leaps into the rapid current; he is carried down by its irresistible
force. Now he dives to the bottom, and there swims and crawls along
where the stream has less power. After two or three trials he reaches
the rock . . .'

Wallace went twice up the Rio Negro, enthusiastically collecting
thousands of specimens of flora, fauna and Indian artefacts. 'My
heart began to beat violently, the blood rushed to my head, [and] I
had a headache for the rest of the day,' he wrote when he found a
new species of insect in his net.

The Amazon was like the Garden of Eden to British, German,
French and American scientists in the 19th century. Wallace, with
Victorian ambition, also imagined how the Amazon could be
'improved'. 'I almost long to come over with half a dozen friends,
disposed to work, and enjoy the country, and show the inhabitants
how soon an earthly paradise might be created . . . I fearlessly assert
that here, the "primeval forest" can be converted into rich pasture

and meadow land, into cultivated fields, gardens and orchards, containing every variety of produce,' he wrote.

Wallace's boat stopped frequently and took three months to reach São Gabriel from Manaus. Our *balsa* stopped only at night and by day we were confined to deck or hammock to gaze at forest across the water. We reached the rapids below São Gabriel, nine days and 279 miles from Barcelos, in such a heavy rainstorm that the river turned white with spray. Red earth washed from the shore at the end of the ten mile dirt road to the town. The *balsa* was too big to get up the rapids and would wait here to be unloaded and to receive empty beer and cola bottles for the return journey to Manaus.

When the sky cleared, I paid the captain, and the other passengers and I carried our few belongings to the bar on shore to enjoy Fantas under the shade of its tin roof. Tables and chairs were arranged around a dance floor between roof poles decorated with fading paper streamers. Chickens pecked across the floor until chased out by a six-year-old boy. A cat was left sleeping.

The bar, at the back, was also a shop stocked with supplies: milk of magnesia, Bic pens, batteries, rice, disposable lighters, tins of meat, powdered milk, aspirins, cigarettes, matches, coffee, cane liquor, soap powder, pressure cookers, jam, razor blades, chewing gum, plastic cups, candles and fishing line.

The boy's beautiful mother, her fine black hair coiled in a bun, stood behind the counter, her bright eyes watching us. Her smile displaying white teeth made to seem whiter by her clear brown complexion.

'Which city are you from?' she asked. 'Not from Rio Grande do Sul? (A state in southern Brazil with many European immigrants.) 'Are you going to work here?'

'No. I want to look around.'

'You must be very rich. Are you single?'

I nodded.

'I wish I was single again. When you're a married woman you just bring up children, stay at home and get old! It's the men who can go out, dance, make love to other women. It's a sad life, being married, isn't it?' she laughed.

The municipal truck gave us a ride into town, along a rutted dirt road through the forest. We entered the town late in the afternoon down a long hill overlooking the white beach and the green forest where the black river cascades over a series of rapids. The astounding view is spoiled only by the concrete-box hotel beside the beach, where visitors stay.

São Gabriel is quite a decent small town, with radio mast, whitewashed church and Mission, streets of wooden houses with tin roofs, general stores and a cantonment of soldiers patrolling the nearby borders with Colombia and Venezuela.

A group of eight loud men from Rio de Janeiro occupied most of the dining room of the hotel. Their small plane, packed with electronic equipment, flew daily up and down imaginary lines two kilometres apart over the forest, prospecting for minerals – uranium, tin ore, iron ore, gold and rare minerals. They are part of the forces changing the Amazon, and like many other outsiders there they want to get their work done, get their money and get out. They keep their watches on Rio time, one hour ahead of local time, and complain there are not even direct dial telephones in São Gabriel. They keep together and are evasive about what they are doing. This has convinced local people that they have come to steal the riches of the land while the inhabitants stay poor.

I sat, after supper, beside the roaring river in darkness and thought about how I should move on now beyond even this outpost of civilisation. Wallace hired a big canoe, paddlers and a guide. But I had not yet been inside the forest and lacked his knowledge and self-confidence. I was frightened by the forest's reputation and intimidated by the fact that 'Indian Areas' are today closed to outsiders not approved by the government. I decided, as a small beginning, to try to get a guide to take me to one of the volcanic cones, covered in forest, about forty kilometres beyond São Gabriel.

Next day, I bought a straw hat to protect my sunburned face and met Maria from the *balsa*, with an aluminium basin full of clothes on her head. Did she know a guide to the volcanoes? She laughed and said there was a perfectly easy and obvious path up the hill at the back of the town.

It was two hours before sunset, and though I was wearing only thongs on my bare feet, I hurried through streets of red earth at the back of the town and crossed a football field below the distant green volcanic cone. This was a start, I thought, as I walked on, anxious about snakes in the grass. I paused to look at a 10-inch lizard striped like a zebra, and jumped back in fright when something crackled: it was a dry leaf from the Brazil nut tree on my right. A narrow trail led up through the grasses and bushes to a whitewashed stone alcove with a picture of Jesus, a candle and an offering of money. It

was the first Station of the Cross: Jesus condemned to Death. I was
worried by the perils of my journey so far and decided to go no
further up the forested hill without shoes on my feet and a machete
in my hand.

The sun was high in the sky when I returned next day, wearing
tennis shoes and holding a long stick in one hand to prod the grass
and the shadows under bushes like a blind man. I felt ridiculous to
be so apprehensive walking on a footpath on the edge of a town. But
I *was* nervous and edged forward, eyes on the ground, hardly
hearing the insects' humming.

'Good morning,' said two women with hoes and machetes,
ambling down the path with a dog. 'Where are you going?'

'To the top?' I replied.

'Are you a priest?'

'No, a foreigner having a look.'

They nodded and continued unconcernedly on down the path.
Their ease and confidence shamed me.

Enormous boulders encircled a clearing at the summit and
statues of the Madonna and Child stood on the tallest rock with two
burning candles and freshly picked purple flowers. Insects hummed
all around in the shade. I looked down on the white church, red
streets and brown tile roofs of the town facing the river. Squares of
brown earth had been recently cleared of forest to build rows of
white houses with tin roofs, silver in the midday sun. Smoke rose
from a few small fires and was lost in the air.

The Earth was forest in all directions to the curved horizon. A
green Earth under a blue sky, I thought. My climb had been only a
very small adventure, but I hoped it had done something to banish
the worst of my fears.

'God made all this to serve us. He put all here for His love of us, so
that we should not lack anything. He made Man intelligent and told
Man to work, to progress, to conquer all the Universe,' Father
Norbeto told me later in his bare, green office back at the Mission in
the town.

Salesian missionaries came to the upper Rio Negro in 1915 and
Tukano Indians came to them for protection from slavers. In return,
the Indians sent their children to the Salesian boarding schools
where the Portuguese language and Western values were, and still
are, instilled. Father Norbeto, originally from Austria, came to the
Rio Negro twenty years ago. 'We want to prepare the Indians for the
contact with the whites which is inevitable, to prepare them for the

shock, for them to defend their rights too. This meeting with the white culture must be slow and harmonious.

'The anthropologists criticise us very much,' Father Norbeto went on. 'They say we are destroying the Indian culture. But anthropologists like to think in theories. The reality is very different. The government wants to progress. The Indians want money, they want gold, they want to progress. They don't want to remain ignorant.'

Their ignorance depends on whether they walk in the white man's world or in the forest. 'The Indian is in his house in the forest. The white man thinks the Indian is a child but in the forest they need nothing and we are the children. The forest is another vision, another world.

'The Indian has a culture of survival. He works to live and when he has food he doesn't work any more. The white man thinks the Indian is lazy but it isn't this. It's a different culture. We think only of money and the more we have the more we want. The white man thinks he is superior. The Indian is put down. The Indian is without value, ignorant, backward. The Indian is humble, downcast and uncertain. He has an inferiority complex because he doesn't have planes and motors. They lose faith in their own culture. They think the white man knows best. This is what destroys their culture,' Father Norbeto told me.

Most of the 3000 people in São Gabriel are of direct Indian descent but have lost their Indian culture. They are Brazilians; lucky if they earn the minimum wage, watching football and soap operas on television, going to Mass on Sundays, drinking beer and Coke and buying processed foods in the stores at double the prices in Manaus. These stores, local government and Church, are operated by immigrants who are more aggressive than the sons and daughters of the Indians, and more accustomed to dealing with money.

I asked each day in the bars and at the boats about going fishing or hunting with a guide in the forest but people stared at me and said, 'It's difficult.' I spoke Portuguese poorly, and was ignorant of the way of life and how to get things done. My energy fell as the disappointments increased.

I was getting nowhere so, on the fifth day, still in São Gabriel, I booked a flight back to Barcelos for the next morning. Then I put on my straw hat, picked up the long walking stick and went out of town for a long walk along the red dirt road through the forest. The sun was high and bleached hairs on both arms glistened with sweat. I was happy to get away from civilisation, to be alone and to hear the birds in the trees beside the road and the constant buzzing of insects.

Black smoke coughed from an army bulldozer grinding back and forth in a new clearing near the town. I came to the well-made road to the airport, built by the Brazilian army, complete with culverts, cuttings, and embankments. Half a dozen cars swept past. When the road forked I turned to the left, towards the border with Colombia, away from the airport. Fallen trees lay all along the road on the right, where the forest had been cut half a mile deep and burned. The smell of smoke hung in the air and the earth was black and bare to the sun.

Charred branches and logs lay scattered between stumps left by the chain-saw gangs. Gaunt, charred tree trunks stood like pencils. Perhaps twelve trees in all the area had lived through the inferno. Their green leaves fluttered at the top of charred trunks, but the bleak land was silent and there were no insects.

Broken branches and the logs would be pushed into heaps by bulldozers to be reburned. The bare ground would be planted with guinea grass to feed white hump-backed zebu cattle. The grass would grow well for two or three years on the nutrients released by the burning. The soil will be exhausted in four or five years and the pasture abandoned when the grass no longer feeds the cattle. This has already happened in huge areas elsewhere in the Amazon and the forest does not regrow in the large abandoned pastures because the soils are too exhausted and depleted of seeds, too overrun with ants and mice without birds, snakes and lizards to eat them and too open to sun and rain for trees to gain a foothold.

To outsiders, it must seem a colossal folly to exchange forest for a few beefsteaks and a field of weeds. Cattle ranching only makes economic sense if the forest is assessed as being of no value and ranchers offset their costs against taxable profits from other businesses. But in Brazil, beef is a national obsession, a symbol of macho independence, of the conquest of the Amazon, and a way for a few people to get rich quickly. Pressure to stop or to slow down the destruction of the forest is resisted by stony-faced anger and by bullets. Gunmen are hired to murder those who challenge. One such victim was Chico Mendes. He was a Brazilian ecologist who organised rubber tree trappers in Acre, in the southwest Amazon, to protect themselves and their forest against ranchers and politicians who try to clear them off. This man fought to protect illiterate

Brazilian farmers who were gaining a basic livelihood from the forest by gathering rubber and *sorva*, used to make chewing gum. He was murdered by ranchers three days before Christmas, 1988.

It rained hard in São Gabriel that evening and was raining so hard when I woke next morning that spray and mist obscured the rapids in the river. Everyone in the hotel said the plane I had planned to take back to Barcelos was certain to be cancelled. I hitched a ride to the airport late in the morning when the rain stopped. The barn-like building had been opened in 1981 by the Brazilian air force to promote, according to the plaque on the wall, 'integration, development and security'. The service includes free passage to missionaries, Indians and foreigners with the right credentials, when there is room.

I was flying only to Barcelos, occupying a seat already reserved for the flight on from Barcelos to Manaus. In Barceles, I would have to wait four days for the passenger boat to Manaus. Cloud broke into blue patches before the 16-seater commercial plane arrived and I was glad for a window seat to enjoy at least one experience that Alfred Russel Wallace had only imagined. '. . . Sailing gently in a balloon over the undulating flowery surface below: such a treat is perhaps reserved for a traveller of a future age.'

We flew very low over where the *balsa* had arrived a week earlier. Trees became mere tufts of green as the plane rose and we seemed to be flying across a plate of broccoli. A thunderstorm filled the sky far to the north of the river. Air vents over our heads suddenly gushed cold steam when air from outside rushed into the heat and humidity inside the plane. The land below us appeared as a deep carpet cut by meandering tributaries and the wide Rio Negro. The forest was still closed, hidden by its green cloak, yet all the time exercising its power to seduce the unwary.

But now Manaus beckoned. I had avoided the city on my arrival in Brazil: now I would perhaps find in it people to help me realise my dream, help me travel the deep, undisturbed forest.

2

Manaus: Island in the Forest

'It is in cities though where landscape taste in Brazil is perhaps most clearly expressed. The concern of Brazil and Brazilians is for the future, not the past. That future in terms of growth and opportunity, appears to lie in the city, generating a preference for the city and its landscape.'

Brazil, John Dickinson.

ON MY FIRST AFTERNOON in Manaus I made my way unbelievingly through crowded noisy streets, astonished by a city that denied its geography and climate. Cold air blew from air-conditioned boutiques that displayed the fashions of Paris and Rio. Salesmen waited, smiling, in shops crammed with duty-free cameras and electronic gadgets from Japan. Yellow Volkswagen taxis raced four abreast to the next traffic lights. Television sets, watches and video cassette players, all made in Manaus, were on offer in department stores for twenty per cent down and monthly payments. Neon lights flashed the names of running shoes and hamburgers. Youths on street corners offered watches, condoms and perfume, and quoted their best price for the US dollar.

My central problem, however, was still to find someone to help me get away from civilisation – an apparently simple ambition that was proving surprisingly difficult to realise. I could not yet imagine myself carrying a canoe and just setting out alone, so my first calls were made to jungle tour offices. There salesmen, each armed with a Coke and a smile, promised to fulfil my wildest dreams of piranhas and snakes, savages Indians and exotic jungles – all in three days, for just US $110.

Three weeks in the jungle, on the other hand, would cost US $600 – of which, or so I was told by a man I met out in the street, the salesman would keep $550. 'A tourist is a foreigner with too much money and no idea how to spend it,' he explained.

My hope in fact was to find someone willing to teach me the way of life in the forest and along the rivers. Admittedly I had met a

Canadian adventurer long before arriving in Brazil, a wrestler of boa constrictors and author of a book on the Amazon, who had assured me that my canoeing dream was impossible. 'Don't even think of it,' Norman Elder had told me as we sat in his large Victorian house in Toronto, a house that was also a museum, an emporium of stuffed animals, mounted butterflies and assorted weapons gathered during his many journeys. The boa constrictors were kept, live, in the basement: if the man had wrestled with these and won, then I reckoned he probably knew what he was talking about. Nevertheless I'd still come to Brazil, and at least I'd been up the Rio Negro as far as São Gabriel, and now here I was in Manaus. So I settled into a hotel and delayed facing the impossible by going sight-seeing round the city. I'd arrived in the week before an official Carnival began, and excitement was already mounting.

But I was a gringo, and gringos stride out too quickly in tropical sunshine, so by the time I'd found my first sight to see I was typically hot and sweaty. Even so, the famous Opera House was well worth the visit, a magnificent grey building decorated with white Corinthian columns and tall windows behind intricate wrought-iron balconies, and crowned by an immense dome of yellow, green and blue tiles – the colours of the Brazilian flag.

The theatre had been imported complete from Europe: girders from Scotland; stone from England; marble and paintings from Italy; mirrors, chandeliers, porcelain and staircases from France; and coal from Wales for the electric generator. Birds and monkeys in the forest were within earshot when an Italian lyric company opened the 700-seat Teatro Amazonas in 1896. How many times since then have men and women looked at this monument of European grandeur to reassure themselves of their performance in the face of the awesome forest?

I hoped to hear an opera or concert, but performances were rare in the theatre and I had to be content with an amateur play on the legend of the dolphin seducing women. Seventy people, mostly friends and family of the cast, sat in the stalls under a high ceiling painted with epic scenes of Drama, Music and Tragedy.

Rubber trees had brought the white man here, and rubber had built this opera house. Rubber, and greed, and delusions of grandeur.

'It took the eye of a civilised man to call attention to these trees. After that the quiet paradise of the primitive became a screaming hell,' wrote David St Clair in *The Mighty, Mighty Amazon*. Soon whole

Indian tribes were enslaved and thousands of Brazilians, fleeing droughts in the northeast, arrived only to be ensnared in debt-bondage gathering rubber in the forest along dozens of isolated rivers.

In the city, the worst of the slavery and brutality became transformed into the civilised life of commerce and culture. Photographs of 'civilised Putumayo Indians with their overseers' won a silver medal achievement award for the British-owned Peruvian Amazon Company at a Commercial Congress held in the Teatro in 1908. The same company's atrocities against the Indians here were exposed by an American traveller and led to a British Parliamentary enquiry to the Putumayo.

'Beatings were meted out most often when a labourer failed to match his daily quota of latex. Many died under the whip and their corpses were fed to the dogs. Others survived in agony for days or weeks, their flayed skins infested with maggots and bloated with infection . . . Women were routinely raped and given as prostitutes for the foremen . . . Indian children, too young to work, were killed in front of their parents, either by drowning or by having their skulls smashed against trees,' summarised Jonathan Kandell in *Passage Through El Dorado*.

But the root of their wealth was forgotten by people in the city. The 'bohemian life of Manaus was superior to the nightlife of Rio de Janeiro', I was told by Mario Y. Monteiro, the venerable historian of Manaus, engulfed by magazines and books in his study where we sipped sweet, black coffee from little cups. 'When people came out of the theatre or the cinema, they didn't go home, to sleep – no, they went to the bars, to the chic French restaurants to drink champagne, French champagne. How I would have liked to have lived here at that time. The high-class people spoke French and their children were educated in Europe. We received French romances, French books, and here in the city the gardens and squares are in French design.'

French led the cultural life, while British engineers laid the sewers and water, operated trams and prefabricated both the Customs House and the Palace of Justice and built a floating quay, thus overcoming the annual 40-foot rise of the Rio Negro.

Men from Europe controlled exports of rubber from Manaus. Their names reflected their origins – Ahlers, Araujo, Dusenschon, Gordon, Scholtz and Zarges.

Araujo arrived at the age of twelve from a small town in Portugal to join his brothers already in trade in Manaus. He apprenticed with another trading house and spent two years up the Rio Negro before starting his own company, sending food and other provisions into the interior, charging high prices plus interest and receiving rubber, *piassava* – for making brooms – and other natural products as payment.

He was a hard, frugal man who lived in a rented house and called his office his home. Yet it was the debt system largely evolved by Araujo that financed both the transformation of Manaus from squalid frontier town to a replica of a European city and the legendary decadence of brothels and drunken revelry.

Champagne fountains flowed at the Babylonian parties of the Austrian Consul, Waldemar Scholtz, former grocery store clerk in Stuttgart. He served beer to the horses in his Rio Negro palace and beseiged Enrico Caruso with cabled invitations to sing in Manaus.

As Mario Monteiro told me, 'When rubber fell in 1912 everyone fled Manaus. The foreigners sold everything and left. Business people here always blame Wickham, that Englishman, who carried the seeds away. But he is not so much to blame. I discovered that businessmen of Manaus were exporting rubber seeds before Wickham came.'

Henry Wickham is famed in Brazil as the man who stole the country's seventy-year rubber monopoly. Wickham told the customs officer in Belem, at the mouth of the Amazon, that his ship was carrying delicate botanical specimens for Queen Victoria's garden. In fact, they were thousands of rubber seedlings for Kew Gardens in London that eventually propagated rubber plantations all over the Far East.

World rubber prices fell when the Amazon monopoly ended. Capitalism collapsed in the Amazon. The white man left undisturbed the remote Indian tribes, as the population of Brazilian rubber-tappers and non-tribal Indians spread along the floodplains of the rivers, subsisting there by hunting, fishing and planting manioc. They intermarried, spoke Portuguese and native Tupi, learned Indian know-how, remained nominal Catholics while accepting the ancient tribal spirits of the forests.

Thousands of their children and grandchildren today live in Manaus, assembling electronic gadgets and ballpoint pens in factories built by multinational companies in a tax-free industrial park that serves all South America.

I talked in a bar to an Englishman, Richard Clayton, who has lived in Brazil for the last forty years.

'Eighty per cent of these workers are women seeing a factory for the first time in their lives, apart from the manioc flour mill,' he told me. 'The impact is tremendous. Manaus is another country, outside the rest of Brazil. It speaks Portuguese but it has different customs, different habits.

'It's different because its access roads are all liquid or aerial and because of the influence of the Indians and its original inhabitants, basically Portuguese. People from the interior have become used to living in tune with nature. They don't have to earn money to eat and they suffer a lot when they come to the city, to Eldorado.

'And another influence is that the male only hunts and reproduces in the Indian society. The women do all the work and the child rearing. Here, they all have to earn money to live. It's extremely expensive, especially in terms of the hours of work needed in order to buy any European-style article,' said Richard Clayton.

Carnival is the season for shrugging off these cares, for singing, dancing, drinking and making love. Girls wear only glitter stuck to their naked bodies and festivities start weeks before the actual Carnival procession.

One night, policemen and barricades blocked traffic from a street near my hotel. Hundreds of people were dancing under bright lights in the street outside the Rio Negro palace, the grey mansion like a French wedding cake built by Scholtz which was now the official residence of the governor of Amazonas.

Drums and trumpets filled the sultry evening with pumping rhythms for the shirtless, sweat-covered youths and their girls. A tanker truck of beer was under siege from heads and arms reaching up with plastic bags for free beer supplied by the state government. Paper cups passed from hand to hand, the people welcoming me, a stranger among them.

Lond banners, hanging over the street, congratulated the state governor on his birthday. Nobody mentioned his retirement after losing the latest election. I wandered with my new friend Mario Monteiro up the steps into the palace. The interior was bare, as if it had been stripped of furniture and carpets before the masses could be admitted. Mario told me that the plain white-washed walls hid murals of the wars of Ajuricaba, the Manau chief who fought the Portuguese in the 17th century. 'There was a governor in the 1960s,'

he explained, 'an Amazonese but he had a Portuguese father and he
was brought up in Portugal, and he was furious when he saw the
panels. "Indians didn't have the capacity to kill Portuguese armed
with iron," he said and ordered the murals painted over.'

From a balcony, I could see a fire engine parked in darkness in a
side street, ready to hose down the street party if people got too hot.
But the precaution was unnecessary. Heavy rain began falling and
only those already drunk or already sweat-soaked kept dancing or
waiting for more free beer.

For me the fun of Carnival came as a welcome distraction from
my loneliness. For several weeks I had drifted like a raft of grass on
the river, blaming the heat and humidity for my lethargy. But then
an article appeared in the newspaper one morning about a Chilean
artist living in Manaus who had spent eight years painting the
portraits of Yanomami and other Indians. So I stirred myself and
went to call on him.

He was, he said, 'a descendant of Robert Louis Stevenson, the one
who wrote *Treasure Island*. I don't know which one. I haven't worried
myself. He came at the beginning of the century.'

Roland Stevenson had come initially on a brief visit to paint
Indians and, like so many immigrants to the Amazon, he had
stayed.

'Depending on the tribe, it can be very dangerous for me when I
paint the portrait of an Indian,' he told me. 'The Yanomami, for
example, if I paint them and later they get sick, then they think I
have stolen their spirits, and they try to kill me with poisoned
arrows. But I've had a lot of luck. They have the easiest faces to
paint and they are the most primitive tribe in the Amazon.'

He fetched a large board painted with a dozen faces of the
Yanomamis. From their facial characteristics, he said, the history of
migration and tribal splits can be reconstructed. 'The face, for the
first time, is telling us something language cannot tell us, because
some Indians have changed their language. The Yanomamis of the
south, for example, cannot understand those of the north. Language
changes but the faces persist.

'With this sequence of faces we are discovering the actual route of
a legendary pre-Colombian road. The road was built by the Incas
with stone markers every twenty kilometres, now hidden by the
forest in an area where the local Indians still speak Quechua, the
language of the Incas.' According to Stevenson the people who
migrated along this road included the Yanomami Indians.

'Are you saying that the Yanomamis are descended from the Incas?' I asked.

'Exactly this. Look at this face,' said Stevenson pointing to his portraits. 'It has features that show it is descended from the Incas.'

Though he had found one stretch of the road, its destination in Macapa was discovered by someone else.

'I take my hat off to him. Do you know who it was?'

'No.'

'It was the English who found El Dorado.'

'Who?'

'John Hemming [Director of the Royal Geographical Society]. He got there before me because he has more resources for research,' said Stevenson. It was here, in 1986–88, that the Royal Geographical Society assembled a major scientific expedition with INPA (the Brazilian National Amazon Research Institute in Manaus). Their archeological work, according to Stevenson, was only a cover for recovering the Incas' gold. 'The people told me the planes arrived light and left heavy,' he said.

Stevenson was planning to explore that remote part of the Amazon himself but he said he lacked the money. In the meantime, he painted pictures of the landmarks of the city, surrounded by a crowd of curious Brazilians wherever he set up his easel.

It was impossible to give much credence to Stevenson's story, though the skill of his portraits of the Yanomamis and his knowledge of their way of life were indisputable. I mostly preferred, in these weeks of uncertainty, to suppress my loneliness by passing afternoons looking at Indian pottery and feather decorations in a museum or reading books about ecology in the library of INPA. But there is an easy-going manner in the Amazon in which people talk to strangers and one night I had a few beers with a young bank clerk in a bar filled with the rhythms of samba.

'Indian of the city,' Chicinho Viana called himself, with a big smile. We became friends and he took me drinking and dancing in the streets during the exhausting nights of Carnival processions and parties.

His family lived in a small house in the city centre and I sometimes took a *tambaqui*, a fruit-eating fish, for the family to barbecue in their backyard on Sundays. Their welcome made my weeks of indecision more endurable, my longing for the forest and my secret dread of it, until the interminable Carnival ended.

By now I had almost been in Brazil for the maximum six months that a visitor may stay, so I had to leave anyway. I'd decided to travel up the Amazon river to Peru, and to try again there to find a willing guide. I was not proud of my inertia in Manaus. Perhaps in Peru, fifteen hundred miles up the Amazon, I would be braver.

I woke on the Saturday excited to be leaving Manaus that afternoon on a ferry up the Rio Solimões, the main channel of the Amazon. I went to say goodbye to a Portuguese friend I had made. He lived in one room in a narrow courtyard lined with wooden houses. Suddenly a man fell into the room through the ceiling, landing on the concrete floor between us.

'He came home full of tea,' said his wife when she rushed from next door. 'He said he was going up on the roof. I told my daughter he was too drunk.' The man was taken to hospital in a taxi with a towel round his head and we cleaned up the blood, broken fan and pieces of furniture. Perhaps shock explained my stupidity later, when I arrived at the river front.

First I returned to the hotel to pick up my backpack and collect Mike, an American who also wanted to get out of Manaus up into Peru. We walked together down to the river and through the jam of people on the floating platform where the long-distance ferries of the Amazon departed.

'God, I didn't think it would be this full!' Mike grumbled when we reached the upper deck already crowded with hammocks, people and luggage. I was aware of someone watching when I put my camera bag in the backpack but took no notice. We hung up our hammocks and put the backpacks in one corner of the open deck.

The journey to the Peruvian border up the Rio Solimões would take one week. I had no idea about the telephone service in Peru so as I had not spoken to my parents for a couple of months, I decided to phone them before I left Manaus. I called England from a public telephone outside the market and returned through the throng to the ferry. Mike, who I thought was watching the backpacks, was standing beside his hammock. We were then called to buy our tickets at the table some twenty feet beyond both hammocks and baggage.

'Where's my pack?' I exclaimed when we returned. It was gone. I checked the ferry, the floating terminal and up the street. My backpack had gone – and with it all my clothes, camera equipment, films, notebooks, address book, reading materials, $2,000 in travellers' cheques, an American Express card, letters of intro-

duction, and driver's licence. I was left with the clothes I was
wearing, a straw hat, hammock, passport, $1,500 in cash in my
wallet, and my open air ticket home.

'Do you know who took your bag?' the policeman asked me when
I told him what had happened.

'Of course not.'

The policeman shrugged, turned, and walked away. Robberies
are too common in Brazil for the police to bother with stupid
tourists. The boat sailed. It would be at least a week before I could
report the stolen American Express items.

'Let's go up to the top deck,' Mike suggested. 'I'll buy you a beer.
You're taking this very calmly.'

I wasn't calm. I was stunned.

3

Rio Tamshiyacu: 'Hi Ho the Jungle!'

'They were two perfectly insignificant and incapable individuals, whose existence is only rendered possible through the high organisation of civilised crowds. Few men realise that their life, the very essence of their character, their capabilities and their audacities, are only the expression of their belief in the safety of their surroundings.'

Joseph Conrad, *An Outpost of Progress.*

SIX GRINGOS WALKED DAZEDLY down a Peruvian city street. The night was dark but the lights were bright, the street empty. Ten tedious days had passed since our leaving Manaus. We had travelled on two over-crowded boats, from Manaus to the Brazilian border with Colombia and Peru, and from there to Iquitos, this city 2,300 miles up the Amazon.

For ten long days and nights the forest wall had passed us, unbroken save for occasional thatched houses set in overshadowed clearings. Now suddenly, at 3.15 a.m. we had arrived in a city and stood in front of a bar with lights and people, amazed by the brightness of it all.

Mike was from America, I from England, the other four were from Denmark and New Zealand. There seemed to be no coffee in the bar, so we settled for beer. A spry Peruvian came hurrying over to the table as soon as we had ordered and sat down. He was holding a copy of *The South American Handbook.*

'Hello, hello, good evening,' he said. 'No, forgive me. Good morning. My name is Freddie. Where are you from? Have you come from Pucallpa? Oh, I see. From Brazil. Yes, yes, welcome to Iquitos. My name is Freddie. If you need anything, if you want anything, please ask me. I am not trying to sell anything.'

We nodded with fatigue, drank our beers and wished he would go away. 'How old are you?' someone foolishly asked.

30

'I am twenty-eight. I lived for nineteen years in the forest and nine years in the city. I have a small office near the Plaza das Armas. If you need anything, if you want anything, please ask me.' He looked at us around the table. 'You are travelling to see the forest here. We have beautiful forest here. Very well, very well. I lived for nineteen years in the forest and nine years in the city. If you need anything, please come to visit. I have a small office . . .' Freddie's friends across the room called him back to finish his beer before the bar closed.

One of our New Zealanders opened his own copy of *The South American Handbook* to read the report about Freddie:

'For those who are tough, Freddie can be contacted opposite the iron Eiffel house; he organises survival courses in the jungle and you learn to build your own camp, find your own food etc. Be warned however: he has to approve of you and your level of fitness and stamina, not you of him. He speaks fluent English. US $400 for 3 (people) for 5 days; longer would be better, mixed reports of his reliability.'

Going with such a guide would be the easiest way for a gringo like me to enter the forest, but I hoped for a better opportunity. I wanted to learn ways of being with the forest, rather than just in it.

The American Express office in Iquitos could do no more than repeat the black market exchange rate for dollars when I asked about getting my stolen travellers' cheques refunded. 'You must go to Lima,' said a more helpful clerk eventually. That was no surprise. Nothing is going to be easy on this journey, I thought, relieved at least to have $1500 in cash still in my money belt. The gods have decided to test my mettle. It was not an ideal situation, but I accepted the challenge.

Next morning, Mike and I booked flights to Lima for the following morning then walked to the main market of Iquitos where stalls run for five miles through the streets. Boys with small trays cried 'Chicklets! *Cigarros*! Chicklets!' A grey-haired man held out copies of *The Political Constitution of Peru* to housewives with shopping bags. They didn't pause or even look at him, but strode on between stalls selling chopped turtles with yellow-spotted paws and heaps of plucked chickens, necks and guts sold separately.

Other stalls sold catfish so fresh they were still gasping, salad vegetables arranged in lines, fruits, bundles of black tobacco, huge snails, pigs' intestines, little live alligators, dried monkey and small *ratos* that didn't have much meat. Stalls were always neatly arranged often with really tiny plastic bags of cooking oil or spices or packets of 'Topless Rice' with pictures of a girl on the beach. People bought only enough for a few meals. Prices were high, wages were low, the climate was hot, and few families had fridges.

We came at length to a long stall selling tree barks and fresh leaves. Mike pointed to a bark that was burgundy-coloured on the inside. 'What is it?' I asked in Portuguese.

'For cold,' said the stallholder, understanding me and replying in his native Spanish. He called to his wife for a bottle of red liquid. '*Chuchuhuasi*,' he said. We drank small cups, feeling the warmth of the brew that he said was to relax muscles and remove arthritic pain.

We sampled next a liquid made from a golden bark. It tasted like pink gin. One dozen barks and two dozen bottles of remedies covered the stall and the generous man became more and more enthusiastic as we asked more questions.

'This is for venereal disease,' he said, pointing to a red furry moss. 'This for liver, this for kidneys, this for skin,' he said, pointing to red stringy leaves, yellow blooms like melon flowers and five-sprigged leaves. All had been freshly gathered in the forest and were to be taken as herbal teas.

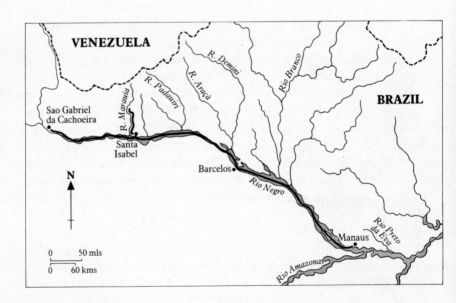

We left feeling pleasantly relaxed and with our heads buzzing. After cups of Nescafe coffee, Mike and I turned from the stalls down wide steps lined with shops. Long fishing nets and yellow floats hung in the shunshine, shading boxes containing hooks to catch all of the more than 1,500 species of fish in the river; six-inch hooks for the enormous *piraracu* and tiny hooks for the barbed *candire* fish that enter the orifices of fish and mammals to eat inside.

We followed an alley down to the river where thirty canoes jostled for passengers across to the water-born city of Belen, meaning Bethlehem. One man asked twenty *intis* – about a dollar – per person per hour. We climbed aboard behind our guide sitting with a big paddle in his hands. He called himself Roy Rogers and asked if we knew Rambo.

Ten thousand people live in Belen, which stands deep in silty water when the Andes snows melt in March, April and May. Roy Rogers paddled his canoe into a wide street. Half the houses were built on stilts and others were rafts. Each had a house number in black and gold and an elevated electric meter box. Two boys fished from the window of their home. A woman sat scrubbing clothes in a basin, legs dangling over the greenish-brown flood water. Laughter and shouting, the squawk of parrots and every murmur of love at night passes from family to family through walls of wooden planking or palm leaves.

We came as voyeurs, peeping at women arguing; at old men in doorways, faces obscured by a hat, sitting on the floor repairing fishing nets; at mothers breast-feeding their babies; at girls playing with younger sisters; at naked boys admiring their urine falling in arcs into the flow of water. People were thin and muscular, lacking the chubbiness of those who lived on the land. Mike took lots of photographs.

Roy Rogers pulled to one side to allow two women and a child to pass in a small canoe. They were selling slices of cake and a purple-skinned fruit which I called chocolate-cake fruit because of its taste. Further along, a mother sat looking for lice in her daughter's straight black hair.

After a half-hour tour, we invited Roy Rogers to go for a beer. The floating bar was called 'El Chicosal', meaning 'small salt', or little joke. Four tables and stools, a long blue counter and a double bed for the family faced floating gasoline stations across open water.

'How old are you?' asked Roy Rogers after drinking a glass of cold beer. Mike and I leaned forward across the table to understand his Spanish.

'Thirty,' I said in Portuguese, conscious that we were now in Peru and trying to adapt to the Spanish.

'You don't look. You look twenty-five. How old are you?'

'Thirty-three,' said Mike.

'Ah! The age of Christ.'

Our companion rented his canoe for five dollars a day, which seemed expensive compared to the purchase price of one hundred dollars. 'Some days I earn enough to pay the canoe rent and have money for me,' he said. He was not married and lived with his family in Belen.

'What do you do when the river is low and people don't need canoes?'

'I work as electrician in the oil business. Very good money – maybe twenty dollars a day.'

Peru had declared a two-day public holiday when a rig struck oil under the forest of Iquitos in 1971. Oil had brought jobs and development, unknown since the price of rubber collapsed, to the jungles of Peru and Equador.

A girl of Chinese descent, grand-daughter of an immigrant during the rubber boom, brought out a box of clothes to sell. She had a bird like a thrush on her arm. Its flight feathers had been clipped and it stood on Mike's hand while he stroked it.

'Delicious with potatoes,' said Roy Rogers.

After a couple of hours, empty beer bottles crowded our table. It was time to pay our bill and climb back into the canoe. We asked about coming back in the evening, when there would be more beers and talk. Roy Rogers nodded, but then said people drank and fought too much at night.

Getting the travellers' cheques refunded by American Express in Lima and returning to Iquitos took twelve days. A woollen bag sat on my knees, stuffed with new clothes and a camera when I returned in the dark. I remembered the market stall in Lima and putting the straps of the colourful bag over my shoulders for the first time. New travellers cheques were hidden in the money belt around my waist.

The motorcycle rickshaw rushed from the airport into the town centre and I laughed to feel the hot, humid air on my cheeks and wondered why I should be so lucky. Everything about this Amazon search had suddenly changed. Lethargy had become energy, resentment had become humour, doubt had become conviction. I had no explanation for this but I knew that from now on, no matter what happened, this journey would be fun.

Once back in Iquitos, I strolled down the street from the hotel, looking for a place to eat supper. By chance, crossing a street, I met a lanky Englishman called John whom I had met briefly in a bar with other gringos before going to Lima. He was a physics graduate and although he had yet to get away into the forest he liked to call himself 'Jungle Boy'.

'Still here?' I asked.

'Yes, I'm going tomorrow. Into the forest. Well, we've been in for a couple of days but now I'm going for a week.' John and a young Dane sat with me in a restaurant while I ordered fried fish, boiled manion (called *yuca* in Peru) and salad.

'You should talk to Julio,' said John. 'He could tell you all about medicinal plants.'

I nodded. 'Who's Julio?'

'We met in a bar. He took us both on a fishing trip.'

'It was good, but too much fish,' said the Dane.

'Why don't you come with me tomorrow? I'm going for a week. You don't have to pay anything. I think Julio worked for a travel company but he just likes to take foreigners.'

'Sure. Great.' I said.

'I'm sure he'll take you. He invited us out to his home to watch a boxing match on TV. It was miles away, just a little place with a thatched roof.'

'And, of course he wasn't there,' I said.

'No, that's right. He wasn't there and the neighbour said he didn't have a television. I don't know.' John and the Dane shrugged their shoulders and drank beer. I laughed.

'You have to get used to eating a lot of fish,' said the Dane. 'Two or three times a day. I mean, even fish for breakfast. For breakfast! A fish head in watery soup . . .'

I was sceptical that the week's jungle trip would actually happen, but checked the location of John's hotel, our meeting point at 6.30 next morning, and bought toothpaste, candles, matches, razor and cigarettes, just in case. And John told me to buy plastic sheeting as well, to keep the rain off my hammock, fish hooks and line, and thirty metres of parachute cord.

A small tin of Nescafe as a lightweight luxury and a pair of thick rubber boots were the most urgent additional items on my own list.

'I have a dread of snakes,' I had explained at my local zoo before coming to the Amazon. 'Perhaps handling some snakes might help.' I was told to stroke an eight-foot boa constrictor.

'That's it, hold the head forward. He's not poisonous but he can give a nasty bite,' said the helpful lady keeper. The creature hugged my waist and I tried to breathe calmly. 'Now we'll wash our hands before we handle another snake. They don't like to smell each other.'

We went to the wash basin. 'Look – a spider!' I said and lifted the creature out.

'Oh my God! A spider!' The lady shrieked and fled.

John introduced me to Julio when they arrived at the hotel after breakfast. Julio nodded. We shook hands. 'Let's go,' he said. We collected our belongings and walked back to the market to catch a river boat. 'Hi ho, the jungle!' exclaimed Jungle Boy John.

We jumped onto the roof of a 45-foot covered canoe just as it was leaving and climbed down inside. Thirty people sat on benches round the sides of the canoe with their bundles, boxes and new cooking pots heaped down the middle. The canoe motored out through a broad street of Belen and stopped at a floating gasoline station to fill up.

An old man, a broad straw hat shading his face, paddled alongside in his little canoe to describe to us the virtues of the orange and purple ice lollies he was selling.

Half an hour later, the refuelled outboard motor was pushing us noisily up the mile-wide river away from Iquitos. The belly of a drunk man, sprawled on the bench, rose and fell regularly as the canoe pitched through the waves. His lolling head tapped the planking of the boat, one arm dangled. Two girls slept beside him. One of them piddled her pants; the liquid dripped onto the floor but she didn't wake.

John settled to reading an Agatha Christie and Julio and I talked. He told me he was a Jivaro Indian, a member of a tribe once infamous as headhunters. Julio had straight black hair and prominent cheekbones broadening his face, but I didn't ask whether he was fullblood Indian or *mestizo* (mixed Spanish and Indian).

He had worked as a tour guide, learned English and had worked as a bartender on a Caribbean island, he said. Now, he was a freelance journalist. I accepted what he said at face value – there was no way to check – and settled to enjoy our week's journey together, already finding him competent and easy-going. In fact he and I would travel many miles together, and he would make me feel completely comfortable in the forest.

The little town of Tamshiyacu was four hours up river and the river bus stopped there. Julio asked the owner of a smaller open canoe going up the Rio Tamshiyacu to wait while we gobbled a lunch of duck stew, rice and roasted sweet bananas. The canoe was powered by a motor up on one bulwark and a long propeller shaft pointing diagonally down into the murky river. A canoe with this arrangement is called a *peke-peke* from the sound of the motor idling.

'We call it tree-vine-river,' said Julio when we turned up the mouth of the Tamshiyacu. Tall trees on both sides made the muddy water seem narrow and dark, but they and the bushes were no longer mere walls of green. My eyes now recognised their differences, slender leaves arranged in rows, leaves like webbed feet, palm fronds, and leaves so small that only the pattern of them all was visible; tree trunks were mottled grey, others were brown and carried flowers, ferns and trailing vines. I pointed to bushes with yellow trumpet flowers.

'It's another medicine. It's used to clean the stomach,' said Julio.

Small clearings had been cut in the forest for houses – little more than platforms protected from rain and sun by large thatched roofs and open on three sides to the breeze.

At sunset, we reached the canoe's destination. Five houses and a large school, with tin roof and blue walls, stood in a pasture with pigs and cattle and children. The last of the passengers got out with their bundles. The captain, Juan, said we would stay at his house overnight.

'What about paying him?' asked John.

'Just help with the food and a gift,' said Julio.

The thatched shelter was open-sided and furnished with a kitchen table, a playpen made out of hanging clothes, a foot-treadle sewing machine and cooking pots on a hearth in a large box of baked mud. Dresses dangled from one of the rafters. A radio and cassette player stood on the table. Five children watched us strangers coming up the ladder into their home.

'I think I'll just go and test the tent. See if it's all there,' said John. 'Actually, I haven't put it up before.' He climbed down again and stood in the pasture, reading the sheet of instructions in fading twilight. Thirty children and five adults, including Julio and myself, watched in a circle.

'The crazy gringo,' announced John, pointing at himself. Julio translated. Everyone laughed.

'All you need now is rain, wind and darkness,' I told him.

Tent and fly sheet were erected in admirably short time. 'Who wants to go inside,' asked John smiling beside the open flap. One boy volunteered. He was six or seven years old and rubbed an eye itching with conjunctivitis. The other children stared and giggled when the boy came out. He smiled, but made no comment.

We placed the last tent pegs. Then John took the tent down and wrapped it away without explanation confirming that all gringos are indeed crazy. We tramped home across the rough grass in the dark.

Juan lit an oil wick and set the smoking flame on the table. The light cast shadows across the floor and made our faces ghoulish. John and I sat with Julio along a wooden railing while he answered the villagers' questions about gringos. Julio's explanations were greeted with muffled laughter and the slapping of hands killing mosquitoes on legs and arms. Suddenly, the railing broke and we fell backwards from the house, luckily landing in the grass below without injury. Even the baby giggled at the gringos.

After that, we sat on the floor in the dark, waving our hands to discourage the mosquitoes. When I became too hot and itched all over I went to crouch beside the river in the dark. Pouring water over my head brought some relief.

Supper that evening was weak rice porridge, served to the gringos without sugar because Julio knew John found the food too sweet. I was glad of the liquid to quench my thirst.

By then, Juan's wife and the three youngest children were already sleeping inside a white mosquito net hanging to the floor like a rectangular box. John took out his tent again and went to sleep in the pasture. I was borrowing a mosquito net from Julio and needed him to set it up for me. Hammocks are not used for sleeping at night on this river. Mine served as a blanket on the floor, with long cotton trousers as a pillow. I wore only underpants and lay sweating and itching inside the mosquito net, hearing hoots and howls, content to be at long last in the Amazon forest.

Mist covered the pasture and the forest early next morning. Tiny water droplets drifted across the sewing machine and table, covering everything with a fine dew. I felt myself to be floating on a raft inside a white cloud.

'Well, what's the plan?' asked John, when he eventually emerged from his tent. Julio offered him a cup of rice porridge. He tasted it.

'It's just too sweet,' he said petulantly. 'So what next? Can we get a boat up river?'

'Maybe,' said Julio patiently. 'There's a river bus at twelve and at six tonight. Maybe,' said Julio.

'What about renting a canoe?'

'It's difficult.'

'Can we borrow a canoe just for today and pay one of the family to paddle for us, if they can't spare the canoe all week?'

'It's difficult. They want to go to their garden in the forest.'

Pasture and forest re-emerged when sunshine burned off the mist. Rice and a pot of boiled fish heads were put on the table for breakfast. A son came in with a few small fish caught in a net across the river. Julio said the river was too high and food too abundant in the flooded forest for fish to be caught with nets or hooks.

After breakfast, Juan and one of his sons gathered up their machetes and a hand sprayer filled with insecticide.

'I'll wear my wellies,' I said, keen to baptise the boots bought in Iquitos with mud in the Amazon forest. I put on the right boot and then saw that something was wrong. 'Well look at that! Bloody hell! I've got two right-footed boots!'

Juan warned us of the spines from palm trees on the path. He wore rubber boots himself but his son went barefoot. Julio and I wore thong sandals. John put on running shoes.

We entered the forest in single file. It was dim and cool. Juan led us along a path through knee-high plants between the trees rising ninety feet over our heads. We could see about a hundred feet across the bushes, short palm trees and dangling vines, until the mass of vegetation closed around us. I walked behind Julio through the alluring stillness, glancing now and then at the ground to avoid tripping on tangles of roots half-buried in dead leaves.

We crossed the trunks of fallen trees over streams and swamps. Shafts of sunlight struck through where these falls had opened gaps in the forest canopy. Julio stopped at the end of one thick trunk when he found orchids growing in its fork. He carefully prised the tangle of roots from the moss growing over the bark and examined the flowers.

'It's like a butterfly,' he said, pointing to the petals. The flowers were strongly perfumed. 'I'll leave it here and collect it when we return.'

It was easier walking barefoot than in thong sandals. In the soft mud on the path leaves stuck to your feet and cool earth squeezed up between your toes. Walking behind Julio, I had no fear of snakes or scorpions but I watched for spines from palm trees and for the sharp knots of roots. Few insects buzzed; we heard only the calls of unseen birds and rustling of leaves under our feet.

After an hour, we walked into a clearing cut in the midst of the forest and surrounded by a wall of trees. The soil was blackened from the fire that had cleared vegetation two months earlier. Cucumbers were growing a foot high amid the ashes and young banana trees came higher than our knees. Juan's son began spraying cucumbers with insecticide to discourage leaf-cutter ants.

The clearing, about the size of a football field, was a gash that would clearly reheal in time, very different from the vast areas cleared elsewhere for cattle. Here the forest would recover this isolated patch as soon as the family abandoned it. Giant trees provide anchor points like the masts of a circus tent, around which smaller trees can resprout from their roots, protecting germinating seeds from burning sunlight and battering rain. Birds and lizards and snakes do not avoid the opening, as they do the wide clearances, but fly or scurry back and forth looking for food.

John and I sat on a log with our backs to the sun, clammy with sweat from forehead to ankle, blinking in the bright light. Flying insects came buzzing round, landing, crawling, biting legs and arms.

'We have to get back,' said John, when we had endured for ten minutes. He stood up. 'We don't want to miss the boat.'

It seemed to me unlikely that the river boat would pass on the river punctually at noon, but Julio could see John's eagerness to get going and turned to set off back through the forest.

'You'll get lost,' warned Juan.

Julio laughed scornfully, replying that he had never been lost in any forest. We started back along the trail, pausing when Julio snatched a green cicada from the leaf of a bush. 'It makes good bait,' he said and pulled off its head.

We walked down a hill, stepping around stretches of mud, and came to a fork in the path beside a giant web of green tree roots.

'This way,' said Julio,

'I don't think so, Julio. The other way,' said John and I together.

'I remember this old tree,' I said.

'No, no, it is this way. You see, here is my mark.' Julio smiled and held up a large leaf that dangled where the stem had been broken. John and I were impressed. Julio led us through the trees, and stopped in front of a tree with a smooth trunk to cut a gash with his machete. A white sap trickled out. 'You mix this with orange juice to clear worms from your intestines. Of course, you have diarrhoea, but it works.'

I walked barefoot behind Julio, watching where he put his feet. Suddenly, I decided I would copy exactly what he did and so learn the way of living comfortably in the forest and on the river. I would do whatever he did; eat only what he ate, bathe for the same length of time, sleep when he slept and get up when he woke. I would become his shadow. This was the only way I could experience the rhythms of life and participate myself, not just be an observer. At the same time, since I was understanding little of what was said in the local version of Spanish, the simplest conversation had to be relayed through Julio, and this brought us even closer.

If he was irritated by my behaviour as his shadow, Julio never showed it.

The noon boat never came. The early afternoon, after boiled fish and rice for lunch, was hot and bright and boring. John sighed with disappointment when two canoes passed upstream without stopping. He took out his Agatha Christie. Julio began helping to clean a fishing net tangled with leaves. I settled to writing my diary. Legs and arms now had so many insect bites that they ached with a pain like sunburn instead of itching.

We heard the put-put of a motor coming minutes before the long, thin canoe came in sight up the river. A neighbour called to the boatman to stop and we ran with our bags to greet the owner of the *peke-peke*. No one asked where he was going. It was enough that he was heading up the river. We would go as far as he could take us and see where we arrived.

There was one other passenger, a man returning home from Iquitos. His two children were waiting on the bank when we arrived several miles upriver, and helped him carry the sack of supplies and a new hammock that he'd brought them. His wife waited under the shade of their thatch shelter. A starving dog watched with tail curled between its legs.

'Julio, what are we going to do about supper tonight? We still have to catch some fish, don't we?' asked John. Julio shrugged.

'John, don't worry so much,' I said.

'Well, what shall we do?' He turned to our guide. 'Don't you want to eat tonight?'

'I certainly do.' Julio smiled. 'But I don't feel like fishing with a line over the side of the boat just at the moment, so there's nothing to be done until we get there. Wherever that is.'

John frowned. 'I wish I could be as calm as that.'

The *peke-peke* dropped us at dusk at two adjoining houses on the left bank. We paid eighty cents each for the journey, and were welcomed on the verandah by a man called Adriano, with a mop of curly black hair. John went out into the pasture to put up his tent. I crouched behind some bushes before darkness.

Adriano boiled bananas and fish for supper and afterwards we sat with some women swatting mosquitoes and enjoying coffee and cigarettes. Smoke discouraged the biting.

It rained hard during the night. Thunder boomed and rumbled across the sky. Flickering lightning revealed grey river and black trees. Rain began again in the morning, soon after we woke and put away the mosquito nets. Low white mist again hung over the narrow river, forest and the pasture. The river had risen six inches during the night.

Adriano ground rice in a hand grinder and made rice porridge and bowls of coffee. He told us there was unlikely to be a canoe going further upstream. Julio and I knew John would be disappointed. He dreamed of making it to the source of the Tamshiyacu river.

'Vile! They make things so sweet,' he exclaimed when he finally emerged from his tent and sipped the rice porridge. 'Did Adriano make a pass at you during the night?' he asked me in English when he thought Julio was out of earshot. 'He asked me if I wanted to sleep with him. And he tried to grope me.'

Men sleeping with men is not uncommon in the Amazon and rarely raises comment. Men and women marry to have children; what happens outside this relationship is of little concern. People are too isolated along the rivers and too near the fecundity of the forest to heed the cold morality of Protestant Europe.

A *peke-peke* arrived when the rain stopped, bringing a cheerful party of neighbours to work their gardens in the forest. The eldest youth carried a large basket on his back, held by a wide strap of bark round his forehead. A huge glass jar inside the basket contained a white alcoholic liquid called *masato*, which would be shared by everyone working in the clearings. Traditionally, boiled manioc is chewed by women, spat out and left to ferment in a bowl. Imported alcohol may be used today to aid fermentation. The result is a beer-like drink tasting slightly sour.

We followed the boisterous party through a tangle of small trees and bushes, where the forest was recapturing an abandoned clearing, and finally arrived at a different clearing. Hundreds of peppers, planted three months earlier between charred logs, were almost ready for their fruit to be taken to the market in Iquitos.

'It's good to plant the pepper when the moon is full,' explained Julio. 'The same with cucumber. Pineapples and bananas, it's good when the moon is in the middle.'

Young plants are sprayed with insecticide to discourage ants and beetles. Julio continued his explanation. 'When women come here during menstruation it's very bad for the plants. The plants die. When a man sleeps with his wife and they make love and the second day they go to the clearing, this also is bad.

'It's incredible but sure,' said Julio. 'It's the same with the chickens. If menstruating women give food to baby chickens, the chickens are dead on the second day.'

Julio said he didn't believe this, then added. 'If I touch the red mahogany tree I will become sick. It's bad. Every plant has a spirit. If a pregnant woman touches any medicine plant, the baby dies.' But she could take medicine prepared by someone else, he said.

'The full moon is a dangerous time because it's easy to become sick. When the women or the chicken get sick they go to the witchdoctor to get well. And they give plant medicines and also work with the spirit because all the medicine plants have a bad spirit and a good spirit.

'You can go to the witchdoctor to check your body. Sometimes he touches your hand to check your blood pressure and they may go to a special place for taking the *ayahuasca*. This drink is made from a vine growing throughout the western Amazon.

'Normally, they drink in the evening, at ten o'clock. Normally, the ceremony of the witchdoctor takes three or four hours. At this time, the witchdoctor checks which spirit has caused the problem. Then when it's finished, on the second day, the doctor says, "Don't drink sweet drink, or salt or grease," or "Don't touch another woman or a man," or "Don't eat fish or cow or monkey meat. Eat this or that – cucumber or banana." If the people break this diet they will die in one or two hours.'

There was no food in Adriano's house when we returned to the

river and it was necessary to catch some fish if we wanted to eat.
John and I fished with worms and he caught a tiny catfish.

'Only good for piranhas,' said Julio when he joined us. He quickly
caught several fish while John and I had only nibbles. There was
still not enough for supper so we bought one of Adriano's chickens
which Julio killed and Adriano cooked for an excellent supper.

'I want to meet the witchdoctor and to take the *ayahuasca*,' John
told Julio.

'Ok, we do it,' he said.

Next morning, I woke with legs, feet and waist covered in a red
rash of insect bites. My body was burning. The itching was so
intense I couldn't think of anything else.

'What are these?' I asked Julio.

'Ticks,' he said. Each tick was the red spot in the centre of a
swollen bite. Millions of these creatures live on the underside of
leaves and grasses waiting for a meal of blood. Julio sent me to the
river. 'Five minutes rubbing with soap,' he ordered.

I dived into the cold water then rubbed soap all over my body and
picked off as many red spots as I could reach. Cool water calmed the
itching but I got out of the river and dried myself when baby piranha
began nibbling toes and legs. Julio rubbed lemon juice over all the
bites. The juice tickled until it dried. Then the itching stopped
completely.

The previous days' visitors spent the morning bringing baskets of
cucumbers and stems of green bananas from their clearing. Their
canoe was loaded by lunchtime.

We started back downriver later in the afternoon, with three
women, a white-faced monkey tied by a string and a hen and her
chirping brood. The *peke-peke* paused at a house to load bananas, a
sack of peach palm fruits, and two bundles of *palmita*. We bought a
yellow fruit, the size of a rugby ball, which Julio cracked open to
reveal white seeds surrounded by a deep pulp tasting like cante-
loupe melon.

The *peke-peke* travelled swiftly down the middle of the river, except
when called to a house. 'When are you coming back?' asked a
woman, handing our captain a small gasoline drum and some
money. 'Make sure it's pure,' she said as the canoe pulled away from
the bank. 'Make sure it's pure!' she called again.

John was very disappointed that we had not gone farther up river
nor into virgin forest. That had been his dream but I didn't think Julio
had ever intended to go beating a brand new path through the forest.

'Do you think this *ayahuasca* business is OK?' John asked suddenly when we were on our way down the river to Iquitos.

'Yes, provided it's with the witchdoctor and with the proper rituals,' I replied.

He scoffed. 'Oh, yes. The rituals.'

I didn't laugh at the rituals. I thought they were probably the safeguards.

4

Rio Amazonas:
Sipping the Vine of Death

'A man could not become a true knight until he had lived in the wilderness. Only a person who had seen his "animal part", who had "died", could consciously live in culture.'
Hans Peter Duerr, *Dreamtime: Concerning the Boundary Between Wilderness and Civilisation.*

'I'VE ALWAYS THOUGHT OF A witchdoctor as a man with a bone through his nose, busy sticking pins in dolls of his enemies,' John muttered in my ear.

Our man wore green flared trousers, digital wristwatch and displayed a plump brown belly. 'Do you know what it's like to be drunk?' he asked.

We nodded.

'Have no fear.'

'Do you want one glass or two?' asked Julio.

'Which is better?'

Julio shrugged his shoulders. 'It's up to you.'

We decided to begin with one glass each and agreed the price of fifty *intis* – about two dollars – each.

'Tomorrow night, Monday,' said the man and turned away.

'What's it like?' I asked Julio after we left the house.

'It's like colour television. You will be in another world when you take it.'

It is to see the other world of spirits that *ayahuasca* is taken by witchdoctors (more properly called shamans in tribal society and *curanderos* in mestizo communities). The Quechua name means 'vine of death' – the separation of body and soul, enabling a person to travel without his body, or to fly as witches reputedly did in Europe in the Middle Ages.

Scientists have isolated the alkaloids that allow hallucinations but they cannot yet explain the exact nature of the visions. For many centuries, tribes throughout the western Amazon have used *ayahuasca* to become telephathic and clairvoyant. Shamans have seen their enemies and divined illnesses. They have worked as healers and sorcerers, restoring the spiritual balance of their communities by banishing disruptive spirits with the help of other spirits of the forest.

The vine itself has a spirit to whom the shaman of the Amahuasi, meaning True or Genuine People, chanted while preparing the potion:

> '*Nixi honi*,
> vision vine,
> boding spirit of the forest,
> origin of our understanding
> give up your magic power
> to our potion
> illuminate our mind,
> bring us foresight,
> show us the designs
> of our enemies,
> expand our knowledge,
> expand our understanding
> of our forest.'

We were staying in a small community on the edge of the forest facing the Amazon river, not far from the town of Tamshiyacu which John and I had visited with Julio the week before. Dom Julio and his wife Dona Tereza were friends of Julio's and invited us to stay in their home for a few days. Their thatched house stood in a line of raised platforms overlooking the miles of river and an island. Mooring ropes held canoes riding the waves. Pigs, chickens and dogs wandered into the shade and scratched the earth under the elevated houses.

A short bridge connected the main platform of Dom Julio's house to the kitchen standing five feet above a pool of mud. 'There are poisonous snakes down there,' said Julio, but that didn't discourage the pigs. A hen sat on her eggs in a box beside the large hearth. She gazed at us with occasional winks while we stood at the lopsided table picking over the rice we had brought, throwing away grit and black, hard grains.

Julio told Dona Tereza that we could eat the usual local foods and she was not to prepare anything special, beyond bowls of coffee from the tin provided. She was relieved. In fact John did not like the sweet rice porridge or fish and rice for breakfast but he kept his comments in English.

Don Julio and Dona Tereza sold tins of evaporated milk, bottles of Inka-colas, beers, matches, cigarettes, and tins of sardines from a counter at the front of the main platform. Only gringos could afford a tin of sardines: it cost the same as seven good-sized fresh fish, but rice and two tins fed the whole family for lunch.

It was impossible not to sleep after a meal in the heat of the day. John put up his hammock across a corner of the main room and swayed back and forth until he fell asleep. Julio said later that our hosts had taken this as a sign that the comforts of their home were lacking. This seemed a bit sensitive. It is normal practice for visitors to bring their own hammock and some food. Hanging up your own hammock had been welcomed in Brazil because it showed you felt at home.

Julio sat carving a frog on a gourd bowl. I slept on a bench. Dom Julio and three friends sat listening to a commentary on the big Sunday football match in Lima. Dona Tereza was sitting on the floor, legs outstretched to cradle her two-year-old daughter while she looked for lice in the girl's straight black hair. Flies and mosquitoes flew in and out. They disturbed Julio's concentration and he stopped carving.

Families came out of their houses when the shadows of trees on the river bank stretched across the grass. The sun was still hot but the light had softened from harsh silver to gold. A few youths, barefoot and in shorts, assembled on a nearby football pitch and dribbled the ball, waiting for more players before placing *intis* bets and starting a game.

I strolled along the path on the river bank counting fourteen canoes out on the half-mile stretch of river to the island. The main Amazon flowed out of sight behind this forest. Some people wore clean dresses or trousers and t-shirts for church while others were stripped to work. They trailed long fishing nets across the river, drifting down half a mile with the current before drawing up their nets.

A girl dipped her paddle in the water holding steady the dugout canoe in the middle of the river. Her brother stood at the back holding a weighted fishing net in his mouth and draped over his arms. He turned slowly, as if looking over his shoulder, and swung back quickly, like a spring released, flinging out the heavy net in a single strong, graceful movement. The net fell in a wide circle over the river and immediately sank.

The boy held the securing rope tightly in his fist. Sister and brother waited for the net to close two or three metres under the water, before he pulled it up into the canoe. They both watched for fish struggling to escape the hem round the bottom of the net, but this time there was none.

The double-deck ferries loaded with passengers cut through the flotilla of canoes, heading to Pucallpa, the next major town, a week's journey up the Amazon. Over them, puffed-up thunderclouds passed in front of the sun, casting our side of the river into cooler shade. The sun gave the clouds a halo, fringing them with shiny white lace.

The canoes on the river had gone home and the football game had ended by the time the sun emerged again. I accepted a neighbour's invitation for a glass of pure cane liquor at his home.

Half a dozen people assembled on the verandah to see if a gringo could swallow their fire-water without a gasp or a cough (which I did).

'You're going to drink *ayahuasca*?' asked one of the audience.

'You are going to be sick,' the man's wife told me.

Oil lamps were lit when the first stars shone in the clear sky. Fires were rekindled to fry fish and boil green bananas and rice for supper and to make coffee for gringos.

'They're not much into knives and forks here, are they?' said John. Actually it was easier and safer to eat rice with a spoon and to pick through fish with fingers, never swallowing until sure you had found all the tiny, forked bones.

Julio rigged up the mosquito nets after supper while John and I looked on. I felt inadequate beside Julio, or the other people, who were all able to improvise solutions to problems, recognise and explain the uses of dozens of forest plants, trees and creatures, and paddle canoes as if they were extensions of their bodies. Such skills and knowledge were necessary to live here comfortably and safely. I determined to learn, but in the meantime felt foolish.

Our host's five daughters went to bed after supper and the rest of us sat in the light of two oil lamps, swatting mosquitoes, sharing cigarettes and warm beer. We tried to break the spells of silence but John and I spoke Spanish too poorly and we were too much the outsiders. Not even a half bottle of rum that John produced from his bag could enliven the conversation. John and I retreated to our mosquito nets, freeing Julio, Dom Julio, Dona Tereza and two men visiting to chat and laugh at the strange ways of gringos.

I lay down, using my towel as a pillow. I could hear the breathing of the chickens, dogs and pigs. During the night these all erupted in barking, snorting and calling several times, waking the neighbours' animals and the babies.

'I think fishermen everywhere like to drink,' said Julio next morning, when several men arrived for cane liquor before going out on the river in the sunshine. It was a little after six. I went to bathe in the nearby creek.

Peruvian pop music on the radio accompanied the breakfast coffee, boiled fish and boiled manioc. The two eldest daughters ate quickly before changing into the grey school uniform skirts and white blouses they had pressed with charcoal-filled irons the day before. A dozen canoes were already on the river, each filled with immaculate girls and boys. The daughters collected schoolbooks and set out in their dugout canoe to join their friends paddling towards the school, two miles downstream.

John and I waited for Julio to organise our day's outing. Hens and dogs crept up the steps to peck and sniff in the house until chased out. They always came back. 'You'd have thought it would be easy enough to prevent the hens from coming in in the first place,' John said crossly.

Julio painstakingly sharpened his machete and then he went half a mile inland from the head of the creek to Dom Julio's garden. Once there, Dom Julio took us to gather what I called chocolate-cake fruit. The yellow or purple skinned *umari* grow to the size of mangos and are valued as a butter substitute and as a snack. The trees planted in small orchards produce two harvests annually which are gathered on the ground.

We arrived home again at noon and had a swim. The manioc from the garden would be enough for the family for a few days. Cash from the sale of *umari* fruits in Iquitos would pay for sugar, rice and other store-bought necessities. Dom Julio could lie in his hammock for the rest of the afternoon, playing with his children and talking to visitors.

Dona Tereza had washed the family laundry by hand in the river during the morning. Shirts, dresses and towels lay drying on the grass. I couldn't think why no one put up a line to help the clothes to dry faster in the breeze.

Late that night, when most families were already sleeping, we went to the *ayahuasca* session. A smoking oil lamp burned in the midst of our circle of five men, casting each person's face into long shadows. We waited cross-legged on the floor facing the *curandero* across a plastic sheet. John handed over a half bottle of rum as a gift.

Our host set out five half-litre liquor bottles, each filled with a different concoction. A smaller bottle contained perfume. He put a crucifix down on the plastic sheet and he wore another crucifix round his neck, beneath layers of an old grey suit jacket, a second jacket and a shirt. Could he be cold in this heat? I wondered.

He laid out a few crumpled hand-rolled cigarettes, a large tumbler and, finally, a brown bottle with the *ayahuasca*. He was sober, jovial and intent about his business. He unscrewed the top of the bottle and for five minutes blew a tune over the opening. When he finished, he looked seriously at the glass tumbler and declared it too big. Dom Julio went home to fetch another.

'When you take it, you must say, "I want to see everything",' Julio told us.

We sat waiting for Dom Julio to return with the smaller glass.

'How long do you have to wait to feel the *ayahuasca?*' asked John.

'One hour.'

We sat in silence, hearing frogs and cicadas in low bushes round the house and the occasional bellow of a cow or bark of a dog. Julio said he would not drink. I was glad. John wanted him to drink, but it seemed to me better that one of us should remain sober.

Dom Julio returned with a smaller glass. The *curandero* poured out a full measure of the thick brown liquid, blew tobacco smoke into the glass and handed it to me.

'Remember the words,' said Julio.

'I want to see everything,' I said in English. I swallowed the full measure in one gulp, as instructed. It tasted unbelievably bitter.

The *curandero* poured a second glass, blew smoke again and handed the glass to John.

'I want to see my true animal spirit,' he said and drank.

Our host handed another bottle to me.

'Drink a little of that,' said Julio. 'It's cane liquor.'

I took a sip and passed the bottle to John. The bottle of perfume came next.

'That's nice. You've got the makings of a derelict,' said John.

Everyone drank the same potions. Then we waited. I lay on my back on the floor, feeling my loud, steady heart beat and my stomach rising and falling. My sweaty hands rested on my chest, occasionally swatting mosquitoes.

I wanted to close my eyes but I feared falling asleep. I stared at the rafters and pin-pricks of blue-grey moonlit sky through the thatch. Hands and arms became heavier and flicked mosquitoes without command. The rafters began turning.

'In the name of the Father, the Son and the Holy Spirit,' said the *curandero* in Spanish.

Julio! Give me the antidote, I thought, shortly before vomiting violently over the edge of the platform.

'Are you OK?' John murmured. Only good spirits are permitted to visit. Bad spirits must be sent away; that is the power and the role of the *curandero*.

'He's OK,' Julio told our host.

I lay flat on my back, wiping sweat from arms and face. A naked woman stood facing me. Elaborate geometric shapes covered her shoulders and breasts. My eyes opened. She vanished. I stared at the sky.

The *curandero* was sick over the railing. I'm not alone. I thought, and closed my eyes.

Soon afterwards, I was looking from above through trees in the forest to a pond or stream with water the colour of cinnamon. I was above the trees but able to see as if only six inches from the surface of the golden water. A dozen frogs hopped over a small rock under the water. I watched them, fascinated by the place and the odd-looking frogs.

When I opened my eyes again, the beautiful place in the forest had gone. I could see the rafters of the roof. The oil lamp had gone out and we were awash in the grey illumination of the moon. Is my animal spirit a frog? I wondered – a creature which I thought of as being ugly, hopping a lot and croaking. This misinterpretation was corrected later. I had become my animal spirit: probably an owl watching the frogs with telescopic vision.

John was lying on his belly, being sick over the side of the platform.

The *curandero* began to whistle and sing slowly the tune he had whistled over the *ayahuasca* bottle calling the spirit of the vine, as the Amahuasi shaman called:

'Spirit of the forest
revealed to us by *honi xuma*

bring us knowledge of the realm
assist in the guidance of our people
give us the stealth of the boa
penetrating sight of the hawk and the owl
acute hearing of the deer
brute endurance of the tapir
grace and strength of the jaguar
knowledge and tranquility of the moon
kindred spirits, guide our way.'

Julio nudged my arm. 'Do you want to drink another glass?'

John said no. I said yes but when I sat up to receive the half glass I realised that it was not possible. I lay flat again, reassured by the droning whistlesong. Its force was friendly to us.

My eyes closed again. I was looking down through the trees on a gravel beach on a river of black water. Two animals, greyish-black with the rounded faces of *capybarys* but the size of zebras, were drinking knee-deep in the water. One shaft of sunlight shone on the animals and all round the forest was tranquil and beautiful. I stayed, looking down.

Julio bent over me. 'I'm going home. Don't give the witchdoctor any more money.'

I opened my eyes and saw John leaning over me, asking a question. I saw Julio bent towards my head. He was not there in the flesh but he was thinking of us. People I did not know appeared in front of me. I looked at layers of cloud travelling across the night sky. The brown silhouette of a frog hopped across the clouds.

I sat up. Our host was being sick again. Dom Julio had gone. An old man was being sick among the bushes in darkness.

Time was expanding and contracting. Hours had become minutes. I sat up, breathing slowly, feeling cold. 'I want to go home,' I said softly to John, who was now lying on his back.

'I want to stay a little longer,' he answered.

I stayed sitting upright, breathing slowly until the effects of the hallucinogen passed and I believed I could walk without the room moving.

'Time to go, John,' I said.

'I'll stay.'

'Are you going to sleep here?'

'No, I'll come back in a while.'

'OK. Julio said not to give the man any more banknotes. See you later.' I stepped down from the house and walked slowly along the path through grey bushes, looking for snakes in the moonlight and hearing lizards scurrying away.

Julio was just finishing putting up the mosquito net when I climbed the steps into the house.

'Thanks for putting up my net,' I said.

He nodded. 'Is John coming?'

'After a little time. Good night.' I crawled inside the net and arranged the edge of the hammock cloth to seal the bottom of the netting. I was glad to be home, away from the mosquitoes. I may have dozed but woke suddenly to be sick again.

Retching on an empty stomach left me gasping, shaking and dripping with sweat. I crawled to the kitchen to rinse my mouth with water and to drink so that if I was sick again there would be liquid in my stomach.

I woke briefly when Dom Julio and his wife slid boxes of *umari* across the floor to take away on the river boat down to Iquitos. John had still not returned and I wondered whether to go back to look for him. He arrived while I was crouched, vomiting again in front of the house, trying not to wake the household with my moans. Afterwards, I stumbled in the dark to the kitchen for more water.

'How are you feeling?' I whispered to John.

'Terrible. I feel terrible,' he said. He had been sick many times and lost his way coming back to the house. We sat on the floor too weary to move. For him, it had been a miserable five hours without visions or any sensations other than nausea.

'It's such a crude drug,' he lamented.

The next morning was grey and wet with the sort of heavy rain that gardeners welcome as a 'good soak'.

'How do you feel?' asked Julio when I awoke and watched him rolling away his mosquito net.

'Good. A bit tired.'

'Do you want to put up the hammock and sleep more?' he asked.

'No, I'm fine.'

He didn't believe me. 'Go take a shower.'

The rain was not inviting but Dom Julio said it would make me feel better. And it did. The black water of the creek, swollen by the rain, had pushed farther in the muddy Amazon, creating a swimming pool of warm water that revived a weary body.

Two days later, Julio and I were in a river bus again, travelling back up the river towards Tamshiyacu, after a visit to Iquitos. 'Jungle Boy' John had flown to Lima, en route to Cuzco by air, and we had two new travelling companions; Juan, a friend of Julio's and a tourist guide, and a young Dutch student.

Blue sky had replaced morning drizzle and we sat in sunshine on the roof of the river bus beside crates of Inka-cola, listening to music on the Dutchman's radio. Infected mosquito bites scarred his ankles. He said $1000 had been stolen from him the day before. For the past year he had been studying 'sociological aspects of tropical agriculture'; learning about the work habits of people in the tropics in order to make them more willing workers for agri-business and more responsive recipients of international development aid.

Was it farce or tragedy that someone barely able to speak Spanish, ignorant of the way of life, lacking local experience of growing food, hunting or fishing, should have the power to manipulate people in an environment of which he understood nothing?

I spoke of my desire to visit other areas of the forest in Peru, especially Madre de Dios, west of Cuzco, and the Manu National Park, which is one of the few nature reserves in the Amazon.

Julio told me he had been to Madre de Dios and knew the rivers. 'We can go together,' he declared with enthusiasm. I nodded but wanted to be more sure of him before committing myself.

We reached the house of Julio's father and stepmother three hours upriver from Iquitos, near where we had stayed before. The house stood on stilts at the top of a long sloping lawn planted with lemon and banana trees and bushes of red hibiscus. No one was home except the parrot – it was called Louro, like all pet parrots in the Amazon. We helped ourselves to boiled manioc and the remainder of a small roasted alligator.

Julio's stepmother greeted the arrival of two more gringos, the Dutchman and myself, with a grunt and scowl when she came home. Julio told the family I was Brazilian and he told me the family was angry because John and the Dane had stayed for a week without thanking them or leaving a gift. I was glad to have brought coffee, cigarettes, sugar, rice and peanuts.

I went to bathe in a stream in the forest, happy to be out of the city again, away from the roar of so many motorcycles with broken exhaust pipes and the crowds of people. The city did provide two comforts I had not yet learned to obtain in the interior: solitude and a respite from mosquitoes. I had not yet learned to wander away in a canoe to be alone, nor had I gained the automatic habit of changing into long trousers and long-sleeved shirt at sunset, and applying lots of insect repellent.

Julio's father was a short, stocky man without his son's high Indian cheekbones and straight black hair. His hair was curly black and the sun had darkened his caucasian face to a deep bronze. None of his children nor his wife's first family lived at home but we met Julio's three cousins, a friend of theirs and an Indian man living and working with the family.

'I have a house in Iquitos, but I don't like. I'm a cultivator of the soil. In the city, people have food but they won't give if you have no money,' he told me and tapped his empty pocket.

When the parents and Julio went to bed, the rest of us set out in two canoes with Juan to the Tamshiyacu Lodge, where tourists paid $30 a night to sleep in the jungle and drink cold beer. A party started on the verandah of one of the houses, with half a dozen Lodge workers telling hunting stories and one man playing a guitar.

Julio's friend Juan got very drunk. He leaned with his head next to mine, like a conspirator, and told me not to trust Julio in money matters. He claimed Julio had stolen money from a tourist while working at the Lodge, and that was why he now stayed at home with his parents. I repeated that Julio wanted to come with me to another forest area of Peru called Madre de Dios.

'You will be with him a long time if you go to Madre de Dios. You must be careful,' he said, handing me the glass and another bottle of beer. I asked if Julio had worked in the Caribbean, as he told me, and if he really had plans to build a cane liquor distillery.

'All lies. He's lying,' Juan said.

I had been in South America long enough to be sceptical of anyone's stories of what they were going to do, where they had been and what they had done. I no longer trusted anyone and kept my money belt round my waist or within reach even when taking a bath.

It did not greatly matter to me whether Julio was telling the truth about working on a Caribbean island or not. (He was. Much later, I saw the stamp in his passport). His knowledge of the forest and his gentle behaviour mattered much more. In contrast to Juan, Julio was considerate over small matters, such as hanging out towels in the sun or putting up the mosquito nets. He was not extravagant even when the gringo was paying for all the meals and beers. More important Julio was serious and uncomfortable in the city although he was relaxed and smiling in the forest.

Juan, the Dutchman and a couple of friends were still drinking, singing and playing the guitar after five hours. The owner of the house and his family had locked up the cane liquor and gone to bed.

I sat disgruntled in the moonlight beside the river watching a small anaconda swim to the shore and slide up the bank. The mosquitoes were fierce, biting horribly and making me more and more angry.

'I've waited long enough. I'm going,' I said. I pushed a canoe away from the bank and paddled away.

In the morning the other Juan in the household, Juan the cousin, a burly man in his early twenties, had promised to teach me to make a throw net, the circular net with a weighted hem. He tied strong cord between two poles on the verandah and, using a hand-held shuttle loaded with green thread, looped and tied fifty knots round a spacer bar called a gauge. He started the second row then passed the netting shuttle and gauge to me. I tied the first knot slowly and badly.

He took back the shuttle in one hand, held the gauge in the other, and again showed me how to keep the thread tight, wrap it round the gauge and tie the knot along the top of the gauge. The manoeuvre took a couple of seconds; holding, releasing and pulling the thread in a harmonious flow like fingers playing a piano.

'He says you must pull the knot hard,' advised Julio from his hammock.

I began again, commanding my fingers to follow the sequence so automatic to Juan's fingers. The nylon thread cut my fingers when I pulled it tight. Knots came undone after I'd tied four or five more along the row. Juan always told me to start again. I lacked the long, hard nails and dexterity even to undo my own knots.

Juan the cousin sat on a stool and continued working on his own new throw net. His fingers worked as if without instruction. The netting shuttle in his right hand weaved between the threads with a speed that seemed to me to be miraculous. If I watched, concentration on my own net was lost and more mistakes were made.

I completed the fiftieth knot and reached the end of the second row later in the morning. Juan tied the last knot to the first knot. Thus the net was made into a circle. He started a third line and handed the net back to me.

The new line of knots had to be kept parallel to the row above; as well as uniform along the top of the gauge and tied correctly, and the strings pulled tight. If not, the rows would be uneven when you reached the end, or the beginning, of the circle. My sweaty, slippery fingers dropped the gauge and the netting shuttle several times. Salty sweat stung in cuts. Thumb muscles ached.

Three hours working on the fishing net was enough. I went into the kitchen to see if I could help Julio's stepmother. She handed me a big wooden mallet and told me to pound a heap of boiled *palmita* (heart of palm) in a shallow wooden bowl. She took handfuls of the creamy-green fibres and squeezed out the water. Half an hour of pounding and squeezing produced a mash of broken fibres that then needed to be crushed, using a granite rock as a rolling pin.

Chopped roasted peanuts were added and everyone sat down to a large lunch of fish, *yuca*, beans, rice and the boiled palmita mash. I was given such a large portion of the mash that I thought after a while that I was eating grass. Everyone slept the remainder of the day except the guide, who left for Iquitos.

Mosquitoes always vanished like Draculas at sunrise, leaving us in peace until the colours of sunset were fading. Seven rows of knots had been completed on the first day and I began again as soon as I woke, while water was being heated for coffee and some extraordinarily bony fish were being fried for breakfast.

I was pleased to be learning a useful skill that might occupy the waiting time that characterises life and travel in the Amazon. Cousin Juan brought out his own completed throw net, eight metres in diameter, containing fifty thousand knots.

Five people listened while he explained the pattern of the circular net that allows it to open flat. He showed us how to double the number of knots in a row after ten lines and to increase again after twenty-five lines. I wrote down the pattern but no one understood my instructions when I read them aloud to double-check.

Julio had the annoying habit of nodding that he understood even when he didn't. He told Juan and the others that I had not understood. But it was not a problem of language. I *did* understand the pattern. It appeared that they simply could not convert the practical task of net-making into an abstract pattern of numbers.

Juan presented the shuttle and the gauge as gifts to me. I felt I was sharing a minor part of his forest life. The thousands of knots necessary to make the fish net would also be tying together a rope bridge over which to enter his culture.

The men of the family went to the clearing after breakfast with machetes and baskets, the women visited neighbours, leaving the house in silence. Julio dozed in a hammock. The Dutchman read a

Spanish-Dutch grammar book. I concentrated on fingers and thumbs and tying knots correctly.

Twenty Peruvian tourists, in new straw hats and bright cotton clothes, walked into the village in the middle of the morning. Their visit to an authentic Amazonian peasant's house included the bonuses of a parrot, a 'Brazilian' (me) making a fishing net, and glasses of lemonade hastily made with lemons from a tree outside the kitchen.

'Is this the Amazon?' asked one of the ladies pointing to the river, the sweat on her forehead making her make-up run.

The group had come to the Lodge from Iquitos the day before and would be flying home to Lima that evening. A few of them looked into the kitchen and declined the offer of cool water to drink. 'Let's go,' some of them murmured but everyone wanted to be photographed with Louro the parrot on their shoulder or outstretched arm.

I remembered a wealthy Peruvian in Lima telling me he wouldn't like the Amazon. 'Why not, you've never been there?' I had asked.

'No, I wouldn't like it. I mean, I'm civilised,' he had said.

Even we ourselves were obliged to return to civilisation on the river bus the next day. A French Canadian sat among the passengers, returning after nine days inside the forest. 'It's enough for me.' He pointed to his legs covered with insect bites. 'You know what that is?' he asked.

Julio laughed.

'Ticks,' I said and explained the treatment of a scrub and lemon juice.

He had paid $135 for nine days, of which his guide received $25. 'He saw many snakes I didn't see,' he said. 'And he was bitten on the ankle by a snake, maybe a bushmaster, but he was OK.'

5

Rio Ucayali: The Great Anaconda

'What is the mystery of the Indians, which inevitably makes them victims?
They have physical beauty and a feeling for the beautiful, even for art, in
their primitive life. They live only for a total and unrestricted liberty,
created for their convenience. Their misfortune is that this degree of liberty
looks like a defiance. It is not; it is the spontaneous, elemental, vital refusal
of everything imposed upon them by nature and man. It is this natural,
untamable liberty that enrages the whites.'

Lucien Bodard, *Green Hell*.

THE HOOTER SOUNDED. The diesel engine revved, shaking the deck.
The *Huallaga* turned in the black river to begin a week's voyage up
the Amazon and Ucayali rivers to Pucallpa, passing the lights of
hotels and bars along the front of Iquitos and the oil lamps of Belen
shining in the dark. Julio and I had agreed to travel together to
Madre de Dios, a thousand miles to the south in Peru. We travelled
as friends, though I was paying all expenses and would give him a
substantial gift when eventually we parted.

We had intended to leave for Pucallpa, where Julio had a brother
we could stay with, on another boat earlier in the week but when I
saw the dirty, battered thing, a floating shoe box, I declined to sail in
such an ugly contraption.

The *Huallaga*, on the other hand, was a relic of the rubber days
and looked like a proper ship with a pointed bow and big black
funnels. She and her sister ship had been restored by German
director Werner Herzog for 'Fitzcarraldo', a film very loosely based
on the life of rubber baron Carlos Fitzcarrald. Both ships were now
sadly in poor condition again; windows and doors were broken or
missing, everywhere was dirty.

'Fitzcarraldo' tells of a man's obsession to build an opera house in
Iquitos. The dream of Carlos Fitzcarrald in fact was principally to
get as much rubber as possible from the Indians in the very remote

area of the Amazon between Peru and Bolivia. He never built an opera house.

One of the guests to Fitzcarrald's fiefdom in 1897 was quick to see the mutual advantages for Church and Commerce from his host's activities. A Father Sala wrote in his report to the Peruvian Government:

'Through terror and moderate punishments, [the Indians] will feel obliged to throw themselves at the mercy of the missionary father, and he in turn will be able, with great charity and prudence, to exercise his divine ministrations on those unfortunate creatures . . . Once a rubber boss has subjugated the ferocious Indian at gunpoint, the time will be opportune for the missionary father to immediately step in and offer him the services and consolations of our Holy Religion . . . By colonising the lands [of the Indians], surrounding and absorbing them, we can obligate them either by force or shame, to accept the customs of civilised people.'

An unofficial partnership the world over between Church, commerce and the military has worked for centuries to coerce Indians from the wilderness to live within the picket fence of civilisation. Colonists have wanted slave labour; missionaries have wanted converts; soldiers and adventurers have wanted to win new lands and riches for themselves. Rubber was the new wealth in the Amazon at the end of the nineteenth century. Thousands of people came from all over the world to find the white latex.

One such couple from London reached Fitzcarrald also in 1897. Lizzie Hessel and her husband Fred arrived on their way to the rubber station in Bolivia that Fred was to manage. Fitzcarrald came to meet them on the river but on the return journey the steering chain of his steamer broke, by accident or sabotage, and the boat was washed away. Fitzcarrald drowned. Lizzie and Fred travelled on by canoe and reached their two-storey home in Bolivia in March 1898 after travelling 4000 miles up the Amazon. Fred worked in the office downstairs and Lizzie managed their home above. Always the Europeans were fascinated by the Indians, though reactions sharply varied. 'The servants are Indians and can only be made to work by the whip. To be kind is no good, they only laugh at you. They are lazy people but I think they are faithful,' Lizzie wrote to her family while awaiting their letters and parcels of London fashion magazines.

'It wants a tremendous lot of patience to civilise the people here; they always have a longing for their old life, they run away for three

months, six months and very often longer. We send after them, and
then give them a hundred lashes; it is the only remedy, of nothing
else are they afraid. If you are kind they take advantage and steal
everything possible,' Lizzie wrote again, in October 1899.

Lizzie died nine weeks later, probably of yellow fever. She was
buried on the river bank. Attempts to civilise the Indians by the
whip or the crucifix ended in the remote Amazon when the world
price of rubber collapsed in 1911. The white men (and their wives)
abandoned the forest.

Indians were left more or less in peace. Greed for gold (yellow,
white or black) and greed for souls may be the causes of most wars
waged by the civilised but they seem inadequate to explain the
intensity of the continuing campaign to eradicate, convert or
improve all naked people. Perhaps their 'innocence', reported by
almost all travellers from the earliest Jesuits to present-day
anthropologists, ignites our jealousy.

'The sunrise! The sunrise!' said Julio, waking me. A white column of
light shone on the water from a bright white halo over the forest in
the east. We were now on the Ucayali river, having passed during
the night the mouth of the Marañón, the other major headwater of
the Amazon. More water flows down the Marañón fork, but the
Ucayali is two hundred miles longer and the latter is considered the
source of the Amazon.

The Shipibo Indians call the Ucayali 'the Great Anaconda',
referring to its broad meanders, and speak of *Ronin*, the cosmic
anaconda of the river and the Milky Way, who lies coiled round the
edge of the world.

On board our boat, one dry bun and a mug of watery rice porridge
came each day soon after sunrise. Lunch appeared according to the
whim of the cook; rice, beans, chicken or a few fish bones in stock
soup and sometimes spaghetti looking like boiled intestinal worms.
Rice with a bit of fish and a mug of lukewarm, sweet coffee arrived at
sunset. Like other passengers, Julio and I bought food whenever we
stopped. We tasted every type of fruit the girls were selling at each
community and Julio pointed to trees and plants that we saw on the
banks telling me their names and uses.

Julio proved to be an ideal travelling companion. Neither of us felt
the need to be always talking or always together. We were still
somewhat reserved, avoiding harsh words that might break our
friendship over trivial matters, but he had invited me to stay in his

house while waiting for the ship to depart and we had celebrated his birthday with a dinner for some of his friends with a birthday cake with candles in a Chinese restaurant. Julio paid a very great compliment when he told a friend I was *tranquilo*, high praise from a people who distrust the hustle and agitation normally associated with gringos.

The hours of the journey merged into days, like trees on the bank merging into the forest. There was no importance to remember which evening we stopped to load heavy boards at a sawmill, nor how many beers we drank sitting in the ship's bow in the evenings, nor how many thousands of insects jumped or flew round the lights whenever we called in at a riverside community at night.

Women nursed their babies and talked with other women, girls looked after brothers, men and youths gambled at cards. One old man, with a face of warts and wrinkles, inspected my fishing net, now nearly three feet in length. He watched me working and took the net in his fingers to peer closely at the knots. 'Not bad, for a learner,' he said with a nod.

Torrential rain fell for hours one night, forcing the ship to nudge in among an island of reeds for lack of forward visibility, and soaking almost every passenger through holes in the roof. Our reward came at sunrise next morning, when every branch and bush and blade of grass of the forest shone as if created anew. I had expected the Indian languages to have many words for greens, like Arabic words for camels and Eskimo words for snow. It was a surprise to discover that the Kayapo, on the river Xingu, use the same word for green, blue and yellow.

'Red is their basic colour. Black comes from the same word as death,' I had been told back in Belém at the mouth of the Amazon by an American missionary nurse Beth-Ann Smith, who had spent fourteen years among the Kayapo.

'Red is a form of protection against the spirit world and so the Kayapo will paint their whole faces red to be protected. For example, when the Kayapo women dream of someone who has died they believe that the spirit has come to visit them and so they will paint their whole faces red after having a dream like that.'

Chilean artist Roland Stevenson had told me also of his experiment with Yanomami children. One day he showed a colour chart to the students at a Catholic mission school.

'What colour is this?' he asked.

'Red,' the children answered.

'What colour is this?'
'Yellow.'
'What colour is this?'
'Blue.'
'What colour is this?'
No one answered.

'They looked, but they couldn't tell you "green",' the artist told me. 'A person born in the forest always seeing green, doesn't seem to feel or sense green. They see all the colours but there's no green.

'When I go in the forest with them,' he went on, 'they stop and point up to a little bird, a tiny little creature up in the leaves. They don't see the forest, but they see the animal. It's a fantastic thing!'

Green becomes the unremarkable background of the forest. This is a great contrast to red, which is the rarest colour in the forest and important to all tribes for painting their faces and bodies. Tribes throughout the Amazon grow *urucu* bushes for their pods of oil red seeds.

Black designs on the body to enhance beauty are also common among the Kayapo and the Shipibo and Conibo along the banks and tributaries of the Ucayali.

The Shipibo used to decorate themselves, their houses and their possessions with intricate geometric designs. These are gifts from Ronin, the cosmic anaconda whose body contains all designs. The custom is fading due to missionary teachings and the influence of the civilised; copies of the intricate designs are destroyed as 'matters of the Devil'. Designs are now applied only to fabrics and to pottery but every person carries a spiritual pattern within themselves. It is this pattern a shaman sees and manipulates at a healing session under the influence of *ayahuasca*.

'Face paintings confer upon the individual his dignity as a human being: they help him to cross the frontier from Nature to culture, and from "mindless" animal to civilised Man. Furthermore, they differ in style and composition according to social status, and thus have a special function,' wrote anthropologist Levi-Strauss in *Tristes Tropiques*.

'You're going to Pucallpa?' asked one of the crew who had been admiring my fishing net. 'Be careful in Pucallpa. There are lots of robbers there. Plenty of people smoking, taking drugs, drinking. Be careful. They take your watch, your wallet, anything. Then they have money for cocaine and drinking.'

I nodded.

'It's very dangerous at night. To go out alone at night, you will be robbed. A knife to your throat. It's nothing for the people on cocaine,' he said.

He dashed away when the ship's engine suddenly stopped, and for ten minutes we drifted in darkness down the river.

Drizzle and mist hung over the river at dawn on the seventh day, and the air felt cold. It was no longer a surprise that the forest along the foothills of the Andes is called 'cloud forest'.

We would be arriving in Pucallpa later in the morning and it was time to repack my bag. I knew as soon as I picked up the bag that someone had stolen something. I searched twice before realising that my camera had gone during the night.

Julio went to tell the captain and returned to say the crew would search the ship. He checked his own bag. The Swiss Army knife 'Jungle Boy' John had given him in Iquitos and his own small camera had gone.

I was bristling with fury. This was one robbery too many! I went to shave and brush my teeth, but there was no water in the tap. Typical. What would be the purpose of buying another camera in Pucallpa, even if available, just to have it stolen.

One of the crew called me to the lower deck. I went, towel still over shoulder and toothpaste spread on the toothbrush in my hand. Three or four members of the crew, Julio and myself started searching in the bow of the ship. I muttered about offering a reward. We searched between boards of lumbar stacked on the lower deck, into dark alcoves of the superstructure, even the pantry of the cook.

'Oh, this is pointless! I want to search the cabins,' I said.

'Then go upstairs,' said one of the crew, probably glad to be rid of a gringo bleating about rewards, police and the Guarda Civil.

Julio found my camera in an upstairs corridor, wrapped in a ball of cloth inside an old sack. The search continued for his camera, even going down into the padlocked hold and searching passengers' luggage. No one complained.

But the Peruvian crew knew what they were doing. A few minutes later the ship pulled into the river bank, and the gangplank was extended. One man and four youths were told to step ashore. None of them carried baggage but they smiled bravely as if they wanted to be put ashore at an unknown spot on the Ucayali river with the mist swirling round.

Bells rang and the ship pulled away from the bank to continue the journey to Pucallpa without the thieves. Peruvian methods worked.

It was good justice as far as I was concerned; though I would have also taken their clothes. I had no doubt that if police had been on board our ship the gang would have been put ashore only after being beaten up.

Unfortunately, we never found Julio's camera nor the money he said he'd put inside it for safekeeping. All the same, I paid a bonus to the crew of $10, in the hope that they would be equally helpful to the next hapless gringo.

The ship reached Pucallpa in mid-morning, with the hot sun shining in a bright blue sky, and moored in a line of boats beyond two sawmills. The population of Pucallpa has more than doubled in the last twenty years, since the road from Lima was opened, allowing refugees from the Maoist guerrillas in the Andes to reach the city, and local peasants coming with hopes of a better life in the sawmills, small businesses, and the beer factory.

'It's like a part of Lima,' said Julio when we took a taxi to go to his brother's house.

Filthy, smelly and squalid, I thought. Our taxi headed down a bumpy street lined with ditches of stagnant water.

The house of Julio's half-brother had five rooms and a backyard full of rusting motorcycle parts and rotting vegetables. Jorge had become so fat since Julio had last seen him that Julio looked at him in silence for a few moments before recognising him.

Jorge operated a motorcycle repair shop in the front room of the house and he and a neighbour were reassembling the engine of a black Suzuki. Julio's sister came from the dark kitchen to greet us and led the way to another brother's home in the next street.

It was a small wooden house, painted pale blue, with three rooms. A big refrigerator stood on the bare earth in the front room along with four steel-framed armchairs wrapped with plastic. Beds and other furniture crowded the dark middle room. A four-week old baby was sleeping on a bench while an elder sister with a squint watched American cartoons on television. Julio's brother was relaxing in a hammock in the kitchen at the back.

Julio pointed to the tin roof. 'This is a rich house.'

His sister spread a tablecloth, set out plates, spoons and small napkins, ready for rice, a couple of pieces of meat, boiled green bananas and potato. Two small parakeets climbed down from the rafters onto the table and helped themselves to rice left on a plate. A mouse walked over jars and tins on a shelf along the back wall.

The family sat in the front room after lunch eating tangerines from the fridge, discussing the robbery on the ship and where we were going, and whether their daughter's eyes could be corrected by glasses or by surgery.

'One day I want to civilise all the animals out there,' remarked Julio later.

'How do you mean?'

'Make them like us. It can be done. In the Indian villages I have seen the birds and the animals. They are not in cages and still they don't run away.'

Did to be 'civilised' mean to be tame?

We walked into town late the next afternoon to photocopy my diaries and looked at cameras to replace Julio's that had been stolen. I offered to buy a Canon camera for $50 as part of my gift to him for all his help but he declined. Over tea and cakes, we planned how to get out of Pucallpa. Julio had been that morning to see a man with a car who sometimes drove to Puerto Maldonado.

'If the car doesn't go, we can travel up the river to Atalaya,' I suggested, hoping to walk two hundred miles beyond the furthest point of navigation to where people said there was a road. Hope and vagueness are two essential qualities of travel in the Amazon.

'No, no. Mafia. Cocaine. It's not possible,' responded Julio.

'I'd still like to travel that route. I don't want to leave the river yet. Let's at least get to Atalaya and we can always fly out from there.' I was also mystified that Julio didn't seem to know the route by road to Cuzco from Pucallpa. After all, he must have followed it if, as he claimed, he'd already been to Puerto Maldonado.

Julio announced next morning that we should go to the river to ask about boats to Atalaya. The *Huallaga* was still loaded with its lumber. We were told Julio's camera had not been found and that the river men put ashore on our journey had reached Pucallpa. It was now said that they were innocent and that the cameras, knife and money had been stolen by a book salesman and his friend who had got off with us here and had disappeared into the town.

Julio asked along the river front, but there were no boats or *balsas* going upriver for at least eight days. Jorge's half-brother owned a *peke-peke* and we took him to a bar to talk business over beers. It was proposed that if I paid for a barrel of gasoline and gave an undefined amount of money, he would take us all the way to Atalaya. The journey would take seven or eight days. We would be able to stop wherever we wanted, camp beside the river and, perhaps, visit native Shipibo villages.

'A mosquito net is indispensable,' he said. 'Do you have a gun? We need for security. For shooting birds.'

Julio did most of the talking. I nodded my head, poured beers and hoped I was understanding the mood of what was being said. The brother agreed to take us but said he could not leave for another week.

We waited the week for Julio's brother, but on the seventh day he announced that he didn't want to go up river after all. By now, Julio and I had been nine days waiting in Pucallpa. It seemed much longer, despite the hospitality of his family. Stray dogs roamed in noisy packs. Julio's niece bawled or pouted nastily if she didn't get everyone's attention all the time. People pissed against the shutters of shops in the town. Fumes and roars filled the house whenever a motorcycle engine had to be tested. Jorge sang songs of praise to God. The Church of god of Peru was very active in Pucallpa.

Like a man with cabin fever in the Canadian winter, I came to detest the way Jorge chewed with his mouth open and spat fish bones onto the grubby table while he talked. My mind was numbed by boredom. I withdrew inside myself, preferring hours making the fishing net to having to see the squalid life all around.

Pucallpa was indeed a culture of poverty – not of poor people but of socially accepted dirt, ugliness, brutality and laziness. It was the town where civilisation ended. It seemed impertinent to suggest cleaning up the rusted motorcycle parts and plastic bottles in the garden, or to plant fruit trees or to keep chickens, or to collect rain water instead of buying it from the man who had a tap.

'The people here have a different mentality,' agreed Julio.

The town belonged to civilised society but, by the standards of civilisation, it was barbarous. When Thomas Hobbes said the savage life was 'solitary, poor, nasty, brutish and short' he must have been thinking of the slums of the civilised world.

I stayed outside, feeling ungenerous to all, thoroughly bored, and continued making my circular fishing net. The only relief to this tedium was that Julio's sister was a good cook, especially of soup. Sometimes I went with her to the early morning market to buy fish and vegetables, washed intestines, eggs and bread for the family. We also went together into the town one afternoon for her to choose a dress as a thank-you gift.

'I want to be with the missionaries,' Julio said mysteriously one evening. I didn't understand, so he explained that he had been schooled by American Baptist missionaries who had replaced his

Indian name with the civilised name of Julius Caesar. This was an act Julio had found it hard to forgive, but now he thought he had overcome his hatred for gringo missionaries. He couldn't tell me, however, how being 'with the missionaries' would help.

One afternoon, we went out to the calm of a lake a few miles from Pucallpa to interview the director of the Summer Institute of Linguistics (SIL) whose campus overlooks the Pucallpa lake.

The SIL operates openly in the United States as a fundamentalist missionary organisation winning souls for a Protestant Christ. They operate in the forests of Peru and Brazil as a language school teaching isolated Indians to read and write and translating the Bible into Indian languages. They have been called shock troops for the host governments. These clean-living Americans are the perfect instruments of the local national policy to absorb Indians and their land into the consumer, wage-labour society.

The missionaries have lots of money, patience and zeal. Best of all, they are gringos – foreigners whose work, if criticised, can be denied by the local governments. Their techniques have included hiding radio loudspeakers in baskets with gifts dropped on Indian villages by parachute. While the Indians gather round the gifts from heaven the missionaries speak to them from the plane overhead, seeming to answer their questions just as the booming voice of God answered Moses.

'It is not difficult to imagine how enormous an impression the mystery of the baskets – in conjunction with the booming voice from the metal bird overhead that answered questions, gave instructions and promised further gifts – must have made on the Auca,' wrote Peter Broennimann in *Auca on the Cononaco*.

Julio was tense even before we reached the campus of the Summer Institute of Linguistics. 'They are killing the Indians,' he said suddenly. He had told me he worked as a freelance journalist (another reason why he wanted an all expenses paid trip to Madre de Dios), so I always questioned him when he made this sort of vague assertion.

'Do you mean with bullets or destroying their cultures?'

'They are stealing pearls from the lake.'

'Julio, where are the oysters in the lake? There aren't any! Why would rich gringos, who have more money than you can imagine, want to come here to steal a few pearls?'

Julio refused to answer my questions. I had pressed him too hard.

Perhaps fortunately, the director of SIL whom we had gone to interview was away.

We waited another week to leave Pucallpa but two more offers of transport fell through at the last moment. I suggested to Julio that we didn't have any more time. 'Either we leave tomorrow by boat or we abandon the river and get out by bus.'

We left by bus next morning, along a dirt road smelling of lemon blossom. In the afternoon, the bus entered a gorge with ferns and vines cascading over 1000-foot walls and pencil-stemmed trees growing up from the depths. The spray of waterfalls spread across the road and seemed to be washing down my cheeks, taking with it weeks of weariness and boredom.

'You're hot,' said Julio, slapping my sweaty bare shoulder.

'No, I'm happy again. I'm smiling again. I'm alive again!' We laughed loudly.

There was something pleasant about being flung from side to side by the swaying of the bus and lurching back and forth against the seat with every jump on the brakes. It was like riding a fairground carousel, going round and round without ever arriving. We climbed up the side of the Andes and, by nightfall, reached bald moors where sheep and llamas grazed tended by shepherds speaking Quechua, the language of the Incas.

Our priority in the morning, after changing buses for some reason in the middle of the night, was to buy thick sweaters in the town we had arrived at and to change from shorts into long trousers. It was a relief to be out of the heat and humidity of the Amazon forest, which boiled your bones no matter how refreshing its frequent cool showers felt on the skin. Suddenly we were cold. I, at least, found the chill invigorating and did not want to have a break, despite the coming sixteen-hour journey to Ayacucho. Julio and I were both worn out but I was afraid that we would get stuck again if we stopped for any reason. Thus, after breakfast of eggs, bread and coffee, we spent a long time trying to get seats on already over-crowded buses and waiting for one bus that was rumoured to be half-empty but didn't arrive because of a landslide.

Julio's considerable patience ended at three o'clock. 'I think we go tomorrow,' he said. We went to find a hotel, but at the first, Julio said, 'Let's try up the street.' We tried several others but they were full or too dirty and eventually we returned to the hotel Julio had not wanted to enter.

'Why don't you want to go inside?'

'Maybe there's another,' he said.

I was weary of these evasive answers. 'I want to know why we are avoiding the hotel. Have you stayed here before?'

'Yes.'

'What happened?'

'Nothing. If you want, we go inside.'

We went inside but the room was unacceptable because there was no way to lock the door.

'It's very expensive,' he said, though the price was the same as the others. 'It's dirty.' His relief was obvious when we left.

We went to one of the hotels we had previously rejected and got a perfectly good double room with balconies looking across the town to the bare hills. I was annoyed that Julio had not answered my question and I decided to speak rather than harbour resentment. 'Julio, why do you not want to go to the other hotel?'

'If you want to go, we go there.'

'No. I want to know why *you* do not want to go.'

'If you want to go, we go.'

'You said you stayed there before. What happened?'

'If you want to go, we go,' he said and picked up his bags.

'No, Julio, listen. When we travel together as friends, I expect people to be honest. I want to know what happened.'

He did not answer.

I took a shower and went out for a walk, feeling totally infuriated. Julio's obstinate passivity was the same passivity that has unleashed the savagery of the white man with sword or shotgun. I would have preferred an open row. Shouting at each other would have been better than this soft absorption of whatever I said. Perhaps unfairly my confidence in him had gone now and I no longer trusted him completely.

Julio was in his bed when I went back to the hotel. He said he had fever, sore throat and aching muscles.

'I'll go for injection,' he said.

'What infection do you have?' I asked.

'I don't know. Something. Maybe flu.'

'There's nothing for flu. It's viral. Take an aspirin and you'll feel better.' I wanted to tell him to take one of his jungle medicines, but kept quiet.

We both seemed in better humour in the morning and caught an early bus towards Cuzco. Julio's flu had disappeared.

*

The mountain road was too narrow for vehicles to pass except at passing places. Several times we stopped face to face with trucks while the drivers shouted at each other until one of them backed up. Both were afraid of reversing and getting too near the edge – if it fell over, no vehicle would stop rolling for a mile to the bottom of the valleys.

Our road joined cobbled sections of the Royal Inca highway that ran 3,250 miles along the spine of the Andes to Cuzco. The Incas had no wheeled vehicles and so their roads went straight up and down the sides of the valleys. Fortunately the modern gravel road tacked back and forth across the steepest slopes.

This was the route of Pizarro and the Spanish soldiers who conquered Cuzco in 1533. They were in search of treasure equal to what Cortez had captured from the Aztecs in Mexico eleven years earlier, and the first gold from Peru was in fact paid as an eleven-ton ransom to free the royal Inca from his Spanish captors. It reached Europe in December of 1533. Four months later the Inca was baptised, then garrotted and buried.

Inevitably his vast golden ransom only increased the Spanish craving for gold. Rumours of El Dorado (the golden man) inspired dozens of Spanish expeditions into the dark Amazon. Thousands of Indians from the mountains were conscripted as porters, but the adventurers never encountered the road nor the city Roland Stevenson had discovered.

Pizarro, on his expedition, became 'so enraged at the Indians inability to tell him where to find gold and spice trees that he ordered some burned, others torn apart by dogs', recounted Roger D. Stone in *Dreams of Amazonia*. What is this fury in us which the Indian can so easily ignite?

It was dark when Julio and I reached the stone buildings and cobbled streets of Cuzco, on the sixth day of our exhausting dash by bus from Pucallpa.

We booked into a two star hotel, in order to enjoy hot showers and comfortable beds. There was no hot water, despite promises. It did no good to be angry or even to ask '*Why?*' We went out for a meal, then climbed into beds heavy with layers of blankets and immediately fell asleep.

The next day, May 19, Julio and I celebrated my thirty-first birthday, with Hawaiian pizza, red wine and beers in a tiny restaurant and cheered by crackling flames in its brick oven.

We stayed five days in Cuzco, during which Julio and I seemed to mend our friendship after our estrangement in Ayacucha. He worked hard to find transport from Cuzco down into the Amazon forest either at Puerto Maldonado or Manu – both on the eastern side of the Andes in an area of Peru called Madre de Dios.

Part of this area of cloud forest and Andean highlands, protected from intruders by its remoteness, was declared Manu National Park in 1974. It is one of the most important reserves in the Amazon basin because of its wide diversity of flora and fauna. Over 6000 square miles of park and adjoining private lands were declared a UNESCO Biosphere Reserve in 1977.

Only scientists are allowed inside the sanctuary. Other visitors must keep to the border along the Manu river. The restriction may reduce the impact of civilisation on the area, but it also betrayed the myopia of our technological age. Where are the painters, musicians or dancers? Does our sense of place come only by counting tree species or giving names to dragonflies?

At best, this remains a partial view. It is unrelated, as Barry Lopez has remarked in *Arctic Dreams*, to the desire 'to know what is beautiful and edifying in a faraway place. Whenever we seek to take swift and efficient possession of places utterly new to us, places we neither own nor understand, our first and often only assessment is a scientific one. Our evaluation remains unfinished,' he wrote of the Arctic. A similar tragedy persists in the Amazon.

It turned out to be possible, though unlikely, that Julio and I would be able to travel up the Madre de Dios river. For now, we were travelling on the first available daytime truck to Puerto Maldonado, where yet another of Julio's brothers lived. Going by road was a deliberate choice, instead of flying, so that we could watch the transformation from grass moorland to tropical rain forest down the side of the Andes. We had missed this in the night travelling up from Pucallpa. And in fact we missed the sight once more, because of delays, and instead spent a dangerously cold night in the back of the open truck without blankets or sleeping bags, since the driver refused to have us inside his warm cab. The 110-mile journey took over forty hours. This speed was considered miraculous – the journey can take eleven days during the rainy season, when there are avalanches.

6

Rio Tambopata:
'Just in Love with the Jungle'

'What is beautiful has always a basis in what pleases us. The sublime, from its association with what is great or violent, is necessarily based to some extent on fear.'

Edmund Burke.

IT WAS OBVIOUS as soon as we reached Puerto Maldonado that Julio did not know anyone in the town; his brother had left the day before, though Julio had telephoned twice from Pucallpa at my expense; furthermore his friends, the people with canoes, on which we were relying to get out into the forest, had all 'gone away'. Julio had lied.

I was furious. How could we travel on the river without transport? Who could give us reliable information? Where could we go to get away from the noise of chainsaws and radios? Had we come to this region of the Amazon all for nothing? I had hoped to recover part of Julio's travelling expenses and pocket money, the return ticket to Iquitos and, already, $120 in gifts, by saving money on canoe and guide. I blamed myself for having wanted to believe what Julio had told me and I was angry to be still dependent on him for Spanish translations. Suddenly, our friendship was frosty again, like the unusually chilly weather blowing down the streets from the snow-capped Andes.

We ate lunch in silence, each waiting for the other to speak.

'Julio, we have a problem. You said you knew people here – guides with boats. But you don't know anyone here. Even I know more about the region than you do,' I said.

'Yes,' he answered, only nodding his head. He wouldn't fight of course, which only infuriated me more.

The next day I took the half-hour flight back to Cuzco to change more dollars for all the extra expenses and to collect the sleeping-bag and blankets left for safekeeping at the hotel. My flight back to

Puerto Maldonado was confirmed for the next morning.

'No, there is no reservation,' said the woman in the AeroPeru office when I went on arrival in Cuzco to double confirm.

'Yes, I have a confirmed reservation. See the ticket,' I said.

'No, the airplane is full. You must go after two weeks.'

Fortunately, the ticket could be transferred to Faucett Airlines, the only other airline in Peru. I flew back the next morning with supplies of coffee, tea, spaghetti, cheese and brandy that were all considerably cheaper in Cuzco than in Puerto Maldonado. After the robbery in Manaus, the expenses of going to Lima, buying new camera equipment, paying for Julio and the prospect now of a lot more expenses simply to get into the forest, I was becoming concerned that my money would not last.

While I was away, Julio had found a guide, Dom Gerardo, who would come himself and bring a motorman with him.

'I want to talk serious with you, Dennison,' Julio said, sitting on the edge of his bed. He had become friendly with a Swedish woman who wanted to go out into the forest for ten days. She could pay half the expenses for that period.

Anna-Maria sat in the shaded courtyard of the hotel. 'The aim is to get into virgin forest away from people,' I explained.

'This is exactly what I want,' she said with the excited laugh with which we were to become all too familiar. Anna-Maria was, she said, a single woman again, happily divorced from a lawyer, with adult children, and paying for her travels third class by renting her flat to the British Embassy in Stockholm.

We visited Dom Gerardo later to pay half the fee and give him money to buy a barrel of gasoline. Where could we go to be in forest undisturbed by settlers or logging? He suggested the Tambopata river, which joins the Madre de Dios river at Puerto Maldonado. It would be easy to bring back Anna-Maria after ten days. We decided to leave early the next morning, giving Anna-Maria, Julio and myself time to buy food, fishing hooks and line, cartridges and a machete.

At least 30,000 people live in the scruffy town named after Peruvian explorer Faustino Maldonado who in 1861 followed the Madre de Dios river down as far as the Madeira Falls in Brazil, where he drowned.

Settlers have been coming to the forest on the east side of the Andes for over a hundred years to collect rubber or to hunt for gold, but the real rush of people started in the late 1970s when the road from Cuzco and the airport ended the region's isolation. Thousands of settlers have arrived since then to earn high wages as loggers, or in sawmills, or working gold claims, or they have cleared the forest and planted manioc and bananas. They are mostly Quechua-speaking Indians from the high, treeless pastures in the Andes or mechanics, waiters, criminals and the unemployed from the cities. The forty-odd stevedores in the port couldn't find four members without criminal records when they wanted to form a union.

Immigrants arrive ignorant of their new surroundings and fearful of the forest after the wind-scoured valleys of the Andes or the dry desert of the Pacific coast. Potato, guinea pig or beef remain favourite foods, though they are all imported from Cuzco and expensive. Fish from the river and *yuca* are popular only among families firmly rooted in the region.

The isolation of the newcomers was confirmed when I went to buy more thread to continue my circular throw net. No shop sold good nylon thread to make fishing nets. Only Peruvian thread which frequently broke. Juan (the fisherman in the home of Julio's parents) had advised using only imported Korean thread. My daily net-making practice had therefore to be abandoned when the

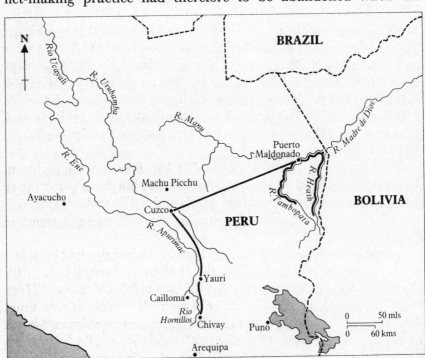

imported thread ended. By then, the net was half-made with about 22,000 knots.

'People don't know the value of the better thread and won't pay the price,' said a shopkeeper. Nets for sale hung in a few stores and these were used by some men, but holes in them were always repaired badly.

Dom Gerardo arrived at the hotel in the evening to report that there ws no gasoline in Puerto Maldonado. The regular tanker drivers, bringing supplies down the road from Cuzco, were on strike for more money. The only gas station in the town was being supplied by the owner's own tankers, which could not keep up with demand. No one knew when gasoline might arrive. We had to wait.

Salvation seemed at hand when Anna-Maria, Julio and I met a six-foot American with big hands and a thick white beard the next evening in a bar. His name was Jim and he wore a camera and a pair of sunglasses on a piece of string round his neck. He'd arrived in town a year before to operate a gold dredger. 'It's inoperative. In fact, it's upside down in the mud,' he said and squeezed lemon juice into his cup of black coffee. 'D'you want to know why I put lemon in my coffee?'

Coming into the city from working in the jungle in Panama, he and his mates would go to a brothel with an orchestra, restaurant and bar, besides the girls. 'Well, I'd order a rum and Coke and put a piece of lemon in. When we came to order more drinks, I'd go quietly round to the kitchen and fill up my glass with coffee and come back and put lemon juice in. Well, you can imagine,' he said in his soft voice, 'after drinking all night the rest of them were so drunk they couldn't get up. And I was just raring to go. You know, I don't like to drink much.'

Jim learned to be a trapper in Alaska when he was eighteen. Later, he went gold prospecting in Canada, taught engineering in Java, travelled for seven years in Africa and got himself sentenced to the firing squad in Sudan after buying sandwiches for a group of starving children.

Buying shrunken heads from Indians in the interior had been one of his other jobs in Panama, he said. 'I often got invited to eat with the chief. The food was good. One day the chief said to me, "Have more. Now you are family, go help yourself." Well, it was soup. Meat at the bottom of a great missionary pot, vegetables and broth at the top. It was pork soup. Sweet. Very delicious. So I dug deep down in the great pot with a long ladle and pulled up a piece of meat

– a whole human hand. Well! So I just took a few vegetables from the middle and rather lost my appetite for the food,' said Jim and he laughed at his tall tale. He had in fact been eating monkey meat.

Jim was a compulsive snap-taker and always had his camera in his hands. 'I've been trying to get a picture of a 'croach. No one believes we have three-inch cockroaches here.' He also snapped what he called, 'the gentry – the mayor and his sidekicks, the judge, the owner of the Coca-Cola franchise, and the rich stall holders with clout'. He charged everyone only thirty *intis* per picture. This was good public relations for a gringo who wanted to start manufacturing gold dredging machines.

The gold, panned in V-shaped pans or dredged and sieved and washed mechanically from sandbanks and gravel beds, is as fine as flour.

According to Jim, twenty to thirty kilos of gold (worth about $2.5–$3.8 million on world markets) is smuggled from Puerto Maldonado to Bolivia or Brazil every week, where the price is fifty per cent higher than the government price in Peru. Smugglers share the profit equally with the owners. Just enough gold is sold at the Peruvian official price, and paid in bribes, to ensure that such local operations are not investigated.

'There is a system of staking claims, but no policing. Officially, to get an intruder off your land requires a run through the bureaucracy in Lima. If your foe has a powerful brother-in-law or other family relation, the gold will all have been taken out long before the cogs of Peruvian bureaucracy have moved an inch.

'Law and order are kept by the shotgun and the machete. Murders are not uncommon. Two men go up the river in a canoe: One man comes back. The police don't interfere. The strongest win.'

Men digging the sand or working the dredging machines earn only four dollars a day and, in theory, all the gold belongs to the owner of the operation.

By contrast, men cutting down hardwood trees earn eighteen dollars a day, using chainsaws up to two metres in length. 'The trees don't stand a chance,' lamented Jim. Sometimes, when a logger has an order for a particular amount of lumber, a tree is cut down and only that amount is removed. The rest is left to rot.

In the garden of a ramshackle carpentry shop Jim shared a little house of bricks and concrete with his Doberman Pinscher. 'We're both bachelors. Well, his nickname is Shniggles, because y'know, he likes to snuggle up.'

Barrels of gasoline and oil and the fridge occupied his front room; bed, water heater and a hot ring for cooking in the other room, and a bathroom. Five ducks and numerous chickens lived outside, scratching in the shade of the banana trees. Jim was waiting for a few geese that had been promised.

He offered to sell the gasoline we needed for a fifty per cent premium. My budget was collapsing. I decided to wait one more day. He invited me for a breakfast of Alaskan sour dough pancakes and we each ate seven pancakes with honey and black coffee. Later, I was sick.

Dom Gerardo managed to buy a barrel of gasoline from the regular supplier and next morning, Sunday, May 31, Anna-Maria, Julio and I enjoyed a last breakfast of fried eggs, coffee and bread in the sunny courtyard of the hotel.

The *peke-peke*, a 25-foot canoe painted blue, powered by a 16-horse power motor, was puttering up the brown Tambopata river under a blue sky an hour later, passing the Hotel de Turistas, whose long verandah faces the town's electricity generating station. Dom Gerardo sat in the bow, his rounded shoulders almost hidden by the upright barrel of gasoline he was leaning on. I sat on the bench behind in shorts and T-shirt, wondering how soon the sun would start to burn me. Anna-Maria and Julio sat together in front of the sacks of food, clothes and mosquito netting. Hugo, the motorman, sat on the side of the canoe with his hand on the handle of the motor. He squinted in the sunlight, face impassive, T-shirt over his head and always watching up the river bank.

The forest along the first few miles had been cleared and replaced by cattle pastures and orchards of orange, lemon and banana trees. Forest still stood at the bends in the river, where the current was undercutting the high red bank hung with fine tree roots like thick horse's tails. Beyond the last pastures, thatched houses stood isolated by miles of high trees.

Birds the size of sparrows, with black and white striped heads, bright yellow breasts and brown backs clung to stems an inch above the river, looked round, then dipped to sip the water. Their call gives them both their Portuguese name 'Bemtive' (good to see you) and their French name 'Kiskadee' (What did he say?).

Black volcanic rock, pockmarked like pumice, lay in seams along the river bank or jutted into the swirling water. Bare branches, whole trees and bushes stripped of every leaf had caught on one of these outcrops, creating a log jam as high as the river bank. The water was silver in colour, bleached by the mid-morning sun that left leaves and trees with a patina of white, as if dust lay over the land. We travelled in silence and Anna-Maria slept. 'There's not much to see in the beginning,' she said, waking when the boat tipped suddenly.

Dom Gerardo pointed to an alligator, but the creature disappeared before I could spot it amid the patterns of sunlight and shade along the muddy bank. He pointed to another alligator which I saw, slipping into the calm murky river.

We reached the Tambopata Wildlife Reserve forty miles up the river after six hours. A staircase up the bank and boardwalk of split black palm led through the forest to the Explorer's Inn. We were too late for lunch, but enjoyed cold beers with Rachel Byers, one of six naturalists living and studying there without charge, in exchange for guiding tourists on walks in the forest.

The 13,500 acre area had been the private hunting ground of eight businessmen in Lima until they decided to preserve the forest as a reserve with a tourist lodge. Legal status as a reserved zone was granted by the Peruvian Government in 1977. The custodian, Peruvian Safaris, is now campaigning to gain additional protection as a national reserve.

Visiting scientists have counted 566 species of bird, 145 species of dragonflies and 1,100 species of butterflies in the reserve. The Inn was a calm place, with cold beers and mosquito netting at all the windows. But even here, surrounded by the forest, two weeks earlier the naturalists' logbook had been stolen. Fortunately, their handwritten reports had been recently photocopied.

'Are you going up to the Colpa dos Guacamayos – salt-lick of the macaws – it's the biggest in the Amazon?' asked Rachel Byers, showing us a photograph of forty macaws feeding at one part of the *colpa*.

'Where is it exactly?' I asked.

'It's finished,' the manager's wife put in sadly, stroking the fine black hairs of her pet spider monkey. 'It fell down.' Birds and animals licked away so much salt from the bottom that the cliff collapsed. The place was said to be four days upstream.

Rachel took us to the medicinal garden where Julio identified and explained the use of many of the plants. Rachel's year studying the hoatzin bird at the Reserve was over but she planned to stay a few months with her boyfriend who lived nearby on the river. 'I'm just in love with the jungle,' she said.

It was nearly sunset when we reached the home of Dom Gerardo's brother, Dom Juan, who lived farther up the river. He welcomed us up the steep sandy bank and helped bring most of our luggage and the food we would need for the night. I handed Hugo a bottle of brandy to mix with lemons and sugar to make *caipirinhas* after the tiring day coming away from the town. Now, I knew, being in the forest also needed long trousers and mosquito repellent on hands, face and feet.

Dom Juan's home consisted of two separate rooms built with poles and palm thatch; a kitchen with a dirt floor and firebox in the right-hand corner, two tables and a collection of tins on a shelf. The other building stood on stilts, and Anna-Maria and Julio put up their mosquito nets on its small verandah; Hugo, Dom Gerardo and his brother and his wife slept inside and I slept up in the loft.

Dom Juan smiled often and had the belly of a man who ate a lot of rice. He had come back from the Ucayali three and a half years earlier to rejoin his family. His wife, Dona Adriana, with cheery face and black hair pinned in a bun at the back, listened patiently to her husband's tall stories and watched the guests' reactions while she cooked rice and opened the tin of sardines we had brought.

Dom Gerardo wrung the neck of a chicken next morning, after coffee and cheese sandwiches at dawn. Dona Adriana served chicken and rice soup an hour later, after which we went for a walk in the forest. Dom Gerardo led the way through orchards of bananas and papayas, their green fruits hanging over our heads, and across his brother's manioc garden into an area of tangled young forest, regrowing after being cleared and burned.

Suddenly, he stopped and pointed. A small black monkey scampered along the path, looked at us and vanished before Dom Gerardo could get the shotgun off his shoulder. 'It likes to eat chickens and papaya,' said Hugo later. He said the monkey picked papayas off the trees, buried them and came back four or five days later, when the fruit had ripened. Seeds are eventually spread in the forest with dollops of monkey fertiliser.

Forest that had never been cleared stood beyond the abandoned garden tangled with bushes, creepers and slender saplings competing for the sunlight. It was dark and cool and humid under the high canopy of the mature trees. We came to the base of a mahogany tree measuring forty feet in diameter across the buttresses. These stood at right-angles to the trunk and reached a hundred feet before the branches began.

We paused in awe at the base of the mahogany tree, then turned right along a lane where the ground had been cleared of all plants but the trees were still standing.

'Road of a petroleum company,' said Dom Gerardo.

Julio said it went to an oil rig but that made no sense. When we came to another huge tree with a window cut through a buttress on its left side, it was clear that we were in fact walking down an old seismic line cut for petroleum exploration.

Beyond the line you had to watch for lianas that slapped your face and for leaves with serrated edges, or with thorns underneath, that cut fingers or could tear clothing.

Lianas hung in clusters, others could be used as ropes, others coiled round trunks or around themselves. Animals, birds and the wind scatter their seeds in the high branches of trees. They germinate in pockets of plant debris and water and drop roots to the ground through which the plants feed and grow high above.

You could see sixty to seventy feet through the forest to left and right because the lack of light kept bushes and plants low to the brown floor of leaves. Only one per cent of the sunlight outside the forest reached the ground where we were walking. This produced a lack of light that was neither gloom nor blackness nor shade, but a quality of light inseparable from the humidity and the warmth of the air surrounding us.

Wee-wee-uh! Wee-wee-uh! The penetrating whistle of the Screaming Pina, a brown bird slightly larger than a thrush and also called the Captain of the Forest. Knowing there was no reason to be afraid was easy, but only long experience would make you genuinely relaxed.

Julio stopped and pointed to a tree standing where nothing else was growing. 'This is *tangarama*,' he said. 'The rubber barons tied Indians here to punish them.' Victims were driven mad by the bites of a species of fiercely territorial ant living in the tree.

The leaf-covered ground is the quiet basement of the forest, with the foundations of the trees, plumbing of the vines, aerial roots and the decaying litter of leaves, branches, seeds, fruits, discarded feathers, dead animals and the excreta of every creature, much of it dropped from the canopy.

Dom Gerardo pointed to the tracks of a tapir crossing a mud puddle and to the burrows of armadillos. We crossed a stream along a tree trunk and walked through several shallow swamps created by recent rains. I gave Anna-Maria a piggy-back ride to keep her white tennis shoes dry, but at the third pool, she took them off and asked if there were leeches before wading through. 'It's lovely, it's cool,' she said.

The path came to a tumble of tree trunks fallen across a stream. Crossing one of these and hoping not to slip off, I noticed a brown line two inches wide along the top of the next trunk. The brown line was tens of thousands of small ants hurrying in two-way traffic side by side.

Many trees lay across the path; some were still solid but most had been eaten from the inside by insects and fungus. Only their hollow bark remained, like snake skins. It is partly the speed with which fungi, roots and insects consume vegetable tissue that accounts for the thinness of the soil, compared to temperate lands where the cycle is so much slower.

Dom Gerardo took us to a lake ringed by palm trees. These lakes lie in old river courses and are some of the most dangerous places for piranhas and alligators. The creatures get hungry in the lakes when flood waters from nearby rivers fall after each rainy season, isolating and confining them.

We climbed along a fallen tree overhanging the water to have a look, then rested inside the forest, where it was humid and tranquil with birds chattering and chuntering. Anna-Marie offered cigarettes, which were good to keep away mosquitoes and, I imagined, to fumigate little bugs inside your shirt. We picked ripe fruit looking like tomatoes and with a lemony flavour, quite refreshing after the two-hour walk.

Dom Gerardo thumped his throat with his fingers, issuing a loud gurgling, 'UUH-AAH-UUH-AAH!'

The call came back from across the lake. We climbed out again along the fallen trees to see the heads of several animals looking up at us out of the water. They were giant otters, no longer common in the Amazon because poachers can sell their pelts for hundreds of dollars. Julio and I had seen four fresh pelts in a house in Puerto Maldonado.

Julio had been looking all morning for an *acaí* palm to cut down so that he could present *palmito* (heart of palm) to Anna-Maria. He found one near the lake and after a few blows of his machete the thirty foot tree fell with a crash. Julio cut out one piece where the stem was green at the top, peeled the layers and handed a small piece to each of us. It has a soft, fibrous tasteless texture and is highly esteemed in the restaurants of Lima and Rio.

Açaí palms are prized in the eastern Amazon for making a rich, purple-coloured drink which tastes so good that a local proverb warns visitors, 'Arrive in Pará, stop, drink *açaí*, stay for ever'.

We could not stay for ever. After lunch at the house, we reloaded the *peke-peke* and puttered up the river again. Thick forest lined both sides, gashed occasionally by an isolated house or a garden planted with bananas. Black volcanic rock emerged more and more from the clay banks until, at mid-morning on the next day, we reached the first cataract. Hugo landed the canoe in calm water below an island of rock.

We faced a new difficulty if we ascended the cataract: Hugo could not return down the cataract on his own when he took Anna-Maria to Puerto Maldonado to catch her plane, as we had planned. Everyone would have to return together to Puerto Maldonado after just one week. Both Anna-Maria and I were surprised no one had mentioned this crucial information before we decided to come up the Tambopata river, though both Dom Gerardo and Julio had said they knew the river. I decided we should press on, come back with Anna-Maria and then plan what to do.

Hugo roped down the baggage in the canoe under a large plastic sheet and swivelled the long propeller shaft up on board. Dom Gerardo tied two long ropes together and told Julio and me to walk on up over the island of volcanic rock in the middle of the river and pull when he pushed the canoe away into the rushing water. We pulled the canoe up through the gushing torrent and clambered like monkeys to keep the canoe out when it caught on rocks. Dom Gerardo had to plunge into the water several times up to his neck and heave before the canoe finally reached calm water at the top of the cataract.

Hugo swivelled the propeller shaft into the water again, pulled the starting rope and steered the *peke-peke* on up the river. I hoped that we would now be beyond houses and clearings but about a quarter of a mile upstream we passed a large tree sawn into lengths. Six people were standing on the rocks when I looked back at the cataract.

We paused for a lunch of smoked chicken and *yuca*, bought from Dom Gerardo's brother, then continued upstream, passing four 'gold mines' during the afternoon. Several feet of clay had been dug from the river bank at one of these to expose a seam of gravel and sand. Two youths, with pick-axes and shovels, loaded wheel-barrows with the dirt and pushed them up a plank to a tray sloping onto a long metal sheet punctured with holes. A man stood picking out pebbles and washing sand through the holes. The flour gold was collected in the sacking on the long tray and the sand and water poured off the end. In ancient times in Europe, miners used a sheepskin instead of sacking to trap the gold – this was the origin of the Golden Fleece. The gold miners in the Amazon could expect to find eight grams of gold from a hundred wheelbarrows per day (worth $102 on the world market at the time).

We continued up the river all afternoon, sighting alligators and kingfishers, turtles sunbathing on rocks and occasionally kapok trees with purple flowers amid the green. It was too late in the afternoon to attempt to press on when we arrived below almost a mile of rocks, eddies and turbulence. Hugo steered towards the beach on a forested island where we could camp.

Dom Gerardo and Hugo cut and collected long stems of *canabraba*, a bamboo-like reed growing in the sunshine along the riverbanks, and we lashed these poles together with vines, making the frame of a shelter to be covered with lengths of plastic sheeting we brought with us. Dry driftwood roared on the fire to make tea and to cook rice, onions and a bit of dried chicken for supper. I bathed and scrubbed scores of tick bites, and rubbed half a lemon over my itching skin.

A gold miners' canoe passed, going up the river behind the island. Dom Gerardo and Hugo watched its slow progress through the rapids, wondering if we would be able to get beyond the rocks in the morning. The extra canoe made the forest seem crowded.

Pink light faded from the eastern sky after sunset and the first planets and stars appeared. The night was too hot for sleeping and later I sat alone on the beach writing my diary by candlelight, pausing often to listen to the river running over pebbles, splashes of creatures in the water and the hoots and cries around us in the dark.

We had slipped away, beyond the boundaries of civilisation. This is the world as it was made, I thought, before we hominids were corrupted with the conceit that creation was for our benefit. Later, I lay naked inside my mosquito net in the sultry darkness, beside my sleeping companions. I panted like a dog with my mouth open and promptly swallowed an insect, alive and whole.

Heavy rain in the night collapsed the plastic sheeting at both ends of our tent and soaked the heap of firewood. However, Hugo sliced off wood chips with the machete, splashed them with gasoline and soon had a roaring fire. He made five mugs of hot coffee.

The river had risen with the overnight rain, submerging rocks that might have blocked our way up the rapid. Instead, we had only the rush of water to fight. It lifted and buffeted us for over an hour, pulling and pushing us from side to side as Hugo steered the *peke-peke* between the rocks.

The gold prospectors had turned up a tributary on the right just beyond the rapids, and had camped there, but Hugo kept to the Tambopata river. Up the tributary, he told us, mosquitoes were so thick the men had to wear face masks and gloves while working for gold.

Two days later, after rounding innumerable bends in the river, we reached a high cliff of orange clay.

'This is the Colpa dos Guacamayos,' said Dom Gerardo. The cliff had collapsed burying the salt-lick as reported. A few macaws flew screeching along the top of the cliff but this was no longer a gathering place.

Dom Gerardo now spoke of a *colpa* down the river near his brother's house. Julio wanted to go back immediately. Anna-Maria wanted to stay. I decided we should camp where we were because, just at that moment, slender herons flew low over our heads on the breeze. We selected a raised beach at the end of an island upstream of the *colpa*, separated from the cliffs on the right side by lagoons of brown water and undulating sands.

Hugo suggested he and I go hunting as soon as we arrived. I put on socks and Wellington boots exchanged in Iquitos for the two right footed ones, and carried my machete behind Hugo with the shotgun. We walked in silence up the beach between the island and the cliff. Hugo waded across into the forest on the island to approach a pair of ducks on the beach, signalling for me to wait, and crept silently to the edge of the trees, about twenty yards from the birds.

A grey hummingbird flew in, hovered in front of my face among the leaves, and darted away. The gun fired with an outrageously loud bang but Hugo missed and the ducks flew away.

We walked on together up the beach, leaving tracks in the sand. In the heat and humidity of the afternoon, when the air was still and silent, I expected to see a dinosaur emerge from the forest and cross the beach, leaving its footprints beside our own. Human history vanished in the sunshine, returning us to a world where time was measured by changes in the design of a leaf and not by the puny mechanics of a wristwatch.

Hugo and I scrambled up the cliff, following a tapir's trail through the bushes. The trail turned right at the top and entered under dense bamboos blown down by the winds. We crawled with heads kept low to avoid the sharp thorns on the bamboo. A little bird flew out but otherwise this place was silent.

The sun had sunk low over the forest when we returned empty-handed to our camp on the beach; time to bathe before darkness. It was best to wear sandals to wade out from the beach in case you stepped on a stingray settled on the bottom. I didn't go far out, then sat down and splashed cool water over head and shoulders to discourage mosquitoes and small flies.

The foothills of the Andes rose as a grey silhouette in the west but after supper the hills disappeared in a sky of grey. Dom Gerardo and Hugo went with the shotgun up the beach in the hope of shooting something. Pencil lines of heavy rain were falling in the distance by the time they returned and the river was already rising again. A pair of macaws flew for cover. The mosquitoes disappeared.

Dom Gerardo announced that he and Hugo would not put up their mosquito nets, but would stay awake all night to keep an eye on the level of the river. Water was already trickling across the beach where Hugo and I had walked.

The rain reached us in the dark, pitter-pattering on the plastic sheeting. I lay with my head outside the netting at one end of the shelter, watching distant lightning and counting the seconds until thunder boomed. For half an hour, it was fresh and cool and enjoyable.

Then the rain really began falling; big drops hitting with a clatter against our shelter. Lightning flashed all around and thunder cracked over our heads as if the sky were tearing. The rain came with a wind, blowing inside our shelter, soaking my mosquito net and lifting it even though it was held down with black-bottomed cooking pots.

Rain fell for half an hour as if the second Deluge had started, surrounding us with such a powerful display of energy that its beauty didn't mask the apprehension we were all feeling.

The river came within a couple of feet of our camp but we stayed put, and at dawn the water had already fallen eighteen inches from the flood mark of leaves and twigs. Grey gloom clung to the trees around us, obscuring river and forest. Hugo went off alone with the shotgun. A bird screamed 'eee-yo-yu, eee-yo-yu' in the mist. Dom Gerardo started a fire with wood chips and gasoline to boil water for coffee and rice porridge – both with the muddy flavour of the river in spate.

We waited for the sun to rise and burn off the mist that surrounded us. Birds began whistling in the forest. Pairs of blue and yellow macaws, with wide wings and long tails, flew over our heads. Parakeets squawked from tree to tree along the flooded lagoon, disappearing in the foliage, re-emerging to fly to the next tree. They were as noisy and excited as we were. I liked to think of them also enjoying the sun and trees and peace of the day after the storm in the night. The mosquitoes were also out in great numbers.

Dom Gerardo, Hugo and I set off into the forest, leaving Anna-Maria and Julio to pass the day together in camp. Her foot had swelled to twice its size after being bitten by a half-inch black ant the day before. The bite had been sharp like a needle but the swelling was painless and would subside after a day. Julio stayed behind mostly because, by now, he had become downright uncooperative. Sadly, I no longer thought of him as a friend but as someone not earning his wages.

'He has complexes, I think,' commented Anna-Maria. 'I have met many like that.'

Hugo carried the shotgun and went ahead, leaving a trail through the forest that Dom Gerardo and I followed as best we could, calling to one another when we lost contact. The explosions of the petroleum companies must have scared away the game, commented my companions when we returned to camp after eight hours of seeing no animals.

Another wet night ruined all the crackers we had saved from our last jungle breakfast and the morning was wet and cold. We had to pack up and return down river so that Anna-Maria could catch her plane to Lima. Rain showers alternated with sunshine but even then the sun remained as pale as the moon. We travelled rapidly down the swollen river, passing our previous campsites and storks immobile on the beaches with their heads tucked in out of the cold. We shot the cataract in a few turbulent minutes of excitement and by noon were again in the kitchen of Dom Juan and Dona Adriana.

I brought out another bottle of brandy to cheer up Hugo who had been soaked and cold all morning without complaining and to keep out the miserable wet, grey weather that depressed us all.

Anna-Maria went down to the river to shampoo her knotted hair.

She returned having fallen in the river in her clothes. 'Typical, typical!' she shrieked. 'I *knew* it would happen. Now everything – ev-e-ry-th-ing – I have is wet.'

Cold, dull weather continued next day, exaggerating our disappointment at having seen so little game. Still, at least the swollen river helped us to travel fast and we arrived at Puerto Maldonado in time to eat lunch and to watch a Tarzan film on the television. People blocked both doors of the restaurant to watch Tarzan wrestling with crocodiles and a leopard and swinging through the forest on a liana.

'Why didn't we see animals like that?' asked Anna-Maria.

'We weren't near a zoo.'

Early the next morning, in the cold shower, I steeled myself to speak with Julio.

'You don't seem to have enjoyed the last week. You haven't spoken to me at all or been very friendly. You said you knew people here but you don't. You said you spent three months on the Tambopata river with some French people but you never once mentioned the rapids or that if we went up with Anna we would all have to come back. I think it's best that you return to Iquitos with Anna-Maria and I will go on with Dom Gerardo and Hugo,' I said.

Julio nodded in silence and we went down for breakfast. I gave him an air ticket to Cuzco, money in dollars (to change in Cuzco at the better rate) to cover travel to Iquitos, hotels and food, and $45 as an extra gift, beyond what I had already paid. This was $5 less than I had promised him but I justified this to myself because we had been away only one week and he had been no help. He left with Anna-Maria to go to the airport. Batteries, matches, fishing line, hooks, and weights were missing from our room after they had gone. I shrugged my shoulders and bought the items again.

7

Rio Heath: Three Men in a Boat

'No journey belongs only to time and place: neither the eye that sees nor the heart that feels is a timetable or a map. Every journey to foreign lands is also a journey through the countries of the mind, and the landscapes of the one flow into those of the other. Moreover, the eye that sees and the heart that feels do not always act in unison.'

Gilbert Phelps, *The Green Horizon.*

'THE COLD WILL PASS, after three days. Then it will be summer,' said Dom Gerardo.

We were travelling down the wide Madre de Dios river from Puerto Maldonado and intended to turn west up the river Heath on the border with Bolivia, named after the American doctor Edwin Heath who explored the region in the 1880s. Later he worked on the railway built to bypass the 19 major waterfalls downstream on the Madeira river. Malaria killed thousands of workers during the five years taken to construct the 227-mile line through forest and swamp. The railway opened in 1912, the same year the price of rubber collapsed. Today, one section of track is operated as a museum and the remainder is the main road to Bolivia.

Dom Gerardo occupied himself on our journey down the choppy river by cutting a wooden plug to block a hole in one of the side-boards of the canoe. And later he caught a dragonfly with a black and greenish body and transparent black wings. He held it out for me to see, then absent-mindedly rubbed a wing in his fingers until it was broken. The dragonfly fluttered to be free. Dom Gerardo looked down at what he had done, broke off the second wing on the same side and threw away the insect. It fell on its back and struggled in the water before being eaten by a fish.

I rubbed my goose-pimpled legs to warm them and bent forward out of the wind to read my book, which was now a romance by W. H. Hudson set in the forests along the Rio Orinoco in Venezuela.

The forest looked less welcoming when the sky was low and grey.

Blustery wind made us glad of our sweaters. Hugo passed forward a few rice cakes for lunch and after four hours he landed the *peke-peke* at the Peruvian border post across from Bolivia. The brown muddy water is the political border between Bolivia and Peru, though the forest is the same and the territory of the alligators extends along both banks. Dom Gerardo presented documents for himself, Hugo and the canoe. I showed my passport.

'Have you any newspapers?'

Alas, I had forgotten their importance for bored officials in the interior.

The government officer nodded his head in the Peruvian equivalent of the British stiff upper lip. Dom Gerardo gave news of people in Puerto Maldonado who had married, died, gone away or had accidents. Later a smiling officer of the Guarda Republicana del Peru wrote down details of our documents in a ledger and reminded us that hunting was forbidden in the reserve on the Peruvian side of the river, though it was permitted to shoot for the cooking pot. He stamped and signed the documents and wished us luck.

We turned right up the Rio Heath just before the flag and thatched outpost hut of Bolivia. Hugo kept the canoe close to the right bank, the Peruvian side, where the cackling of the motor echoed on the wall of trees. The *peke-peke* moved slowly through the brown water, even out of the full force of the current, giving us time to enjoy our surroundings.

Swallows skimmed over the water catching insects. The little Bemtive birds with black and white striped heads looked at us and flew from stem to stem ahead of us. A five-foot alligator stayed immobile at the water's edge a few feet away.

'Look, there's another,' said Dom Gerardo, pointing to a black alligator. These are the larger species growing up to fifteen feet, but rare in the Amazon today because of poaching for their skins.

Later, after passing a few houses and clearings, we reached a settlement of civilised Indians on the Bolivian side. 'If we stay there, they would steal everything,' said Dom Gerardo, with Hugo nodding.

A more serious warning was given to the British explorer Colonel Fawcett in 1910. 'You can't get up that river. The savages are so bad that it's certain death. They are in their thousands,' said Peruvian officials when the colonel arrived on the Heath to survey the boundary between Bolivia and Peru. Fawcett did not shoot back when Guarayos fired arrows at his canoes. Instead, his men sang popular English music hall songs and one of them played the accordian. The warriors ceased fire and Fawcett crossed the river to meet their chief. 'I could think of only one way to show him friendship. I placed my Stetson on his head and patted him on the back. He grinned, and all the surrounding braves roared with laughter – in fact, they laughed at everything, funny or not. Then bananas and fish were produced as gifts for us, and friendly relations were firmly established.'

Fawcett died looking for a lost city in the forest of Matto Grosso in Brazil in 1925. Today the Indians have vanished from the Rio Heath, except for the settlement Dom Gerardo and Hugo did not want to visit.

There were no beaches for a camp on the Peruvian shore so Dom Gerardo suggested stopping at the riverside house of a friend of his, Daniel Cruz, who welcomed us for a supper of rice, fried deer meat and sliced bananas, crisply fried like potato crisps. We were all hungry. The meat was the best I had eaten in months.

Talk over coffee turned to the price of dentists and the merits of gold or silver amalgam fillings, to the problems of obtaining secure land titles, and to the prices of radios and batteries. Then Dom Gerardo started storytelling but he spoke so quickly and with so much slang that I understood only that they were stories of jaguars, alligators and gringos.

The water level of the river fell two feet during the night, leaving mud smeared on the leaves along the bank that dried in the sunshine next morning. We thanked Señor Cruz for his hospitality and set off again up the river. Dom Gerardo sat in the bow, as usual, spotting submerged trees or other obstacles and pointing out the alligators and turtles still hidden to my eyes.

Alligators stayed motionless when the canoe came close. Their irregular shape and olive-greenish colour merged so well into the light and shade along the clay banks that even when you spotted their yellow eyes watching you the rest of them sometimes remained invisible.

Turtles were more timid. Three blackish-green turtles, sun-bathing in a line on a silver tree trunk, jumped off and disappeared into the water when the buzz of the *peke-peke* came near.

'Further up, let's go and kill one,' said Dom Gerardo, raising his heavy eyebrows greedily at the idea.

Blue butterflies, with wings the size of small birds', flitted between trees along the water's edge. Burgundy-red and black dragonflies whirred back and forth over the calm, brown water.

Bumble bees the size of Brazil nuts buzzed round our heads.

Hugo sat on one side of the canoe, gripping the steering rod and watching the water as we crossed and re-crossed the narrow river, always keeping to the insides of the bends. The river turned so often and so sharply that we could see only a very short distance ahead or behind. Did the forest close over our heads too, after we had passed?

Solitary egrets, as slender as swans, watched the canoe coming up the river and kept ahead of us, flying in three or four short glides from tree to tree along the banks. Each bird escorted us through its territory and returned to its first perch after we had passed.

We watched for monkeys and iguanas up in the trees. Leaves shaking suddenly might be caused by a monkey peering at the canoe or fleeing through the branches at the strange noise of the motor. A single stem dangling in a curve, unlike a twig or branch, might be the tail of an iguana.

By keeping alert and watching for movement and irregular shapes, even a gringo could spot a boa constrictor coiled in branches over the water or a family of *capybary* at the water's edge twenty feet from the canoe.

Thin, brown lines of termite tunnels ran along many of the branches and down tree trunks, reaching out from big termite nests attached to trees like bulbous kitbags. Termites build their long dark tunnels by mixing mud with their saliva. They digest raw wood with the aid of protozoans living in their gut. They provide food for fungi and roots and together recycle the forest's nutrients.

Ferns, orchids and other tree-dwelling plants covered the trunks and branches of many trees, feeding on rainwater, dust and the debris of dead leaves and insects. The weight of these can topple trees. Don Gerardo pointed to one tree, the smooth trunk of which literally repels such burdens. The man-wood tree, as he called it, looks like a sculpture of green wax. Its smooth bark is a tight skin that wrinkles only where the green branches grow from the trunk, and peels off easily in layers like greaseproof paper.

Dom Gerardo named many trees and birds and corrected my many mistakes. Too much schooling and book-learning had dulled my powers of observation and my memory for details of colour, shape and pattern. Unlike illiterate people in the Amazon, I could not learn by merely seeing, hearing and remembering. The name of an insect was only fixed in my mind if I first wrote it down and then learned the name from the paper. The identification of a tree was only lodged in my mind if I divided tree from branches and leaves and deliberately observed their shapes and colours and learned them by rote.

Big colourful birds were the easiest creatures to identify. The macaw's curved beak and long tail distinguished it even when its brilliant red and blue, or blue and yellow, plumage was obscured by glare. The macaw's tail feathers are especially valued by Indians all over the Amazon for decorations. To the Auca in Ecuador, a macaw tail feather is a gift of welcome. Macaws are strong flyers, able to go sixty miles in a day, searching for food. They seem to mate for life but also gather in flocks so large and noisy that we could hear the birds long before we spotted their splashes of colour, high in the branches of the biggest trees.

Turning a corner in the afternoon, we saw a woman waving to us from a hut in a large clearing on the Bolivian side. Dom Gerardo suggested going to see what she wanted.

'Nothing,' replied the stout woman outside the thatched shelter. Her husband came to shake hands. His shirt had been repaired so often it was impossible to tell which was the original cloth. The woman wore her hair in a long pigtail that was starting to go grey and wore a dress mended with half a dozen different patches. I handed round cigarettes, a welcome luxury. Their house was the last on either side of the river, said the man, clutching his cigarette in his crippled right hand. The woman sent their two teenage daughters, both of them wearing tight denim jeans, to fetch drinks and *farinha* for us.

The brown drink they brought tasted like cocoa and was made from a palm nut gathered in the forest. I offered cigarettes again, to everyone's delight, and Dom Gerardo explained why we had come and where we were going. The conversation meandered as much as the river, turning from talk of getting three or four kilos of gold out of rivers in Brazil to the quantity of fish in the Rio Heath and the restrictions on hunting and logging in the reserves.

'How is a man supposed to live?'

'There's no justice,' added Dom Gerardo, after he had told them the Tambopata Reserve was trying to expand its area.

The family gave us three large cucumbers and we handed eight oranges to them.

'Thank you for your visit. Good luck to you,' said the man, shaking hands again. We promised to call on our way back if we had shot any game.

We left Bolivia and continued up the river. Soon the sun was touching the tops of the tallest trees. It was time to find a campsite before sunset but we inspected and rejected six beaches before spotting a small thatched shelter just inside the forest on a bend in the river. Hugo steered to the shore and Dom Gerardo jumped out.

Three temporary shelters, used by people gathering Brazil nuts in the season, stood just inside the forest. We cleared the ground of fallen branches and empty Brazil-nut cases and lit a fire in front of one of the shelters. Big ants, with a painful bite, were crossing the floor of the largest shelter but they had all gone home by the time we brought up the luggage and food from the canoe. Unfortunately, we had left the kettle at Daniel Cruz's house, and the lid of the largest cooking pot, kept overnight in the canoe, had apparently been stolen. Dom Gerardo boiled water for tea and coffee and we ate tinned sardines and rice for supper in twilight.

There were few mosquitoes just inside the forest, allowing us to relax in the dark. Hugo and Dom Gerardo sat together and talked and talked. I wrote my diary until the candle burned low. Our three mosquito nets were erected side by side in the shelter, with the gringo in the middle. This was the driest place but I lay between two friends who never stopped talking. Clanging tin mugs woke us in the night when a creature rummaged through our camp, knocking over tins of coffee, milk and sugar.

'A fox,' said Dom Gerardo in the morning, showing the cleaned-out sardine tin. The visitor was more likely to have been a *paca*, a catlike mammal that prowls at night. Dom Gerardo later presented me with a two-inch curved *paca* tooth and told me to wear it round my neck for good luck.

We ate coffee and crackers for breakfast. I collected the discarded wrappers and put them in the fire. 'It's beautiful here because there is no rubbish,' I said.

My companions nodded. 'Yes, yes,' they agreed, though this would not change their habits.

I kept the cigarettes and oranges separate from our general food supplies and handed out these luxuries myself. Saying 'help yourself' would have resulted in a two-day feast followed by a two-week famine. My companions would not think of making luxuries last, but neither would they complain about their lack. Abundance and scarcity surrounded us in the forest. My attempts to husband our supplies or clean up our mess belonged to an alien philosophy.

When we reached a small stream cut through the right bank of the river, 'The *pampas* – grasslands,' announced Dom Gerardo, pointing up it.

Red Howler monkeys were shrieking at each other, far away. We camped nearby in a patch of grass between the forest and the riverbank; clearing away fallen branches, cutting lianas dangling from trees, building the frame of a shelter with saplings and securing plastic sheeting over the top. Our activity stirred up thousands of insects that crawled and flew round and round us with a humming, whining and buzzing so persistent we seemed to be living inside a beehive.

I went for a bath in the river and stood in underpants thigh-deep in muddy water, pouring it over my head and shoulders to discourage the clouds of tiny mosquitoes. I washed my clothes and put on long trousers, long-sleeved shirt and mosquito repellent, then passed the bottle to Dom Gerardo and Hugo.

We ate a delicious lunch of rice with a little of the fried deer meat Daniel Cruz had sold us, an onion and cucumber salad with salt and lemon, and coffee and cigarettes. Bees buzzed loudly round our pots of salt and sugar or got trapped under the plastic sheeting. I had foolishly bought clear instead of blue sheeting, and they drove themselves to exhaustion, flying up and down, trying to escape through the clear sheeting.

Hugo and I retreated inside our mosquito nets to read an old newspaper or a book. Dom Gerardo caught seven white piranha and cooked them in a sauce of onions and garlic, with rice and salad, for supper. He baited a night line and in the morning hauled out a stingray measuring three feet in diameter. He tied the fishing line to a tree and left the fish to die on the mud. The flesh was too chewy to eat and later we cut only a small part to cook for supper and threw the rest of the carcass into the water.

'Is it OK to bathe here?' I asked when I saw the blood in the water.

'Of course,' Dom Gerardo assured me.

I washed on the other side of the canoe and got out quickly.

We set off to the *pampas* after breakfast of coffee and potato and onion salad.

Hugo led the way through the forest carrying the shotgun. Dom Gerardo followed, cutting away overhanging vines and leaves. I walked behind him, carrying extra shotgun cartridges and slashing from side to side with my new machete, bought in Puerto Maldonado. The forest became so silent that Dom Gerardo started talking as if in self defence, naming tamarind, rubber, man-wood and other trees.

A sudden howl came from a tree up ahead. Hugo fired the shotgun. A small black monkey fell to the ground but it had gone by the time Hugo reached the foot of the tree.

The forest ended abruptly after a mile and we walked into a vast area of rough, open grass still wet with dew. Termite mounds as tall as men, and short black trees dotted the savannah. In Africa you would have expected elephants and giraffe to be grazing there.

We walked a mile north towards a line of thick palm trees, then turned right to enter a wood of small trees, bracken and moss. A stream of crystal-clear water flowed through pools stocked with trout-like fish that gulped and splashed at the surface.

'Rich, isn't it, Denny,' said Hugo when we sat on moss on the bank. A kingfisher, a San Martin pescador, flew over the pool in front of us and perched on a branch, to watch us watching him before darting away.

Hugo looked hungrily at the fish. 'Fried,' he said with a whistle, 'with rice and spaghetti.'

We came back to the pools, with fishing line and hooks, at the same time the next day. Hugo broke open a termite tunnel on a tree trunk and threw a handful of the insects onto the water.

Dom Gerardo cut a fishing rod from a sapling, tied a short length of line and baited the hook with dried deer meat. As soon as the hook dropped into the water, he jerked up the rod and pulled in a fish.

'How beautiful,' he exclaimed when there were five fish struggling on the bank.

'It's too easy. Do it without meat,' I said.

Hugo laughed and to humour me dropped his line with a bare hook into the water. He caught a fish within ten seconds.

I sat on the moss bank, delighting in the cool, bug-free air and the gentle tumbling of the water flowing through the pools.

'It's enough,' said Dom Gerardo, when they had caught twenty fish in less than half an hour. They caught five more then stopped. Hugo cut down palm fronds and made two small baskets to carry home the fish. Dom Gerardo collected dry sticks for a fire. We grilled three of the fish over green stems and sat licking our fingers after the meal with the self-satisfied smiles of greedy schoolchildren.

When we got back to camp beside the river, Hugo fried more fish to eat with cold rice for breakfast inside our mosquito nets. Once again, the camp was alive with buzzing bees and wasps, tiny mosquitoes, big black triangular flies with infuriating persistence and sharp claws, flying ants and crawling ants, beetles.

Later in the afternoon, when the noise of insects had begun to quieten and the sun shone with a yellow light on the leaves, we heard a loud squealing, whining call from downstream.

'Otter,' said Hugo. Dom Gerardo began tapping his throat with his hand, as he had done once before, mimicking the gurgling, gargling call. A reply came immediately from about 130 yards along the bank. Dom Gerardo called again. One otter, almost black, bounded along the shore towards us. Dom Gerardo called again but his voice was tiring and the sound became choked. Another otter surfaced in the river and barked a call. The otter on the shore looked from Dom Gerardo to its mate in the river and, after another bark, turned and slipped into the water.

Hugo lamented that otter hunting was illegal in Peru. 'It's not fair,' he said.

We retreated inside the nets once again until Dom Gerardo hooked a three-foot catfish with bright orange tail and greenish back. The big hook had caught just inside the mouth. Hugo tried pulling it out, and when he couldn't, cut out the hook with his machete while the fish snorted loudly. Dom Gerardo grabbed the long whiskers on both side of its mouth and pulled the stranded fish back down into the water where it disappeared. 'No good to eat,' he said.

Suddenly I felt deeply depressed. I could never be happy here, I thought. Hugo boiled water for coffee or tea with crackers for supper. I looked across the river and tried to enjoy the glow of the evening sunshine on the forest. Near sunset, the light always seemed to radiate from each leaf individually. But even the sight of two red and blue macaws flying up the river did not lighten my spirits. It was not just the insects, nor the lack of music and books, though I did miss them, nor the alien ways of my companions. It was the forest itself. The forest made me feel so diminished and powerless. Our existence counted only as much as that of the ants or orchids or trees, and no more. Our daily schemes and dreams, so powerful inside civilisation, were as empty as echoes in the forest.

Colombian writer José Eustacio Rivera wrote of this despair in *The Vortex*:

'Where is the solitude poets sing of? Where are those butterflies like translucent flowers, the magic birds, those singing streams? Poor fantasies of those who know only domesticated retreats! . . . No cooing nightingales here, no Versaillan gardens or sentimental vistas! Instead the croaking of dropsical frogs, the tangled misanthropic undergrowth, the stagnant backwaters and swamps . . . At night, unknown voices, phantasmagoric lights, funereal silences. It is death that passes, giving life . . . warning whistles, dying wails, beasts belching. And when dawn shows its tragic glory over the jungles, the clamour of survivors begins again . . . The sadistic and virgin jungle casts premonitions of coming danger over one's spirits. Our senses confuse their tasks; the eye feels, the back sees, the nose explores, the legs calculate and the blood cries out, 'Flee! Flee!'

I did indeed want to flee. The forest was too oppressive. The civilised mind can be fascinated by the abundance, variety and adaptation of hundreds of thousands of forms of life, all interdependent and self-perpetuating, as if the forest, river and sky are components of a machine: it can admire but it cannot belong. I wanted to get back to Puerto Maldonado and out of the forest as quickly as possible. Such was my instinct. But I could not allow myself to be so afraid, just because the forest did not return my gaze. I determined to stay the number of days we had already decided and lay sticky with sweat in the refuge of the mosquito net, surrounded by the awful droning of insects.

We went to bed as soon as it was dark. I took half a lemon inside the net with me to anoint any itching, and my flashlight to spot intruders. Hugo and Dom Gerardo blew out the candles when they finished talking, leaving us in a blackness filled with chirping cicadas, the roar of Red Howler monkeys far away and shrieks of 'Wee-he-he-he-! Wee-he-he-he!' abruptly starting and stopping.

'Bonk-bonk-bonk-bonk,' came a baritone call.

'A toad,' said Hugo in the dark. The sound came nearer, just behind us in the undergrowth. Bonk-bonk-bonk-bonk-bonk, repeated twenty times. The forest was waking up while we settled to sleep.

Two days later, we were camped on a beach farther up the river. Mist hung over the tops of the trees. Red Howler monkeys roared nearby. Dom Gerardo was already cooking spaghetti for breakfast when I got up. Hugo had gone off with the shotgun.

We heard six shots and when Hugo came back he threw down a female Howler monkey on the sand near the fire and helped himself to coffee. The dead monkey was the size of a small child, with thin arms and legs, long tail and golden orange-red fur.

Hugo told us he'd shot two other monkeys and left them to be collected later. He made up the fire after the breakfast and held the body of the female over the flames to singe the fur before scraping it off with his knife. The heat of the fire tightened the skin and muscles of the monkey, pulling open the mouth as if it were screaming and contorting hands and feet as if they were grasping or clinging.

Hugo took us back to the foot of the tree where he had shot the monkeys. One Howler had fallen from the branches and was dead on the ground. It was a big male, with loose folds of skin and fur around its chin where the amazing noise is made. There was a smaller monkey, also dead, caught over a branch forty or fifty feet above our heads. Hugo hung the male in a low tree.

We walked on inland through dense vegetation of saplings and tall plants. As usual, Hugo went ahead with the shotgun and Dom Gerardo and I followed. Dom Gerardo cut a wider path with his machete than before, chopping lianas and palm fronds, breaking stems of young saplings and notching the bark of trees with the machete. I believed he was afraid of getting lost.

Hugo tiptoed towards a crunching sound like that of a horse eating oats, while Dom Gerardo and I paused beside the curved fins of a massive tree covered in lichens. A chorus of birds gave warning cries. The crunching stopped and the creature moved off through the vegetation.

We walked further, entering darker forest where the ground was more open.

'There's nothing, nothing,' said Hugo and Dom Gerardo together.

Hugo walked a short distance farther and fired into a tree. A body fell to the ground. We reached Hugo standing beside another male Howler monkey. It was wounded and groaning slowly.

'Kill it! Kill it!' I exclaimed.

Dom Gerardo looked at me and laughed.

Hugo was telling us how he had seen the monkey and fired the shotgun.

'Kill it now!' I said, lifting my own machete. The monkey groaned again and blood was coming from its wounds. Dom Gerardo struck the monkey twice on the head with a stick. Its groaning stopped. Hugo picked up the monkey by the tail and dragged it as he walked, followed by Dom Gerardo with the shotgun. The monkey was groaning again, very softly now. Dom Gerardo glanced at me staring at him and struck the monkey a third time. The groaning stopped and didn't start again.

We walked back through the forest in silence, smearing monkey blood on plants, stems, logs and dead leaves, to the tree where we had left the other Howler monkeys. Hugo took off his boots, climbed up an adjacent tree and knocked the dead young monkey out of the tree where it had been hanging, its tail wrapped round a branch.

Back at camp, Hugo singed off the fur of the four dead monkeys on the beach and cut up the bodies. He built a second fire and a grill on which to cook the joints of meat over a slow, smoking fire.

Some travellers have protested that monkey looks too human to be eaten but I put these thoughts out of my mind. I ate rice and chewed one limb of the baby monkey: the flavour was like that of dark turkey meat.

Hunting, other than in order to eat while travelling, was forbidden in the Reserve and broke Dom Gerardo's word to the Peruvian officer on the Madre de Dios river. But Hugo was delighted to have monkey meat to take back to his family. He had taken what was available.

Smoking the meat continued all night and the fire died at dawn. The weather had changed next morning and it was too cold even for insects. A grey sky threatened rain. We stood on the beach in our sweaters, eating chopped-up monkey in a gravy with potatoes and onions for breakfast. It was time to go back.

Mist was rising from the warm river and fine drizzle was blowing in the wind when we started downstream after packing up our camp. Hugo kept the canoe in midstream, where the current was strongest. Tree-falls on the river are most likely on wet windy days and trees falling on canoes is a surprisingly common and fatal accident. We passed *capybarys*, alligators, turtles, flocks of parrots, macaws and river birds during our swift descent, pausing at one previous campsite to retrieve a fishing line which had been snagged on a heavy bush but was now exposed by the falling water level.

The canoe hit logs in the river twice during the morning, waking Dom Gerardo, who was supposed to be watching for obstacles. The advantages of the *peke-peke* motor with its long propeller shaft were obvious; Hugo could push down the steering rod, lifting the shaft clear of the water every time we went over a submerged tree.

We stopped for lunch on a beach where Dom Gerardo collected several dozen turtle eggs to take home. We were so cold, with purple feet and hands, that he began dancing like a chicken to keep warm. He danced round and round, bending over, arms apart and lunch bowl in one hand. He had worn the same green trousers, red T-shirt and blue sweater every day.

The rain stopped but we were cold all afternoon until we reached the home of the Bolivian family we had visited on the way up. Their welcome was as warm as the mugs of hot coffee they gave us. The wife brought a basket with half a dozen large cucumbers and set it beside Hugo without comment. He took the cucumbers and brought back smoked monkey limbs.

'Many thanks, gentlemen,' said the husband. He invited us to sleep but Dom Gerardo said we must reach the mouth of the river that night.

Less than a quarter of a mile downstream, however, we saw a crude shelter on the Peruvian side and he suggested camping.

'Let's keep going,' I said, wanting at least to camp out of sight of the Bolivians. Beyond several bends in the river, we came to a small shelter on the Peruvian side and two well-made huts in Bolivia. They looked deserted, without a pillar of smoke though it was late on a cold afternoon.

'Hello, hello,' we called as we climbed the steep muddy bank.

The door of one of the huts was barricaded with a table. Thin mattresses on the beds inside had been rolled up. No dogs came barking from the trees and there was nothing valuable except a few dozen dried corn cobs tied in pairs dangling from the roof under a shelter.

The ashes of the fire were still warm; evidence, we decided, that the family who owned the hut had gone down river that morning, taking their shotgun, cooking pots and radio with them in case of thieves. We were uneasy about sleeping the night and decided to boil water for tea while we waited to see if anyone arrived.

'If we don't take anything?' suggested Dom Gerardo.

'There isn't another shelter half so good.'

No one came and, after tea, we put up the mosquito nets and went to sleep.

In the morning, I left six shotgun cartridges and a note inside a tin trunk in the house: 'Thank you for your hospitality in your house for one night. Nothing stolen,' I wrote in Spanish. This was not true, because Dom Gerardo took half a dozen dry cobs of corn as we were leaving. 'For seed. There isn't this in Peru,' he said.

I nodded wearily but laughed half an hour later when he came back empty-handed and angry from an orange tree in an old garden on the riverbank. 'Someone has taken all,' he exclaimed.

It was another grey day, with a chilling breeze. We spotted *capybarys*, alligators, turtles, river birds standing like statues on the beaches, and a boat with a television crew and a dozen gringos, with another boat bringing their baggage behind them.

The Madre de Dios river looked a mile wide when we emerged from the mouth of the Rio Heath. The grey water and huge sky restored light and distance to our senses and we sailed out between high trees lining the banks.

I was glad to be out, and looking forward to fried chicken and chips and a cold beer. Insect bites and minor cuts on my legs would heal quickly. So why did it feel good to be out of the forest? Three men in a boat had travelled for nearly two weeks where order, morals and the value of human life vanish like a rainbow. We had found no Heart of Darkness. More awesome than the collapse of good or the triumph of evil is the place where neither exists.

Neither snakes nor jaguars would make me anxious again in the forest. These fears, that I had felt for many months, were replaced by a humble respect for a place in which all the thunder of civilisation is absorbed like the sound of one bird falling dead.

When we returned to Puerto Maldonada, where extra clothing, books, naturalists' notes and a diary had been left at the hotel for safekeeping, we arrived to discover that Julio had stolen everything – though the fishing net had had other admirers who might have taken advantage of the situation. Hotel staff said Julio and Anna-Maria had had a problem with her ticket and returned to the hotel after my departure with Dom Gerardo and Hugo. Julio had left me a long letter.

I read Julio's letter, saddened to be falsely accused of having not given him enough money to fly to Iquitos via Lima. His other accusations were more just. They added up to the charge that I was just another ignorant, arrogant gringo.

The hotel owner accompanied me to the police station across the street and after several hours and a bribe of $10, I received a *denuncia* against Julio giving details of his crime. It serves as a warrant for arrest, though in Peru that service requires another bribe.

'Don't trust anyone!' warned the officer.

The theft of my diary was the greatest loss. It had no value to Julio and I assumed he took it to read what I had written about him (nothing nasty) and to hurt me. There was a chance, when he calmed down, that he might deposit my belongings and the diary with the other items left for safekeeping at the hotel in Cuzco, for which I held the receipt. When I arrived in Cuzco I discovered that Julio had been to the hotel and claimed most of what we had deposited; including a beautiful poncho bought to keep warm in the mountains and a large cloth decorated with Shipibo geometric designs. However, he had at least returned my diary.

The discovery of this robbery in Cuzco sent me into a fury that not even a fall of snow on the hilltops around the town could cool. I was angry at Julio for wrecking our friendship and for stealing from me. I was equally angry at myself for reigniting his hatred of gringos, that had begun when the Baptist missionaries took away his name. And I was angry most of all with the hotel because I possessed the only receipt to all the belongings. They had no right to hand over anything without the receipt. After some arguing, and threatening to go to the Tourist Police, the owner of the hotel agreed to pay me $50 in compensation though the items could not be replaced.

'You know, normally we don't take Peruvians because they are too dishonest. I allowed your friend only because he was with you,' said the owner.

Anna-Maria wrote to me months later, having returned to Iquitos with Julio. She was amazed to hear of the thefts and remembered the beautiful brown cloth Julio had given to his family.

My plan now was new: to go back along the Royal Inca highway to the bridge over the Apurimac river and to walk from there to the farthest trickle of melted ice – the source of the Amazon. But on the night before departure, I was overcome with extreme fatigue, aching bones, sore throat and chills, and lay shivering, sweating and groaning all night. I was sure it was malaria but wanted to wait for the specific symptoms before getting a doctor or taking tablets.

Malarial fever never developed and the flu, or altitude sickness, passed after a few days. However, it was followed by a bout of mild food poisoning. The two illnesses in one week left me too weak for a month's hiking in the Andes above 15,000 feet. It seemed best to shorten the walk by starting from a town called Yauri near the Apurimac river. From there, the walk would be only sixty-two miles and up to 16,700 feet to the source of the Amazon.

8

Rio Hornillos:
In the Birthplace of the Amazon

'Man only exists for the purpose of proving to himself that he is a man and not an organ-stop! He will prove it even if it means physical suffering, even if it means turning his back on civilisation.'

Fyodor Dostoevski.

SNOW WAS COVERING the courtyard when I looked out of the little window above the door. Just my luck, I thought, to be in Room 13 along an outside balcony of the Tigre Hotel in Yauri. The room was unheated and I climbed back under layers of blankets in the sagging bed to sleep another hour.

'I want to see the source of the Amazon,' I had told a fellow passenger, called Jesus, coming in on the small bus the day before.

'Not checking the rocks? Looking for gold or silver?' he asked, as we lurched along the cart track over the misty moor, and the woman beside me was sick into the plastic bag in her lap.

'Of course not. Just to see the birthplace. Just that.'

'You mean it?'

I nodded.

'You're crazy,' he said.

I shrugged my shoulders. 'I know.' The woman threw the plastic bag out of the window and smiled.

Now the need for breakfast drove me out of bed. The man behind the only stall open down in the silent market dunked a used tea bag in a mug of boiling water and added a little sugar from a paper sack. The tea wasn't hot (because of the lower boiling temperature of water at this altitude) and it was best to hold the mug in both hands and sip very quickly. Two rounds of flat bread and two mugs of tea provided my breakfast.

Snow was falling again when I returned to the hotel to put on the native style cloth bundle I had acquired, holding sleeping bag, plastic sheeting, cheese and notebook. My shoulders had never before felt the weight of a bundle carried across the back in the peasant manner and I was not certain how well they would take it. I found it best to walk bent forward.

I was no longer self-conscious of my appearance, as I had been in Cuzco seeing the Hispanic Peruvians smiling at all the dressed up gringos. I like dressing up really, especially in practical, colourful clothes. I wanted to appear less strange walking alone in the Andes, so I had dressed like the local men, in thick trousers, heavy poncho and mutli-coloured woven cap with earflaps (called a *chullo*) under a sun hat. Fingerless wool gloves, wool sweater and jacket under the poncho kept me warm, and thick socks and suede boots protected my feet. A small woven shoulder bag also under the poncho carried camera, boiled sweets, balloons, and a supply of dry *coca* leaves and the special ash to go with them.

Coca leaves (not cocaine) can be bought legally in every street market in Peru and Bolivia and exchanging leaves is common practice between friends and strangers in the mountains.

'*Coca* is the daughter of *Pacha Mama* (Mother Earth), born as a sacred plant with the power to drive away evil,' explains Lynn Meisch in her book about the Inca countries. Indians 'sacrifice the leaves to *Pacha Mama* during sowing and at other times to protect the crops'.

Coca was a divine plant to the Incas and permitted only to the nobility. In the 16th century, the Spanish encouraged all Indians to chew the leaves, to make them work harder with less food, and to make personal fortunes from the trade.

A few leaves chewed with a piece of alkaline ash, release a tiny amount of cocaine that numbs cheek and gums and gives a boost of energy while suppressing hunger. It's ideal while walking or working at high altitude and the Indians often measure distances by the wads of *coca* to be chewed on a journey.

I decided to leave Yauri despite the storm. Snow muffled every sound up the deserted white street and was falling so thickly that I stopped to put on a plastic sheet cut in the shape of a poncho over my bundle and layers of clothing. I looked back along the track, only a quarter-mile from Yauri, but the houses had already vanished.

Hills worn smooth by ancient glaciers emerged from the mist when the snow eventually stopped. Several men in ponchos and cowboy hats muttered 'good day' as they rode towards Yauri on bicycles. I was not certain this was the right route but the ground sloped slightly to the right, as if approaching a greater valley, and the track had to meet the river somewhere, I hoped.

Snow melted, revealing tough, yellow grass on which lonely flocks of alpacas and sheep were grazing, watched by women wrapped in blankets or pairs of children in sweaters with *chullos* pulled down over their ears.

I walked slowly, taking steady breaths, and reached a fast-flowing river of milky-white water. This was the Apurimac, whose name means 'Great Speaker', a reference to the 1,300 foot gorge 145 miles downstream, that I had avoided by starting from Yauri.

The sun shone through layers of creamy cloud, melting the snow from the lower slopes. Sheep with a few lambs, mules and brown llamas nibbled the green shoots amid dead grasses. A flock of alpacas approached along the road, with coloured woollen tassels in their ears. Each colour belonged to a different owner. Alpacas have woolly sideburns and shorter necks than llamas and it was not difficult to tell them apart.

I stopped after a few more miles and sat on a rock to make a cheese sandwich; slicing the cheese with my machete and enjoying just sitting looking over the bleak land that looked so much like where I was born: the Yorkshire Dales in wintertime.

Soon the road dropped into a shallow canyon, rejoining the river beside abandoned terraces and roofless houses. My feet ached mildly and I knew from experience not to walk farther on the first day out. I carried no tent and hoped to stay with shepherd families or to sleep in barns. But on this first night, solitude was preferable. Long months always with people had taken their toll.

An overhanging rock on the bank beside the road provided a small dry cave, enough for sleeping if I curled up. Admittedly the cave could be seen by anyone coming up the road, and they might ask questions or invite me to their home or steal something, but it would be dark within two hours and perhaps no one would come.

Paper from my notebook and dead grass were too damp to burn so there would be no hot tea or soup for supper. I sat comfortably under the rock eating another cheese sandwich, and looked over the river, out through a cleft in the wall of the canyon to far-away hills. They were rounded like broad shoulders and still white with snow. What a luxury to see landscape after my months in the trees. Clouds descended and the snow-covered hills were gone.

The ground under the rock was dry and sheltered from the wind. I laid the poncho on top of a mattress of cut grass and climbed fully clothed into the sleeping bag, still wearing the *chullo* to keep my ears warm. The purling of rushing water and muffled bonks of boulders rolling along the river were the only sounds. The land was sleeping. I was alone, with the mouse that fell next to my head and scurried over the sleeping bag in the middle of the night.

Crisp cold air at dawn next morning kept me sluggish until warmed by the sun. I chewed *coca* and walked slowly for a couple of hours through the canyon beside the river.

The weather by mid-morning was ideal for walking; overcast, no rain, with patches of blue to keep you cheerful, and a breeze echoing the river along the canyon walls. I stopped to take the weight of the bundle off my shoulders and to eat a cheese sandwich. Children across the milky Apurimac were throwing stones in a game like quoits, while their sheep and alpacas grazed within calling distance. Two small blisters and a sore spot had appeared on my feet but they were quickly padded with pieces from an old T-shirt.

The stony road turned away from the river after six miles and climbed up a side valley with high sides falling into a gushing stream of clear water. A snow-capped peak appeared far away beyond an opening in the wall of the valley. There, somewhere, was my destination, the source of the Amazon river.

I reached a community of thirty tin-roofed houses after two hours steady climbing, and looked in the dark doorways of several grocery shops before seeing a plastic-topped dining table and two crates of soft drinks.

'Do you have hot water?' I asked in halting Spanish. 'Is there tea?'

'No, there's soft drink. There's *chicha* (a soft drink made from maize).'

'How much?'

'Six thousand *soles* and two thousand *soles*.'

I thought of my budget of twenty dollars – 300,000 *soles*. 'Yes, *chicha* please.'

'Come in, come in,' said the young woman and went out of a back door.

Two girls stood in the low doorway and watched me release the bundle from my shoulders and sit at a table. They watched closely when I took out a matchbox from my pocket and began blowing up one of the balloons I had bought in Cuzco to give to children along my journey.

'You want?' I asked. The tallest girl nodded. The four children each took a balloon and went outside to play. The woman fetched a plastic jug of *chicha* and a bowl of potato and gruel. 'Where are you going? Where have you come from?' she asked.

I told her I was going to the birthplace of the Amazon.

'It's a beautiful place further up,' she said.

Chewing *coca*, I walked steadily up and up the valley, beside the stream. Snow lay only in a few shaded places and when the valley opened dramatically into a bowl several miles wide, the hillsides were yellow with the grass and dotted white, black and brown with llamas, alpacas and sheep. The narrow river flowed through a gorge to the right of the track which continued straight up the hillside over huge flat rocks and short grasses nibbled by the animals.

It was a tiring climb to the top. I shifted the bundle from shoulder to shoulder, breathing deeply and steadily with my mouth wide open. The sky was blue. The sun was bright. I sat for ten minutes at the top to get my breath back, and looked down into the next valley. A few grass-thatched houses and a long building with a shining tin roof stood in a cluster surrounded by walled animal pens in the bottom. I wanted to sleep outside again but, when the road reached the settlement, my feet turned towards a break in the village wall.

A young man who had been sitting in a doorway wrapped in jacket, scarf and cap, reading a book and listening to music on a radio, approached and asked where I was going and where I had come from. He was a schoolteacher and his name was Ascencio. He called the school director, called Juan, and they invited me to supper and to stay the night. 'We don't get many visitors,' said Juan. Both had come to the isolated school from towns after graduating as teachers a few months earlier.

I gave them a handful of tea bags and Juan boiled water on the kerosene stove behind a curtain of blue plastic dividing his office from his bed and a table. He made soup, and when it was ready he cleared the schoolbooks from the only table in the whitewashed room and laid a white tablecloth. The soup was a gruel of potatoes, peppercorns, the *moraya* that I disliked and a piece of dried meat. They didn't explain why, but they made me eat separately while they waited, listening to an Ecuador versus Peru soccer match on the radio. It was difficult to remember that it was Saturday night.

'We're lost here, no?' remarked Ascencio.

We had tea again after they had eaten and sat at the table talking about the valley and the school. Sixty-nine children were enrolled, aged six to fifteen but twenty of them didn't attend because they had to shepherd their family's flocks. Classes started at 10.00 a.m. and finished at 1.30 p.m., to allow the children who walked up to five miles over the hills to get to and from school in daylight.

'Do you teach Quechua?' I asked. It is estimated that half the people in the mountains in Peru speak only Quechua but until 1975 Spanish was the only official language, used for all business of the government.

Juan said there were no books in Quechua (the Incas had no written language) and that the language was greatly mixed with Spanish.

'It is not a proper language,' he said.

They told me there were no longer fish in the river because of pollution from the copper, gold and silver mines scattered in the remote, high valleys.

We went to our beds when it was dark and cold. Juan laid three sheepskins on the wooden floor and I spread plastic sheeting, poncho and sleeping bag on top and slept fully clothed, still wearing my *chullo* and having a cold nose all night.

Next morning, Juan made thick pancakes with onions for breakfast with tea and gave me rice and pancakes to take for lunch. I left teabags, a heap of milk powder, *coca* leaves and ash, and some balloons for the children. I offered Juan money but he refused to take it.

'Meat is expensive,' I said.

He shook his head. I hoped he was not offended.

The night's frost had already melted. Flocks of sheep and llamas were out on the hillsides and lambs and ewes cried across the valley as I followed the track up the hillside. I was soon taking small steps and panting hard with mouth open like a goldfish to suck in more of the oxygen-poor air. The road eventually levelled off by a cemetery on the snow-covered hilltop and I sat down on a gravestone for a rest.

What a bleak place for a cemetery; eternal quiet and eternal wind. Jagged, snow-capped mountains crossed the horizon to the south, three days' walk away across a saucer-shaped, windswept moor, and many small valleys where the wind whistled. This is the birthplace of the Amazon; snow and ice melting on the mountains and hills, water from mosses and soggy gravels trickling into streams.

I popped a boiled sweet in my mouth and started down the slope, following what looked surprisingly like a bicycle's track through the snow. Undeniably there was contentment to be found in such desolate places. But why did I feel a comfort in this treeless landscape that I had never felt in the forest?

The moors and mountains are just as unforgiving of mistakes as the forest. The climate is harsher. Little grows and there is little to eat. But I did not feel engulfed here, alone on a hillside with the cold wind buffeting my ears.

The road divided at the bottom of the sweeping hillside, beyond a half-abandoned settlement near the Apurimac river. A kerosene tanker truck passed with men and women on the roof heading towards the whitewashed, tin-roofed houses of Cailloma, seven miles away. My feet and shoulders ached and the town was too far off my route to be worth visiting. According to my map, the longest headwater of the Apurimac lay in the mountains on the south side and not towards the town to the west.

The mountains themselves were hidden behind white hills in the foreground when the road dropped into the valley of the Rio Hornillos. This little river, the longest headwater of the Apurimac, flowed hidden in a gorge running like the gash of a knife across marsh pasture in the bottom of the valley that I reached the next day. I sat in the sunshine halfway into the valley, content to sit. The black summit of Mount Chungara rose with such clarity in the thin air that it was difficult to believe that it stood twelve miles away. A small settlement lay on one side of the valley, with goal posts for soccer, a school, basketball court, walled animal enclosure and a few stone houses gathered together to face the empty land.

I coaxed myself on another three miles before stopping for a rest where the road ran parallel to the Rio Hornillos, hidden now by great granite boulders deposited by ancient glaciers.

There is a hypnotic rhythm to walking that is hard to break, even when you are tired. Legs work with a steady pace, freeing the mind to wander the land, to see details of flowers and grasses fluttering in the breeze, formations of rocks and shadows of sunlight in gullies. There is time to think about them. Changes come step by step, like dabs of shape and colour on a painter's canvas. Walking alone and in silence, you become part of the landscape through which you are passing. Sense of one place is carried into the other when snow-capped hills sink into closed valleys of yellow grasses and flocks. You take with you memories of the passage like a river carrying rocks and sand and melted snow down the mountain.

The sun was overhead when I paused again, this time to eat an orange. Long-tailed rabbits scampered among the outcrops of rocks as I climbed to inspect a huge square boulder around which a shepherd's shelter had been built. The walls were well built and the gaps closed with sods of earth and grasses. I circled the shelter and animal enclosure twice looking for the entrance before realising that the low doorway had been expertly concealed. Another shelter, with a grass roof, stood two hundred yards away across the flat moorland, surrounded by more walled animal enclosures.

This shelter was the size of a large doghouse, with a low entrance partly closed with stones. It was smaller inside than a double bed, with a cooking hearth at one end, and with just enough headroom to stand up without touching the smoke-blackened grass roof. The ashes in the hearth were cold. I waited for my eyes to adjust to the dark and to the shafts of light shining through chinks in the walls. The room was bare, except for a few dust-covered bottles in an alcove and a nest of dry grass where the shepherd dogs probably slept.

I decided to stay and collected dead branches from an ankle-high bush that grew nearby to make a fire to melt snow. The shelter could not be seen from the road, there were no footprints in the patches of snow and the grass round about was short, so it was unlikely that anyone would arrive.

Half an hour later I was sitting in the sunshine enjoying mugs of tea with powdered milk and vanilla biscuits for lunch. My spirit soared on the silent wind over the valley. This land, and myself in it, belonged to geological time, to a slower-turning wheel on which ambitions of daily life were forgotten. All the world seemed part of creation, within it and making it. In this age of scepticism, I hesitate to call these feelings mystical, but for a time I enjoyed peace. As Byron wrote of such fleeting moments:

> I love not man the less, but Nature more,
> From these our interviews, in which I steal
> From all I may be, or have been before,
> To mingle with the Universe and feel
> What I can ne'er express, yet cannot all conceal.

Asparagus soup from a packet, bread, cheese and several mugs of tea provided a delicious warming supper, though my clothes probably reeked with smoke from the fire. The air chilled as soon as the sun sank behind the hills and their shadows crept up the far side of the valley. I brushed my teeth, washed hands and face, and prepared for night by blocking the doorway of the tiny shelter with stones and a piece of plastic sheeting. Poncho and sleeping bag provided my bed on the floor. I got inside fully clothed and fell asleep almost as soon as I closed my eyes, content after the beautiful day and hopeful my feet would not ache too much tomorrow.

In the morning I put some tea bags in a plastic bag as a gift and left them with a note in Spanish: 'Sir, many thanks for the bed for one night. I am a gringo travelling to the source of the Rio Hornillos (beginning of the Amazon). Around here is so beautiful. Thank you.'

The path through the valleys to the big mountains veered away from the gravel road, making walking much easier. Soft turf led across a flat-bottomed valley. The footpath entered a gorge and this widened after several miles, where a stream came tumbling down a narrow valley from the left. After sitting awhile in the sunshine, I turned left up the side valley, to cut across the moors instead of doggedly following the stream through each gorge.

A flock of twelve wild vicuna darted across the hillside near a large abandoned settlement where stone walls had collapsed and roofless homes sheltered only weeds. These deer-like animals are prized for their silky-soft hair. Vicuna were protected during Inca times and are protected again today but they remain rare.

It was good to be out of the valley, walking slowly across bare gravel, clumps of mosses and stunted heather-like plants. I felt myself to be standing on the roof of the world, looking over the panorama of valleys, hills, grasslands and mountains where the Amazon is born. Sometimes there was a faint path or a few cairns, but mostly I followed my own imaginary line, dipping into small valleys and climbing up the far sides. I was now at the foot of the snow-capped mountains seen three days before and could look back across the moors and valleys to the cemetery on top of the white hills.

I walked carefully as my body tired, especially when crossing areas of waterlogged fine gravel, sticky like wet concrete. I slipped twice and was fearful of twisting my ankle. My solitary figure would be swallowed by the grandeur of the scenery and the wind would absorb every call for help. As in the forest, the possibility of death was with me as closely as my shadow.

The last of my energy was consumed late in the afternoon walking up a long gentle slope towards a chapel and cottage. Four black dogs with golden eyes came barking and bouncing down the slope but didn't come near to bite.

'Good afternoon,' I said in Spanish when a woman looked over the wall of an animal enclosure.

She smiled. 'Where have you come from? Where are you going?'

I explained.

'Yes, yes,' she said, not understanding. 'What are you going to do?'

'I'm looking for a place to sleep,' I said.

She shouted at the still barking dogs, threw a stone at them, and invited me inside the shelter of the enclosure. The woman had been spinning wool with a hand-held spindle and mending a pleated blue skirt in the sunshine, sheltered from the wind. She spread a black shawl on a rock and told me to sit down.

'Where are you coming from?' she asked again. 'Where do you sleep?'

'May I sleep in the church?'

'It's locked.'

I offered the plastic bag of *coca* leaves. She accepted it eagerly and with a grin. 'Do you take?'

'Yes, it's good for walking.'

She nodded, folded a few leaves and put them in her mouth. 'You have such a big bundle, what are you selling?'

'No, no, I'm not selling. I have a poncho, sleeping bag and food. Where can you buy anything round here?' I asked, waving an arm to the hill on the horizon.

'You don't speak much Spanish?'

'No, English and Portuguese.'

'Here, we don't speak English. Quechua and Spanish.'

'Of course.'

'Do you have a camera?'

I took it out.

'No, no – I must change my clothes,' she exclaimed, smoothing her ankle-length pink skirt and patched long-sleeved jacket. 'Where are you from? From Chile? You're not Peruvian.'

She nodded when I told her of my land and asked about her flocks, if there were many llamas and alpacas. I didn't know the Spanish or Quechua for sheep, pig or horse so I baa-ed, snorted and whinnied until this kindly woman stopped laughing and told me the names.

'In the morning, where are you going?'

'Up the Quebrada Apacheta – the longest source stream of the Rio Hornillos.'

ght on the Rio Tamshiyaku, Peru, after a late afternoon thunderstorm. Guide Julio Cesar fishes for piranha.

Above: The Sale[s]
Mission church [and]
boarding schoo[l at]
Sao Gabriel da
Cachoeira, on t[he]
upper Rio Negr[o,]
Brazil, were fou[nded]
in 1914.

Left: A family o[n the]
upper Rio Negr[o,]
Brazil, going ho[me]
with a pig and t[he]
family dog.

Top right: Powdered milk to fish hooks; a general store sells on credit a few of every item. Sao Gabriel da Cachoeira, upper Rio Negro, Brazil.

Middle: The congested terminus in Manaus, Brazil, where long-distance ferries await passengers, and where all my luggage was stolen on the boat to Peru.

Below: Fresh turtle meat to disposable razors – everything is for sale somewhere along eight kilometres of stalls in the main market of Iquitos, Peru.

Above: A family paddles home in the late afternoon on the calm Rio Negro, Brazil. The man sits in the customary paddler's position with knees tucked under the bow bench. Canoes are essential transport for everyone outside the towns. The forest on the Rio Negro is shorter than on brown water (silty) rivers because of the lack of nutrients in the underlying geological formation.

Above: A family of rubber-tappers (*seringueiros*) on the Rio Negro, Brazil. Families leave their main homes to collect the white latex in the forest during the four-month season before the rains come in late April.

Right: By the Tamshiyaku river, near Iquitos, Peru, a mother watches her daughter making clothes for the grandchildren. A sewing machine, an outboard motor and a radio are considered to be the most desirable luxury goods.

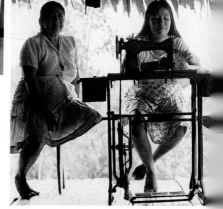

Below: Trees of the Amazon forest holding themselves up by leaning on each other and not through a deep and extensive root system. Soils, varying in fertility throughout the vast region, are thin because of the rapid decomposition of vegetable matter by fungi and insects. Large sections of forest along the rivers can fall when the bank collapses during rains or floods; as has happened here on the Madre de Dios river, Peru.

Top: Trees and bushes of the flooded forest are adapted to stand in water during the rainy season. Lago Janauacá on the Rio Solimões, Brazil.

Middle: Few leaves escape the appetite of thousands of insect species roaming all levels of the forest.

Above: Black water perfectly mirrors the flooded forest. Lago Januacá on the Rio Solimões, Brazil.

Top: Yanomami chief, Renato, wearing his best clothes, sunhat and chewing tobacco, manoeuvres the author's little canoe in rapids below a waterfall of the Rio Marauiá, Brazil.

Above: With sleeping bag and food in his bundle, the author reaches the top of the pass at 5100 metres (nearly 17,000 feet) in the Andes, southern Peru. The melting snow forms the Quebrada Apacheta, the source of the Amazon 6500 kms. (over 4050 miles) from the Atlantic ocean.

Left: Sitting at the top of a forested volcanic cone behind Sao Gabriel da Cachoeira at the start of my journeys.

Top: Leaving the Yanomami land with chief Renato and Domingo, and the four Brazilian diamond prospectors, at the second waterfall on the Marauia river, Brazil.

Above: So many insects visited the author's camp beside the Rio Heath, Peru, that eating meals inside the mosquito net was like being inside a beehive.

Right: Wearing a shirt with the tiger from a different continent Peruvian guide Victor Hugo prepares to roast a red howler monkey shot on the bank of the Rio Heath.

Below: Gilberto bathed and decorated after a day's fishing. He must live in the village and work for his father-in-law for two years before marrying the chief's elder daughter.

Above: Robi, the chief's middle son, wears a simple pattern, painted with the o red seeds of the *urucu* tree cultivated throughout the Amazon by Indians to decorate themselves and t possessions.

Left: Their visitor was a constant curiosity to Yanomami children and parents. The sons of Chie Renato and his brother-in Gabriel were ever present observers and playmates

'Do you want to sleep here tonight?'

I nodded and she handed back the bag of *coca*, gathered up her spinning and mending and led me to a lean-to shack at the back of her own home. 'Wait here,' she said, then swept the floor and sprinkled water from a metal bucket to keep down the dust.

The shack was one room, with stone platforms for sleeping across the ends, a narrow stone bench along one wall and a machine-made wooden table that must have been brought on the back of a pack animal. I held out a handful of teabags when the woman brought sheepskins for the bed. 'I'll make hot water,' she said.

'Do you have food to cook?' she asked when she came back with the kettle of hot water.

'No, I have bread and cheese. If you have food – soup – I'll pay, of course.'

'You want soup?'

'Yes please, but not with *moraya*, I'm not accustomed.'

'You have bread?'

I gave her half the bread in my bundle. 'I have milk powder.'

She fetched a mug to be filled. 'Do you want rice soup?'

'Yes, thank you.'

The sun was low and weak in the sky. I sat with my knees shivering, though I was fully dressed in poncho, and gloves. Flocks had come back and were settled in the walled enclosures. It was bedtime as soon as it was dark, after a bowl of rice and potato soup. I heard the dogs bark and a man's voice some time later, but I was soon asleep, bundled as usual in the sleeping bag.

Two men came to talk while I drank a bowl of tea in the morning. Both of them had arrived in the night, one of them had come with five cows over the pass from Lari and would be returning after a few days. He said it was a journey of twenty-two hours and that the top of the pass was knee-deep in snow. The stream beginning at the top of this pass was the longest headstream of the Amazon.

'It's a beautiful place here, no?' he asked.

The cheery woman brought a bowl of soup with a cracked bone in it. All three people were disappointed when I told them my camera did not give instant photographs. The woman never smiled again and accepted two handfuls of *coca* leaves with a stern face – even though I offered to mail photographs later to Lari.

The path from their cottage passed along a black lake edged with ice, then climbed the shoulder at the end of the valley. I halted abruptly at the top, as if slapped in the face, and had to sit on the rocks of a cairn for a few minutes. Silence was the shock; no sounds at all. Nothing. Everything in the valley had stopped, even the wind, and the water in the stream.

I walked on, down through scattered flocks, watched by children or groups of women, and after four miles came to the mountain that blocked the end of the valley. Streams entered from both sides. An expedition from National Geographic in 1971 had planted their flag in an icy ridge above the Carhuasanta stream on the left side. The path I was following turned up the right side into the narrow valley of the Quebrada Apacheta. According to the map, this stream is the longest headwater of the Rio Lloqueta which flows into the waters called the Hornillos, Apurimac, Ene, Tambo, Ucayali, Solimoes and Amazon.

I sat on a rock for ten minutes, enjoying the relief of not wearing the bundle on my shoulders, and listened to the trickling water from snow and ice melting in the sunshine. Once I started from here, I would have to hurry to reach the summit and get down on the Pacific side before night fell on the snow on the summit. The sun was already high in the sky and though the distance was only about thirteen miles the way would be exhausting. I decided to get going.

The way became much steeper after two miles, when I jumped across the stream to follow a path on the left side of the valley. I walked with my mouth open and stopped every twenty paces to catch my breath, and sat many times with eyes closed to block out the dazzling snow and to relieve the strain. I chewed *coca* and could feel the boosts of energy and the numbing of my aches and fatigue.

The air in the valley was so clear that distant rocks and ridges of snow looked to be near. I was happy to be deceived, tramping up that long slope, looking at the top of the mountain that never came nearer. All sense of time was lost. Eventually, I was walking through slushy snow covering the valley down from the rim of the mountains, and I stopped for a long rest where the Apacheta river emerged for the first time from under the snow.

My breathing slowed after five minutes and I could hear water running under the ground. Now, the mountains were no wider apart than the sides of a ravine. I walked with one ear bent to the snow, listening to the stream flowing under my feet. I knelt in the snow farther up the ravine and began cutting a hole with the machete. The work left me breathless and dizzy when I stood up.

Donkle-donkle-donkle, came the sound of bells from the top of the ravine. Two dozen llamas, loaded with sacks, were approaching down the track.

'Good day, sir,' I said in Spanish to the first of two men walking with the animals .

'Good day. Where are you going? Where have you come from? What are you selling?' he asked, pointing to the bundle with the bulky sleeping bag.

'Nothing. I came to see the source of the Amazon. Exactly here,' I said. They looked at me as blankly as their animals, then nodded resignedly.

'Do you want *coca*?' I asked, holding out the bag to them. They said they had come up from Lari on the other side and were heading to Yauri. We shook hands and they were soon out of sight, though the donkle-donkle of the bells round the necks of the llamas sounded for several minutes, until it too was swallowed by the silence.

I climbed back to the hole in the snow, knelt and reached through to fill my mug with water from this stream that began as trickles of meltwater and flowed from here over 4000 miles across the continent.

I climbed more slowly than ever up the last part of the ravine, panting so hard I couldn't swallow, stopping every four or five paces to catch my breath and feeling very unsteady. I was stepping so slowly and resting so often that I seemed hardly to be moving at all, when a large iron cross emerged above the snow. It stood above a large cairn, marking the *apacheta* – the sacred spot at the top of the mountain pass. I stood with eyes closed, when I finally arrived, waiting for my breath to quieten and my heart to cease pounding.

Three horsemen stood in front of me when I opened my eyes. Their faces were round and dark and broken by smiles and the white of their teeth. Their laughter was a mixture of surprise at meeting a solitary gringo and relief at themselves having reached the top of the 16,700 foot pass. We exchanged greetings and then they were gone, down the path towards the Atlantic.

How many days would a bottle take to float from the snow and ice in this narrow pass, down through the forest to the mouth of the Amazon, so wide that a boat in the middle sees no land? Approximately three months, I thought. And the message in the bottle? People scratch their names on walls and nations leave their flags in remote places, even on the moon. Each is insisting: 'I have been here.' No bottle for me, therefore. Even without a written message the statement it made would be vainglorious.

It was already late in the afternoon with a chilling wind blowing through the mountains. Shadows were growing across the snow and I was much too tired to think seriously of climbing to the summit of one of the white mountains rising on either side. So I threw a rock onto the cairn, then started down the Pacific side of the pass, away from the Amazon. I had descended a hundred yards before realizing I'd forgotten a trophy for my collection of stones from the sources of rivers. I climbed back to the cairn and searched until I found a little brownish slab lying a few feet inside the watershed of the Amazon.

The path on the Pacific side of the Andes plummeted into the gloomy canyons of the Colca river, 125 miles from the coast. I walked with knees bent and shoulders leaning into the white escarpment for fear of falling sideways down the mountain. The path widened into a track below the snow, then plunged down valleys of brown cliffs and across pastures of coarse grasses. The sun set and daylight faded into the blue-blackness of a moonlit night. Eventually, I reached the bottom of the valley 6000 feet below the mountain pass and walked into the village of Lari feeling like a returned pilgrim.

Originally, I had planned to go home after reaching the source of the Amazon. But now, my search seemed far from complete. I felt thoroughly trained and invigorated by the experiences of the previous months and was eager to get back to the forest; this time alone, in my own canoe.

I travelled from Lari in the back of a truck and by bus to Arequipa, back to Cuzco to collect some belongings, and then down to Lima. The flight to return from Lima to Manaus, in Brazil, passed through Iquitos. A two-day stopover gave me the hope of catching up with Julio or at least visiting his family. It was almost the end of July when the plane arrived two hours late in the familiar heat and humidity of the Amazon. That night I reached Julio's house at 10.30 p.m. carrying a flashlight and a machete.

The house had a new frontage – paid for with money obtained from somewhere or other – but the door was not padlocked. I battered until a woman appeared. 'Julio isn't here. He's gone up river to Tamshiyacu,' she said.

I told her he had stolen my property.

'He'll return tomorrow. Come tomorrow.'

'If I come tomorrow, I'll bring the police,' I said.

The woman fetched her husband and I walked inside. Walls and furniture had been rearranged and we sat round a table covered with Julio's boxes.

'There's nothing here,' said the husband.

'Well, I'd like to look.'

The husband said Julio had returned with Anna-Maria but that she had now gone. I showed them the *denuncia* against Julio from the police in Puerto Maldonado and started opening drawers and Julio's boxes. I found my map of South America, letters, papers, fishing line. Fishing net, poncho, Shipibo cloth and a shirt were still missing. I handed the husband a letter for Julio and said I'd go up river to see his parents the next morning.

Unfortunately, I missed the river bus, which left punctually, but from a new place. The annual snow-melt in the Andes had passed and the river had fallen at least twenty feet since March. People in Belen were walking where they had paddled canoes five months earlier. Streets had been cleaned of the mud and debris from half a year's flooding. Ground-level shops had been cleaned, repainted and stocked with groceries, shoes, drugs and crates of beer.

That evening I met Freddie, the guide who had introduced himself to me five months earlier. He was searching for Julio and claimed Julio had stolen $280 from a Dutchman in a tour group with his brother. Freddie claimed Julio denied the charge but had offered to replace the money.

Our combined anger was hotter than the sultry night; we talked of buying revenge by having Julio's arms or legs broken. The talk was serious. Revenge costs little money in South America and is more effective than the police. However, I wanted Julio to be ashamed, not a victim of my thuggery. And in any case I gained neither, for I flew empty-handed to Manaus the next morning, frightened by my own resentfulness.

9

Manaus:
The Macaw and the Butterfly

'Man's power over Nature often turns out to be a power exerted by some
men over other men with Nature as its instrument.'
C. S. Lewis, The Culture of Technology.

IN MANAUS I STARTED my first morning back in Brazil by walking
through boatyards and bars beside the Rio Negro, asking if anyone
knew of a canoe for sale. It was Sunday, when most Manaus families
go to the beach, or stay home watching television or flying kites
above the tin-roofs and power lines.

'Are you a Paulista?' asked a youth, breaking away from a football
game in the street. I laughed and felt complimented that someone
thought I could be Brazilian. Paulistas – people from São Paulo –
are known for their pale skin, while the equally pale-skinned gringos
are recognized by their clothes and their assertive way of walking.

'I'm looking to buy a canoe,' I told the youth, knowing that my
Portuguese accent would instantly mark me as a foreigner after all.

'A canoe? Maybe I have a friend who want to sell. Let's go there
and you pay me ten per cent commission when you buy, O.K.?'

Ten minutes later were looking at two large canoes moored down
at the end of an alley between slum houses on stilts over the water.

'Well?' asked Emidio Viana, the man who had built them. I
learned later that he also worked as a night watchman and his wife
worked as a seamstress.

'They look very big for just one man,' I said. 'Could you build
something smaller?'

'Smaller? Yes.'

Emidio agreed to build a ten foot canoe for $36 within five days. I
went back that evening with half the money. 'This is a dangerous
area for gringo with money,' he said when we met near the bus stop.

There was not much I could do if he skipped with the money but I asked for a receipt all the same. Emidio could not read or write but, fortunately, his brother-in-law was with him and he signed the slip of paper.

'Only one condition. I want to work with you to build the canoe.' Emidio frowned.

'I just want to learn how the canoe is made. You don't have to pay me,' I explained. We agreed to meet at a boatyard across the inlet early the following morning and I left giddy with excitement to have accomplished so much on my first day in Manaus.

Canoe-building was delayed a couple of days due to a shortage of wood at the sawmill, Emidio said, but the craft was ready to be painted on the fifth day. Its construction was simple; Emidio used an adze to shape points on both ends of a flat board held with his toes. Two pairs of boards were planed and nailed to build up the sides and he shaped two small boards to close both ends. Gaps were stuffed with rough cotton from the Kapok tree and caulked with a white paste.

'It's a very little canoe,' said many men in the boatyard. I worked with Emidio and listened to the comments in silence. People asked the price of the canoe and a few offered to buy it from me. Everyone thought the gringo was mad for wanting to travel into the forest alone. 'Aren't you afraid?' they asked.

I planned to be away five weeks and bought food, cooking pots, mosquito net and fish hooks and line even before the canoe was finished. I continued work on a new fishing net each evening, hoping to be able to take it with me. Where to go? Friends from my earlier stays in the city answered questions about the smaller tributaries and kept quiet about my foolishness in wanting to be alone.

In the meantime, my money was running out. Prices had doubled in five months and the exchange rate with the US dollar had not quite kept pace, so that hotels and meals were starting to feel expensive. Less than $100 remained in my money belt after all the robberies, extra flights and Julio's expenses.

I decided to paint the canoe yellow and bright green, the colours of the Brazilian flag and the colours of two common butterflies.

'What's the name of your canoe?' Ernesto asked. He and his wife operated a simple tourist lodge on a lake near Manaus and we had become friends during my first visit.

'I don't know. It's just small and light, so maybe I'll call it *borboleta* – butterfly,' I said.

'Butterfly? Don't you know that's slang for transvestite?'

Ernesto had twice paid deposits to carpenters to build large canoes to transport tourists at his lodge and twice they had disappeared with his money. I took him to see Emidio and he ordered a 32-seater canoe.

My canoe was ready for its trial on the Rio Negro a couple of days later, when the paint dried thoroughly. Emidio presented me with a paddle and I climbed carefully into the canoe to sit at the front, tucking my legs under the seat. A few trickles of water leaked through the caulking as I backed the canoe away from the shore and turned down the calm inlet. The canoe seemed remarkably buoyant though the waves came within a couple of inches of the gunnels. The sun was half-down in the sky and the afternoon wind made the air seem fresher. I paddled on either side of the canoe, keeping it gliding straight down the inlet and out onto the windswept Rio Negro.

The canoe rose and fell like driftwood on the surging swells of black water, pitching and rolling in the troughs between the waves. Water splashed over the sides as I ventured farther from the shore towards a floating gasoline station. Within an hour the canoe was back at the boatyard and I felt defeated and weary from fright. The canoe floated too low in the water; its internal space was too small. *Butterfly* would be a good canoe for fishing along a calm river but it was much too small for long-distance river travel.

Emidio nodded his head when I told him. The canoe would have to be sold. Emidio now suggested building a 13-foot canoe which would displace proportionately much more water than the smaller canoe. But I did not have enough money to pay Emidio until *Butterfly* could be sold. Meanwhile, even modest meals and the clean Hotel Iguacu were taking dollars every day from the last $50 in my money belt.

I would have to forget the canoe and leave the Amazon unless someone bought the boat within a few days. When Ernesto heard this, he said he would buy *Butterfly* himself and immediately took the money from his wallet. Emidio promised to get the second canoe built promptly but, first, he had to finish Ernesto's canoe. The work would take two weeks, he said. I could do nothing but wait. Ernesto invited me to stay at the lodge in the forest and I earned my keep for a week by helping with the dozens of young tourists, each experiencing the Amazon in two days.

The Hotel Iguacu was full when I returned. My money was almost all gone. 'You have a hammock, no? If you want to sleep in the basement, and take a shower and have breakfast in the hotel, then O.K.,' said the father of the family that owned the hotel. I had stayed with them before and the father called me 'godson'. They had even offered to lend money when I arrived from Iquitos with little Brazilian currency on a Saturday. Cobwebs were soon swept away in the basement and I told the chickens pecking in the corners to stay outside.

Emidio reported delays in completing the big canoe for Ernesto because of a shortage of boards at the local sawmill. After a week, the owner of the Hotel Riomar, where Ernesto operated his business, invited me to stay at his house. 'Eat meals in the hotel,' said Armando. 'It is not often someone comes here, learns Portuguese, travels as far as you have, asks so many questions or really wants to go into the forest. I want to help,' he said.

Help came from many people eager to share if I no longer had money for meals or beers or entertainment. I was relieved and grateful to them all to be able to stay in the Amazon for a few more weeks.

At last, Ernesto's new canoe was ready, and Emidio started work on the new canoe for me the next day, even though inflation in the meantime had pushed up prices at the sawmill. The canoe was ready in three days and then we went together for a few beers to celebrate.

'I am a poor man, sir,' began Emidio, flushed with several beers. 'I have nothing. You see my house. But, sir, I have my word. When I say the canoe will be built, then it is built,' he said.

My host Armando asked, 'What colour will you paint your new canoe?'

'Paint? I've no money for paint now.'

'But what colour, if you had?'

'Red and blue,' I said, 'the colours of a macaw.'

Armando laughed. 'Then buy your paint.'

During the weeks of waiting in Manaus, I had attended a one-day public meeting about Balbina – a hydro-electric dam nearing completion nearby. The project highlights many of the current conflicts in the Amazon – development and conservation, Indians and Brazilians, science research and technological achievements.

'Balbina means a better life, with more tranquillity, more comfort and security for Manaus. Balbina is one of your most important conquests. And guarantees the future for you, your family, your city,' claimed a prolonged advertising campaign in newspapers, and on radio and television.

'Who is not in favour of Balbina is against you,' was the campaign's slogan.

Even Brazilian scientists have to establish their patriotism before they dare criticise industrial projects in the Amazon. The Balbina dam is no exception. At the public meeting pale-skinned Paulistas in particular had first to state that they were Brazilians who loved their country.

Balbina is needed to power industrial growth in Manaus and will replace expensive imported oil, its proponents assert. But when one thousand square miles of forest are flooded, the rotting trees may poison the water with hydrogen sulphide, claim opponents, as just one example of the probable ecological damage. Also, electricity from Balbina will be expensive; the lake will cover the same area as another enormous hydro project in the Amazon but for technical reasons will produce only five per cent as much power.

Today the Balbina dam is almost complete.

About 2000 Waimiri-Atroari Indians and a few Brazilian families have been removed from their traditional lands to make room for it. These same people were 'pacified' in 1975 by National Indian Foundation (Funai) official Sebastiao Amancio after they had killed three Funai officers and another Brazilian during the construction of a road through the area.

O Globo, Brazil's biggest newspaper, quoted Amancio as saying: 'The Waimiri-Atroaris need to learn their lesson, to learn that they did something wrong. I'm going to act against them with an iron hand. The chiefs will be punished and, if possible, deported far away from their lands and their people. In this way they will learn that it's not right to kill the civilized.'

The newspaper further reported that, 'according to Amancio, his first duty was the protection of the workers constructing the road. Secondarily, he would attend to the reinitiation of contact with the Indians: 'I'll go with an Army patrol to an Indian village and there, in front of everyone, I'll give a beautiful demonstration of our power. We'll shoot machine-gun volleys into the trees, we'll explode grenades and make a lot of noise, without wounding anybody, until the Waimiri-Atroaris are convinced that we are a lot stronger than they are.'

Newspapers in Manaus carried news of another tribe during the weeks I waited for my second canoe. Yanomamis were accused of massacring gold prospectors 420 miles north of Manaus. Newspapers reported that armed Yanomamis had attacked the unarmed prospectors. Photographs showed the survivors and stories quoted Federal Police, Army and FUNAI officials blaming missionaries for inciting the Indians.

Several thousand Yanomamis in the border area between Brazil and Venezuela remained some of the most remote tribal Indians in the Amazon until the 1960s. Since then, missionaries, prospectors and soldiers have brought the Bible, clothes, steel tools and disease.

Headlines dropped to single paragraphs when the Indian massacre story was revealed after a week as the deaths of four Indians and two prospectors. FUNAI, headed by regional superintendent Sebastiao Amancio, ordered the removal of all whites from the area, but such interventions are known to be a two-edged sword. The ban keeps out missionaries and anthropologists who would help the Indians protect themselves, but nothing stops gold miners from paying bush pilots to fly them back after a few months.

Efforts to survey and safeguard Yanomami land in Brazil have failed. Official excuses include shortage of money and people. In fact corruption and mismanagement have eaten up the funds. Lack of will is the main reason for endless delays and broken promises. Even the internationally-famous Xingu National Park was bisected by a road in 1971.

Brazilians know the Yanomami lands are rich in gold, silver, diamonds, tin ore, uranium and other high-value materials. Politicians, businessmen and soldiers voice the almost universal opinion in Brazil that the industrial development of their nation cannot be slowed or prevented for the sake of a few thousand 'indios' who are 0.2 per cent of the population. This assumption underlies all the rhetoric and all so-called laws to safeguard Indians. It is neither new nor limited to Brazil.

'What good man would prefer a country covered with forests and ranged by a few thousand savages to our extensive Republic, studded with cities, towns and prosperous farms, embellished with all the improvements which art can devise or industry execute?' asked Andrew Jackson in his inaugural speech as President of the United States of America in 1829.

'How can we settle their land claim and still maintain our own standard of living?' asked a Canadian journalist about Canadian Indian land claims still in dispute after forty years of struggle. Brazilians ask the same question and argue that, because their white people are so much poorer than white North Americans, their need for development is so much greater.

'We will take every care with the Indians. But we will not permit them to impede the advance of progress,' declared the Brazilian Minister of the Interior in 1970.

'No one should expect Brazil, with its riches, with its potential, with its determination, to be a second-rate country . . . We have a different vision of ourselves,' said President José Sarney in 1986.

I asked a carpenter working in a neighbouring hotel what he thought about the conflict between Indians and Brazilians. 'It is the Indians' land, it is their gold,' he said. 'But what are they doing with it? Nothing. And the prospectors work hard in conditions like hell. They make themselves rich and help the development of our country.'

Perhaps there can be no solution as long as the white man believes he is more highly evolved than 'primitive' people. Even Canada, a country without a population explosion, without great poverty, without the need of massive land reform to share wealth, has not been able to settle its Indian land claims. Only thirty years ago Eskimo villages were being moved south to force children to white schools. Even today, petroleum and logging rights are sold by the government on Indian lands which are still disputed.

For whatever reasons, Indians are deemed not to be using the land and therefore it is forfeit. Even when parks have been made for Indians – and there are several dozen reserves in the Amazon today – their boundaries are not respected. When a white man wants a road, he takes the most direct route across land he sees as 'empty'.

We may not want to admit it, but change in the Amazon is inevitable. Civilisation (whatever that is) has always grown at the expense of forests. The forest that once covered Europe – encouraging Hansel and Gretel stories – has been turned by civilised people into a few fields and an urban wilderness.

Clearing trees may be inevitable; squandering them is not. The real tragedy in the Amazon and other areas of forest devastation is that the forest is being destroyed for quick cash and is not being replaced by settled communities and sustainable agriculture. Brazilians blame their enormous foreign debt – though debt repayment has nothing to do with cattle ranching, except where logging of hardwood trees precedes general clearing and burning of forest.

'The forest is an asset – it should be an economic asset not just an asset,' João Rego, a timber merchant and businessman in Para, in the eastern Amazon, said to me.

'Do you think it right that people starve or a country reneges on international promises just because they want to keep the green forest in front of them?'

'And when the last mahogany tree has gone?' I asked, something Senor Rego forecast would happen within five years in the eastern Amazon.

'If you ask what will happen if we run out of mahogany, I don't think it's going to be a tragedy. There will be other woods.

'I would rather take my son to see one mahogany tree in a sanctuary and tell him, "We made money from that tree, we made furniture from that tree." I think it all boils down to economics,' said João Rego.

People in industrial societies today seem to find economic arguments irresistible. Yet the ecological argument for preserving forest is that ranching is unsustainable and therefore bad economics. Logging tropical hardwoods without replacing them is also bad economics. And in recent months, mercifully, the need for wiser stewardship of an invaluable resource has slowly been gaining support in Brazil.

My own thoughts about the forest were still evolving, and had changed from anxiety to anticipation during the months of travelling. The uses to which the forest can be properly put depend on one's vision of it. My own glimpses of the forest were still very incomplete. Leaving the advertising campaign for Balbina portraying a man shivering in Manaus for want of electricity, I was eager to paddle away from civilisation, to be in the forest alone, and to learn from it.

10

Rio Preto da Eva: Paddling Inside the Vast Body

'Hunting in my experience – and by hunting I simply mean being out on the land – is a state of mind. All of one's faculties are brought to bear in an effort to become fully incorporated into the landscape . . . To hunt means to have the land around you like clothing. It means to release yourself from rational images of what something "means" and to be concerned only that it "is". And then to recognise that things exist only insofar as they can be related to other things.'

Barry Lopez, *Arctic Dreams*.

I HAD HOPED TO paddle away from Manaus before the city awoke and boats disturbed the flat clam of the river, but the sun had risen by the time my food and equipment were loaded into *Macaw* on the day of departure. The first five miles would be the most hazardous; passing the floating harbour, the port of long-distance ferries, the second port of the river buses, and the fishng boats, barges and speedboats crossing back and forth all around the small canoe.

Water poured over the bow when the canoe caught the wake of a passing boat. A second wave crashed over the stern and swilled around my ankles. However, Emidio had assured me the canoe was big enough, and sitting farther back lightened the bows, allowing it to ride higher in the water. Water still spilled over when speedboats chased by, but after a couple of hours of steady paddling I was no longer fearful of sinking. I kept about 150 yards offshore from the shipyards, sawmills, oil refinery and naval patrol ships along the bank of the Rio Negro, and so benefited from the current without getting into the choppy water farther out on the mile-wide river.

Manaus stands ten miles up the Rio Negro from its meeting with the Amazon (or the Solimões as the river is called before the Rio Negro enters) and the sun was high in the sky by the time I entered this junction. The Meeting of the Waters, where telecommunications dishes stand on the high bank, is famous because the silt-laden Solimões and the black Negro flow side by side without mixing for ten miles down the Amazon. Indeed, when the Spanish Jesuit Cristobal de Acuña came down the Solimões from Ecuador in February 1639, he saw the two rivers as master and servant and noted the supremacy of the white over the dark. 'The new river does not wish to become subject to [the lighter Solimões], without receiving some marks of respect, and it thus masters one half of the whole Amazon . . . At last the Amazon, not permitting so much superiority, forces it to mingle with its own turbulent waters, and recognise for a master the river which it desired to make a vassal.'

Pink dolphins broke the surface of the water, swimming with the canoe for half a mile, until I reached people picnicking and fishing along a beach. I stopped at the far end of the beach beside a fishing boat whose crew was sleeping on the deck. Commercial fishing is big business on the Amazon, but is being damaged by the deforestation along the floodplains. Many fish rely on fruits and seeds when the rivers flood these forests in April, May and June.

The fears of the morning had taken away my appetite. I stretched my legs, then sat in the shade on the bank and ate three oranges. Three boys arrived in a canoe. One of them fished with a circular throw net while his companions lit a fire. My own net, sixteen feet in diameter, fell in a heap in the water when I tried throwing it. I needed help and walked to the boys to ask them to teach me. They were eating a *tucanare* grilled on green sticks over a small fire.

'Have you had lunch?' asked one of them. I was invited to eat and crouched down beside them to pick a piece of the succulent fish from the paddle. We scooped *farinha* from a bag with our fingers and when it was finished I fetched more from my canoe and some oranges.

'Are you Colombian?' the eldest boy asked me.

'English,' I said.

They nodded blankly.

'How do you throw the net?'

They demonstrated how to secure the cord around your waist, grip the weighted skirt between your teeth, drape the net over both arms and hurl it, all with one fast turn of the body.

I had a go. 'You need practice,' they said and gave me a fish for my supper before paddling away.

I set off too. Cattle pastures and occasional wooden houses lined both banks of the river and far to the south plumes of smoke were rising from fires clearing the forest for more cattle pastures. The smoke from these fires can be so thick that some regional airports close during the dry months of August, September and October, when tens of thousands of fires release millions of tons of carbon into the atmosphere, adding to the greenhouse effect. Fires so large that they can be seen from space are sad beacons of an advancing civilisation.

The river was quiet in the heat of the day. I paddled sleepily on. It was time to make camp when the harsh sunlight changed to a softer light two hours before dark. I stopped where there were large trees, little underbush and no houses, dogs or cattle. This was my first night camping alone and it was almost dark before all the strings of the mosquito net, the hammock inside and plastic rain sheet over the net, had been adjusted and securely tied.

Fishing, cargo and double-decker boats loaded with passengers, and *balsas* loaded with freight trucks, were passing close to the shore on their way up river to Manaus, so I emptied the canoe and padlocked it to a tree with the chain.

I took a bath and had a fast supper of bread and lemonade before thousands of mosquitoes came out whining and biting, invisible in the twilight. They peppered the outside of the netting around the hammock and it was a reasonably pleasant game, before I fell asleep, to kill the mosquitoes that got inside.

I slept on a beach the next night and drifted on down the river in the morning, eating bread and jam and drinking river water for breakfast. The day was windless at first, making me glad of my hat as the sun rose higher in the sky. I paddled with strokes as automatic as walking, and so far with only a few blisters on my hands. I passed a settlement with the popular name of Belo Horizonte, meaning Beautiful Horizon. The house looked across the river to a cattle pasture and clumps of Cecropia trees.

'Entrance forbidden to persons without authorisation. Subject to armed enforcement,' read the sign at a cattle ranch I paddled past just before noon.

Another sign on the river bank announced 'New Life Farm' and a black youth with muscles like Hercules came down to the floating jetty. I called out asking the distance to the Rio Preto.

'Where are you going? Have you had lunch? Do you want a glass of milk?' he shouted back.

I hadn't had fresh milk for many months, so I went ashore. Hercules lived in a freshly-painted wooden house at the top of the bank. Hammock, table, and shelves with radio-tape recorder and school books furnished the first room, separated by a cloth partition from the tidy kitchen where his sister was cleaning pots. I accepted a second glass of milk and, when the brother-in-law came, they asked me again who I was, where I was going, where I had come from and what I had in the canoe. There was nothing to hide, so we went down to the canoe and I pulled back the plastic sheet.

'What's in here?'

'Food.'

'All this for two weeks? You have a camera?'

Every gringo carries a camera and it was foolish to deny it. They looked at the camera and handed it back. 'Do you have a receipt? Do you have documents?'

'Are you police?' I asked, feeling my neck tense.

'Something like that.'

'Let me see your papers.'

'We have ours. Where are yours?'

My passport was in Manaus, in case of an accident with the canoe, and I showed them a photocopy. One of the pages had Peruvian immigration stamps.

'You lied. You said you were English. This says Peru,' said Hercules.

My explanation produced a demand for papers with a Brazilian stamp. I said, 'You have no right. You think I'm a thief, but you are the people searching my belongings. Oh! I'm leaving.'

I moved to untie the mooring rope. Hercules suddenly grabbed me round the waist. 'Calm, calm, calm. We'll go to the police.'

We returned to the house but they wouldn't let me inside. Hercules fetched a white rope and told me to be silent. But he couldn't resist asking me questions. 'If you are a tourist, why aren't you travelling on a big boat? Tourists don't have canoes, thieves do. Foreigners already stole my canoe.'

'You see nothing on a big boat. It's better with a canoe if you want to meet people,' I said, anxiously watching Hercule's large hands play with the rope.

'Why don't you have a little motor?'

'I don't have the money.'

'Why not?'

'Because it was stolen.'

'Where did you get the canoe?'

'I had it made.'

'It's bad to lie,' he said. 'You're going to learn. The police will make you repent the day you were born. You'll learn that you cannot travel like this. Can you swim?'

'Yes.'

'Good.'

The brother-in-law set off along the riverbank ahead of us and Hercules and I returned to my canoe. He sat at the back and I paddled upstream. We were silent until Hercules said. 'A man has to be very careful here. Boats are passing day and night. You can't trust anyone.'

'Exactly,' I said. 'I'm alone. Two men demand to search my canoe. What am I to think?'

His anger seemed to turn to doubt with each stroke of the paddle. 'If there's a problem, the policemen will send you to Manaus. If not, you will go freely,' he said.

And what about the white rope? I thought.

A stocky man in black shorts appeared at the door when we arrived at the policeman's home about a mile upstream. He questioned me and I told the family, who had gathered, why I was in the Amazon and why I was going to the Rio Preto da Eva. The brother-in-law arrived. We went down to the canoe and the policeman asked what was in each sack or box but he didn't search.

'Gun?'

'No. Only a machete.'

'Alcohol?'

'No.'

He saw the throw net and I said I'd made it. 'Do you know how to throw?' he asked.

'I'm learning.'

He picked up the net and threw it to open beautifully over the water. 'Well, I think it's very good that you've come,' he said. 'I wish you good luck. Do you want to leave now or have a coffee?'

We went back to the house and I blew up balloons for the three children. Hercules went off without apology or good wishes. His brother-in-law sat in the house and smiled when he saw the balloons. They were not an ideal gift because they burst on rough splinters in the wooden walls. 'What animals do you have in your country? Is life better here or in your country?' asked the policeman. 'You can't go round dressed only in shorts in your country, you have to wear smart clothes all the time,' he answered himself with a smile.

It was too late in the afternoon to paddle much further. I asked

several people along the water's edge if they knew somewhere to
sleep but, just as the Indians always told the early Europeans that
Eldorado lay just a little further downstream, they said the ideal
place to camp was a little further on. Only bare cattle pasture and
thick Cecropia trees lined the bank for an hour downstream while
the sun sank in the sky.

Finally I paddled in towards a clump of man-wood trees on the
edge of an island of pasture and bushes, drawn by their deep green
trunks shining in the late afternoon sun. Leaf-cutter ants were
climbing and descending one of the thin wax-like trunks, but two
sticks under the rope securing my hammock provided an underpass
for them to continue up and down with their awkward loads. The
ants chew leaves and use the mush to cultivate gardens of fungus,
part of which they eat. One colony may remove up to forty tons of
soil while excavating their underground nests.

It was too late to cook a meal after the boxes and sack had been
carried up the bank so I decided to practise throwing the net. It
opened like the skirt of a swirling Dervish on the first throw, but
brought in no fish. On the second throw, the net caught on
something under the water. There was no choice but to strip and
dive. To avoid being swept away by the current I pulled myself
down under the water by holding the net. The net was free after a
dozen dives.

I padlocked the empty canoe as night came, shooed away cattle
and sat in my hammock inside the mosquito net, enjoying rice left
over from lunch, and lemonade. I could see at least five miles up and
down the river and feel the cool evening breeze. The moon was full
that night, painting everything in grey light through which boats
passed, flashing their searchlights along the river bank and
occasionally up at my solitary hammock hanging between the trees
and my canoe padlocked to a tree trunk at the water's edge.

Just a smudge of dawn's light showed in the east when I reloaded
the canoe and drifted with the current while eating breakfast.

Downstream, I left the black waters of the Rio Negro and paddled
into the Rio Preto da Eva: it was narrow and lined with thick bushes
and with trees so overhanging the water that they made the river
seem enclosed inside the forest. I felt as if I was paddling up a vein
inside a vast body. Isolated houses stood in small clearings and, a
mile up the river, men and women dressed in bright clothes crossed
in canoes to a school for Independence Day celebrations. It was
September 7, also the day the Amazon was opened to non-

Portuguese shipping in 1867, allowing ships of all nations to sail up from the sea.

Both hands were aching after four day's paddling. I peered into the forest, looking for a place to camp away from the houses and clearings. A youth sat fishing in a canoe up the river and I paddled up to ask him for bait. 'How is the fishing?'

'Bad,' he said, with a dozen small fish in the bottom of the canoe. He handed me an eight-inch fish with three harpoon holes in its side. 'I'm going home,' he said but stopped after he'd paddled a short distance and called back to ask if I had a place to sleep.

'I have equipment to camp,' I shouted.

A dark inlet ahead was barely wide enough for the canoe to enter over and under trees lying across the stream. It was cool and musty inside the forest, like an empty church. The inlet led to a silent little lake with trees standing in the water. Brown rings up the tree trunks showed how high the flood water had reached in June. Dead leaves covered the ground, clear of undergrowth, and it was all hidden from the river. I put up the rainsheet, hammock and mosquito net and ate a lunch of crackers and pâté from a tin, then went to sleep.

Splashes of fish as they fled from predators broke the silence on the river when I went out to fish late in the afternoon. I caught nothing and lost a hook and some bait to a piranha biting through the line. I bathed and returned to my lakeside.

It was easy to start a fire by burning a small piece of rubber inner tube. I made oatmeal porridge with cinnamon and tea for supper. By then, daylight was gone and insects' *zzeeeeoorrr zzeeeeoorr* heralded darkness. I retreated inside the mosquito net and lay in the hammock hearing the Screaming Piha's penetrating whistle.

All became black, hiding even the trees to which my hammock was tied. Sounds seemed closer and clearer in the darkness. I heard a smacking splash as a fish leaped. Howler monkeys roared. But silence fell abruptly on the forest whenever a predator came near. A cry, a growl, or the comforting chatter of mating calls would begin again when the danger had passed. I could lie safely in my hammock and wonder how different the land must be when a creature 'sees' by smelling or listening or touching.

The moon had risen when I woke in the night and peered over the edge of my hammock. In the grey light of that forest tree trunks had become pillars as thick as legs, standing at every angle like a painting of black geometry.

Termites built tunnels during the night across the boxes of food and up inside my hat under a plastic sheet. Most of them fell off with a good shake or fled when exposed to light. Bigger, black ants took over the hat for themselves. Scout ants were always investigating across the floor of the forest and on the twigs of bushes, and twice I cleaned them out when they found the tins of sugar and jam. Ants have been calculated to be the most populous creature in the forest.

Minnows, tiny *tucanaré*, with the distinctive three vertical black stripes on their sides, and oval fish, with black lines along their sides, swam back and forth along the edge of the inlet while I sat munching crackers with jam and sipping sweetened black coffee. I could not watch them, nor hear the splashes of bigger fish in the lake, without becoming obsessed with hunting. Fish will fry in my frying pan today, I resolved, despite past failures.

The desire was more than merely a physical appetite. The forest overwhelmed my senses and I needed to respond. How would I ever become comfortable there if I remained an outsider, eating from tins and packets?

Little fish in the inlet would be perfect bait, I thought. I sewed a net from spare mosquito netting and tied it to the forked end of a long sapling. The fish didn't go inside the net as planned, though I crouched on the bank for nearly two hours. Scattering cracker crumbs on the water made the fish swim away.

The sun had not yet risen when I packed up camp after two days unsuccessful fishing and short walks in the forest. I paddled back out into the river. Ripples from the canoe spread across the calm water in broad arcs. I tied up to a half-sunken tree, a short distance upstream, and sat with fingers trailing in the warm current, looking at a dead tree stump, stripped of bark, gnarled according to its nature and the work of woodworm, beetles and woodpeckers. What species with tools could make a finer sculpture? Light streamed down the trees and a kingfisher of metallic green flew along the water's edge. Women and children passed in a big motorised canoe. I waited, munching crackers and jam and coffee, until the clatter of their motor had vanished up the river.

The blisters on my hands had healed and the canoe was easy to paddle up the slack water along the right bank. Ducking under overhanging branches, I still knocked insects, leaves and sometimes flowers into the canoe. It was best not to touch anything, but to flick it off legs or arms or to shake your head wildly. Tiny sticks fell between my legs. Each was a pattern of browns and as thin as a matchstick. Only when one of them arched and walked away did I realise they were animal not vegetable. Fish bait, I thought.

An iguana jumped from a branch with a splash that rocked the canoe. It was easy to imagine a snake dropping into the canoe, so I started carefully scanning the branches as we glided underneath.

Blue-black birds the size of thrushes, with long tail feathers and yellow eyes, watched the canoe coming up the river and flew ahead or circled over the water, guarding their territory.

Dragonflies abounded along the banks. Most were burgundy red with black-rimmed wings and black eyes. Six stood together on a stem in the shade. Others flew over the water and hovered in your face and darted to left or right. Is it for the aerobatics that Auca Indians call the whiteman's helicopter a dragonfly?

The river opened into a lake. Black tree stumps dotted pastures where grass had been planted and a few cattle were grazing. It took more than an hour paddling round the shore to reach the entrance to a second lake. A signboard stood on the bank: 'Festa Dia 12 – party Saturday'. Houses showed through the trees.

Forested hills bordered the second lake and many valleys entered. Around midday, a tower of smoke rose in the sky several miles away like a gathering thunderstorm and charred leaves settled on the water. I paddled past several headlands and beyond the last house before landing on a beach on the edge of the forest and making camp.

Sunken trees and bushes provided too many snags to let me use the throw net. So, leaving water to boil on the fire for tea, I went into the forest to find a straight pole with which to hang up the net between trees standing in the water. Maybe a fish big enough for bait would be caught. In the meantime, there was rice porridge for supper.

It was soon dark. Sound replaced sight, slow-croaking frogs along the edge of the water, booms and rumbles of distant thunder, cries of birds, whizzing of insects all round, and the growls of an animal sniffling my camp.

I jumped up with fright when I heard a human voice in the dark. 'Who is it?' I called and pointed my flashlight towards the lake. A man, with a shotgun on his shoulder, a youth and a boy were walking on the beach. Their flashlight shone on the canoe and at me. 'What are you looking for?' I called out, with more bravado than I was feeling. But I didn't understand the man's reply. The strangers walked along the beach and back and disappeared round the headland.

A man coughed in the gloomy shade of the palm trees behind my hammock next morning, but no one appeared. I went for a walk along the beach after my usual breakfast of porridge and coffee, and crouched at the edge of the trees listening to dry leaves rustling and fruits being cracked. Patterns of shadows and tangles of bushes hid the sources of the noise until they were betrayed by their movement. Half a dozen black wild pigs stood thirty feet away eating fruits on the ground. The pigs ran off when they caught my scent or saw my T-shirt and vanished in a moment.

Kingfishers and a brown partridge-like bird flew among the saplings growing on the beach. Two orange-headed caterpillars, each six inches in length and as fat as cigars, were moving up one stem. Their bodies were like black velvet, with yellow belts and orange slipper-like feet. I peered closely. One of them snapped its mouth at my nose. These were caterpillars of the Sphinx moth, I found out later, and famous for being able to transform themselves into replicas of the heads of small vipers if molested. 'The enlarged triangular head, prominent eyes, and swaying motion faithfully duplicate the appearance of the real thing,' wrote Adrian Forsyth and Kenneth Miyata in *Tropical Nature*.

A strong onshore wind in the afternoon made the tranquillity of the lake seem more remarkable. The canoe entered slowly as I dipped the paddle in the flat black water. Forested hills rose steeply on both sides. I and my canoe might have been entering an oil painting.

Three bats came so low over the water towards the canoe that I ducked to avoid them as they passed. They circled several times before landing on dead trees standing in the water just in front of the canoe. Their camouflage was so perfect that they became invisible on the tree trunks, though I had watched them land.

A man arrived in a dugout canoe when I returned to camp. He came up the beach to talk. I offered coffee and lit a fire and he rolled a couple of cigarettes of coarse tobacco and sat talking.

'It was a big surprise, yesterday, seeing you at night,' he said. He had come with his neighbour's children looking for turtle eggs buried in the beach, as the full moon had just passed. The man looked to be forty years old, the age of a grandfather in the Amazon, with nut brown complexion. His wife had died some years earlier and he lived alone in a house around the headland.

'Yes, there are caymans here,' he said when I asked. He was on his way to the Saturday party down the lake and carried smart clothes in a plastic bag in his canoe. *Festas* are important and regular events, bringing scattered communities together to dance, to drink, to gossip and to make love in the woods at the back of the dance halls. Married women may only dance with other women or their husbands or brothers. Despite the excitement and the drinking, fights are rare – unlike such occasions in the city.

I asked about the forest on the far side of the lake, where a brown clearing had been cut from the green.

'It doesn't belong to the army. They're farther up the lake but the land has been restricted.' That hadn't stopped him cutting down the few hectares I had asked about and clearing the land with fire. 'There's no one to say. A man needs land to plant rice and manioc,' he said. He assumed I was from southern Brazil or from São Paulo and asked when I'd arrived. We finished our coffees and cigarettes and he paddled off with a wave.

I paddled down the arm of the lake in the morning, while the right slope was still in shade and the air was cool, for a walk in the forest. Socks and Wellington boots would protect my feet. The compass was in my trouser pocket and I walked up a long path, machete in hand, to where an *itaúba* tree lay felled and cut into short lengths. The reddish-brown wood is valued for boat-building because it is durable in water, though heavy. The trunk of the tree was hollow and termites came scrambling out when I poked it with the machete.

The trail ended farther ahead in bright sunshine where another felled tree had crashed down, tearing and pulling lianas and orchids from the branches and opening a gap in the forest to sunshine.

In the dark forest beyond the tree gap, I watched the ground in front of me, pausing often to listen for the rustle of leaves and cries of alarm from birds and watching for a plant or palm frond to shake when all else was silent. I looked into the branches, black against the sky, hoping to see monkeys peering down or a solitary sloth clinging to a branch. Even my sense of smell was alert to the reek of decay and the places where the air was cooler or smelt of new growth. I had never gone this far inside the forest before on my own. I left markers every twenty paces, breaking stems of plants and letting them dangle. I cleared fallen branches and rotting palm fronds out of the way with the machete and struck tree trunks before climbing over them, to test if they were solid or had been eaten from the inside.

Suddenly, Howler monkeys started screaming. I halted slowly and turned my head from side to side, trying to judge the direction and distance from where they were calling. The monkeys were some-where behind me, a quarter or half a mile away. I decided to go to find them, but the forest had changed when I made my way back from marker to marker. Bushes and burrows in the ground and fallen trees appeared so strange that I couldn't remember whether I had passed on the left or the right. Markers that had seemed so obvious walking in were now hidden. Notches like small plaques on darker bark disappeared in the confusion of light and shadow.

I paused often, then stopped beside a broken palm frond and could find no other marker. A shaft of light a short distance along a natural trail between trees caught a spider's web. That was not the way. A branch too high to have climbed over and tangled with bushes on the ground blocked a second direction. I went back to the broken palm frond and stood observing every bush and tree, hoping for a clue to the way out. The sun shone in an opening where a tree had fallen. I went to it, being careful not to lose my orientation to the broken palm frond marker. The tree had been cut down but there was no trail through the surrounding bushes.

Fear was rising in my stomach. Where was the sun when I entered the forest? What direction had I come from? Where was the compass? Why had I not brought food? My reading of the compass and the position of the sun did not make sense. I could not have come past the spider's web. Had I by-passed the fallen tree branch?

No signs. No signs. Sweat stung my eyes and trickled down my back. I searched again for a clue, though by now any broken twigs and scuffed leaves might be only where I had already walked.

Be calm. I must not twist an ankle.

The forest dipped towards the lake and I hurried down the slope towards light beyond the trees. Vines caught my feet and could not be cut. I slipped and fell in haste towards the trail that had to be in the light just a few paces beyond the bushes.

Not a tree, nor anything else, was familiar when I reached the bright sunshine beside the lake. Open water was half a mile away on the right but the mouth of the inlet looked different. Fallen trees lay rotting along the shore. There was no red and blue canoe nestled into the bank.

I walked almost to the closed end of the inlet then turned back, skirting dense bushes tangled in full sunshine, climbing fallen trees, peering along the shore at every opportunity. I moved hastily and ripped the seat of my trousers and tore a pocket on a branch. It was easy to understand how someone could become frantic here. I thought of leaving my clothes and machete on the shore and swimming to search more easily for the canoe. Water stung the cuts on my face when I crouched to drink, making me realise how hot and scared I had become.

Blue plastic sheeting tied between trees was blowing in the breeze up the lake when I rounded the next headland. It was the rainsheet in my own camp. The canoe had nudged under an overhanging branch. I looked briefly at the possessions that represented my security, then returned up the trail passing where pihas had screamed, passing the felled *itaúba* and reaching the tree gap where I had stepped beyond the trail. Like getting back on a horse after falling off, I needed to go back at once. I also needed to understand how I had lost myself in the forest. An explanation was simple: the broken palm frond had been the last marker before the tree gap and the tree gap itself had been the marker to the trail, but I had forgotten this.

What an advantage to be a bumblebee, able to remember its route of a mile or more visiting flowers in the forest I thought.

I returned to walk in the forest later, hoping to see the Howler monkeys that screamed at dawn and at dusk. I stood with eyes closed to 'see' the forest by smell. What was the smell of each tree and plant, the scent of pig or *capybary*? How different would be the forest if our *picture* came by smelling or hearing, like the ant and the bat? Where is reality if we study it through restricted senses?

On the last afternoon, I listed quantities of food eaten, equipment used and additions and clothing changes needed for a solo journey. Next time, I intended to go much further beyond the frontiers of civilisation, which in the Amazon stretch along its major rivers and dirt roads. All the experiences and learning of the past year seemed only a preparation for this further search. After all, I hoped to visit Indians still retaining their traditional way of life. How else could there be any understanding of the contrasts between the white man and the Indian than when they both stand, side by side, in the forest?

In the meantime, I was broke and would have to return home to earn and save more money. Modest living and the considerable extra expense of robberies and air travel had emptied my money belt. Perhaps a short time outside the Amazon would be a tonic after my year's immersion.

A boy was paddling out from the flooded forest when I returned to the campsite along the narrow Rio Preto.

'Going fishing?' he asked.

I nodded.

'It's really good here. The *igarapé* (literally canoe path) is full. Look here. One good fat *tucanaré* and one *lebré*.' The latter was a long flat fish like a carpenter's saw.

'Could you give me a piece of fish for bait?' I asked. The boy cut a filet from the *tucanaré* and gave it to me, then paddled away down the river.

After setting up camp and lighting a fire to make tea, I returned to the lake with excitement and baited a hook to catch supper. I threw the line in many places and sat silently in the canoe. There were many splashes but never a nibble on the line.

Next morning I paddled down to the store on a floating platform near the mouth of the river to await the boat to Manaus. It sold one of everything, including a refrigerator that ran on bottled gas. 'Are you not afraid to go alone in the forest?' asked the owner, the father of the boy I had met.

'I am afraid if I see a cayman or a big snake. But I am not afraid to stay in the forest. I go with much caution, and respect the forest,' I said, sitting on a sack of *farinha* inside the store.

There were seven children in the family. Two teenage girls and the two older boys came back from school after midday and stood watching me scrubbing my frying pan and kettle. I gave their mother the frying pan, leftover vegetables and fruits, and received a fish stew with *farinha* at lunchtime. The eldest boy, twelve years old, asked his questions when the others had gone to eat. 'Where are you from? Where do you sleep? Aren't you afraid to go in the forest?'

'Are you?' I asked.

'Yes,' he said.

'Why?'

'The snakes, caymans and nasty creatures. Do you have a gun?'

I shook my head. 'I don't hunt and a gun is not much good against jaguar or snake. They see you before you see them.'

The girls settled down to cleaning the cooking pots in the afternoon and the boys went fishing, taking the shotgun.

When the regular boat to Manaus arrived my little canoe, the *Macaw*, was hauled onto its roof. The captain laughed with delight as I climbed on deck.

'I saw you,' he said, 'paddling down the Amazon from Manaus. I said there's a gringo.'

'How did you know a gringo?'

'The clothes, the hat, the canoe,' he said. The captain had been running to the Rio Preto for three years and before that was up the Rio Negro, and he was happy to talk about waterfalls, settlements and Indians up its tributaries.

He ordered a milky drink made from palm nuts and offered rice and *piraracú*, fish stew, at suppertime. But by then I'd shared banana porridge with a young couple, baby daughter and parrot returning home from a visit to the husband's uncle.

The boat criss-crossed the river, called by waving white shirts or flashlights shining in the dark to pick up passengers and boxes and sacks of *farinha*, peppers and fruits such as pineapples, papayas, *graviolas* and *genipapos*. The journey took fourteen hours and we reached Manaus in the dark. Half the passengers stayed on board until dawn when porters arrived to carry off the boxes of produce to market stalls. (The captain takes a commission and delivers money and empty boxes on his return journey.)

Everything cost money in the city. I could no longer afford even a taxi but went back and forth with one box or a sack at a time on the buses to get my belongings into the city centre. Emidio the boat builder promised to look after the canoe for the few days before I left Brazil and Ernesto said he would take the canoe out to his lodge to use and to look after until I could return. Unfortunately, he neglected the canoe and it rotted.

'You're as thin as Saint Sebastian,' remarked the mother when I took a watermelon to the family I'd met in my first week in Manaus.

Armando, owner of the Hotel Riomar, generously invited me to stay at his home, provided meals and paid the taxi fare to the airport. I left with $15 in my money belt. On the way to the airport, the driver handed me an envelope containing $20 and a note: 'Hope to see you soon. Ernesto and Luzimar'.

11

Rio Negro:
Slow Boats to Santa Isabel

'What a sight! All Nature, living and lifeless, reasonable and un-
reasonable, surges together, like towering storm clouds, hither and
thither; it is black oppressive Nature with only here and there a lightning
flash from God – a flash of Providence, rending the clouds.'
William Shakespeare, *King Lear*.

THE AMAZON RIVER was rising when I returned to Manaus and the heat
of February at the end of Carnival, just in time to samba for a night with
Ernesto, Luzimar and their friends amid six hundred other frenzied
people at a club. I had been away for five months working in an office
and came now with $3000 which I was confident would be enough for
my planned travels in my own canoe.

Emidio Viana's six children watched with delight when we
assembled a big kite in their kitchen, on stilts, out over the mud of the
estuary. Emidio had just returned in his big canoe from the interior
with dried fish, fruits, live pigs and a goat to butcher and sell.

'You missed Carnival,' I said.

'Oh yes, but it's no fun without money. So what to do? It's better to
be out of the city,' he said.

I sent out for beers and soft drinks and Emidio and his wife Maria
spent an afternoon showing me how to make a gill net for fishing across
small bays and streams. Emidio agreed to build a 15-foot canoe with a
square transom within a week. This would allow me to take it with me
on the once-weekly ferry up the Rio Negro to Barcelos the following
Thursday. He gave me two *cupuaca* fruits, which I took to Dona Isabel
to make into a dessert for Sunday lunch with all the Viana family,
whom I'd met on my first visit to the city.

It was important for me not to miss the ferry to Barcelos. The
Amazon was steadily rising now, fed by melted snow from the Andes,

but the Rio Negro, fed by rainwater, would continue to fall for a few more weeks before the rainy season began, flooding every river, flushing out fallen trees, undermining the banks and making travel miserable and dangerous in a canoe.

Prices had doubled with inflation in five months but, perversely, the dollar exchange was better than ever, making even the high prices cheaper in dollars.

My hotel room filled day by day with packets of spaghetti, coffee, sugar, rice, crackers and tins of jam, meat, tomato paste and oatmeal. Gifts for the Indians included machetes, fish hooks and line, harpoons, mirrors and combs.

The new canoe was ready within five days. I took Emidio, his brother-in-law and a neighbour for beers to celebrate. Emidio said he had actually bought the canoe ready-made from the brother-in-law because there was a shortage of lumber at the local sawmill and he knew I didn't want to wait another week. They had cut off two feet from the new canoe to make a square stern on which to mount the *peke-peke*. The canoe was therefore deeper and broader than usual in proportion to its length. This may be what would save the canoe from capsizing several times on the journey ahead.

Emidio advised buying a 5.3 horsepower motor. Prices varied up to 50 per cent and after hunting between the stores, I bought a Suzuki motor, a six-foot-long propeller shaft, nuts, bolts, and the tools to secure them together.

The passenger fare to Barcelos had increased, but this did not seem to diminish the number of passengers hanging their hammocks on the two decks of the ferry. The captain agreed, after negotiating, to charge a single fare for my equipment and canoe, which was lifted into a large unfinished hull being towed to Barcelos for fitting out. There was less chance of being robbed on this boat to Barcelos, because almost all the passengers knew each other, but I hid my boxes under other people's baggage and I kept watch.

A boat came alongside while we were waiting to leave Manaus. Hercules, who had arrested me five months earlier, stood on board. He was surprised and embarrassed and pretended not to recognise me until I smiled and asked how he was doing. He'd left the farm for the softer job of working as a deckhand on the boat.

'Is it better in the city?' I asked.

'Certain! More chances for chasing girls.'

We left Manaus two hours late with both decks crammed with

people, heaps of sacks and boxes from their shopping sprees in the city, and the hold and lower deck stacked with crates of beer and sacks of animal feed.

Officers of the Port Captain stopped the ferry within a mile up the dark river and turned us back to Manaus. The ship was overloaded, unlicensed, lacked fire extinguishers and life jackets, and there were said to be problems with the documents for the hull we were towing.

We passed the next day, a Friday, waiting on the boat. No one expected to leave before Monday. I settled to making a fishing net and chatting with people who came to watch. A well-dressed woman, with big brown eyes and soft hands, said she wanted to learn to make the net – though it clearly wasn't fish she was hoping to catch.

'She's yours for the taking,' said a grinning male passenger.

Two men also asked to learn how to make the fishing net; one was a *garimpeiro*, going gold hunting in rivers beyond São Gabriel da Cachoeira, theoretically an Indian reserve and closed to outsiders. The other man was an Indian from one of the rivers beyond São Gabriel. He said he was returning after putting his son into college in Manaus. He was dressed like a poor Brazilian, in long, scruffy trousers, T-shirt and plastic sandals, but his straight black hair, broad cheekbones, lack of facial hair and quiet and calm face marked him unmistakably as an Indian. He was a shy, softly-spoken man who would stand watching in silence no matter how desperately he wanted to make the fishing net, and wait until I offered it to him. Then he'd work for an hour or more, while I watched for mistakes, and finally he'd leave the net when he'd had enough.

He said he was going up the Rio Demini, a tributary on the north side of the Rio Negro near Barcelos, to help his mother-in-law settle on new land. He told me about the people, crops, houses, fish and animals and waterfalls on the Demini, Araca and some other rivers. It was clear from what he said that people on these rivers were non-tribal Indians, who had lost or abandoned their traditional culture and become poor Brazilians of Indian descent, living as separate families, selling rubber and tree gums in exchange for provisions from the city, and hoping one day to buy a battery-operated television to watch soap-operas and football matches.

We left Manaus the second time late on the Friday night, with just as many passengers and no extra life jackets. By dawn on the Saturday morning, we were marooned ten miles upriver with a cracked engine valve. A message was sent down with a passing boat and we waited all day tied to the bank with Brazilian pop music from competing tape recorders playing on the two decks. The greasy food made me feel sick but the beer in the bar was cold and I fell into conversation with a big white man with a bushy moustache and double chin. Senhor João had arrived from the state of Minas Gerais twenty-five years before and was now the administrator in Barcelos of FUNAI, the government agency responsible for Brazil's Indians. He was reading a Portuguese edition of Alfred Russel Wallace's *Travels on the Rivers Amazon and Rio Negro* written in 1853.

'Nothing's really changed,' he said with laughter and a shake of his hand. He asked where I was going and what I was doing. I said I wanted to make a journey up one of the tributaries and asked about the rivers. He told me about people and waterfalls. 'Be careful of the Indians. They're no joke,' he said, It would be illegal I knew to venture into an Indian Area so I had to be careful where I said I was going. Official permission would be refused to an independent traveller.

I asked about the Calha Norte Project – meaning Northern Ditch or Moat – along Brazil's 4000 mile northern border. 'It's a craziness of the military. It's their idea. They're donkeys, so this is what we get.'

The purpose of the Calha Norte Project is to enable Brazilians to occupy and develop a wilderness area covering 14 per cent of their country. Airports and roads will allow greater access preventing illegal coca plantations in the forest, and allowing the mining of minerals to feed Brazil's huge industrial society and bring schools, medicine and diseases to the Yanomami and other Indians.

'And the future for the Indians?' I asked Senhor João.

'Bad.' He then warned me about the other well-dressed white man on board. 'Military,' whispered Senhor João.

That man had already told me his occupation was secret. I had assumed he was a geologist. 'I arrived twenty years ago, I like the women here and I've never left,' he had said.

Later that day I asked the military man about the Calha Norte. 'It's to stop the cocaine plantations along the border. The Americans are paying,' he said. 'It will help the Indians by bringing medical services to them.'

'And the missionaries?'

'Aah, the missionaries. They are not what they appear. They're mining for gold, using the Indians as slaves. They are all Germans. They want to make their own territory. They're not really priests at all.'

The ferry reached Barcelos two days late. With help from one of the passengers on the ferry, and a tip to the caretaker, I was able to sleep there on the deck of the official boat of the town of Barcelos and to store my belongings in a lockable cabin. My priority was to paint the canoe and to assemble and test the *peke-peke*. The canoe was soon painted blue with scarlet trim but, despite assurances from the salesman in Manuas, the motor and propeller shaft would not fit together. We needed a mechanic with a lathe. The town mechanic, with a lathe in his workshop, was sick with malaria but he came the next day to have a look.

'The canoe is too small, the motor is too big, the canoe will sink, the jaguar will get you. It's not possible,' said the mechanic in the helpful way of South Americans.

'What to do?' I asked somewhat annoyed.

The work of drilling a wider hole to fit the motor shaft took only one and a half hours but it was three days before this could be done and the *peke-peke* assembled on the canoe. The motor started with the first pull of the cord, sending the canoe bounding over the waves.

I met the manager of the sawmill in Barcelos who lived in a brick and stucco house painted pale green overlooking where the boats moored on the river. His brother owned the mill, he said, but he was seventy years old, in ill health and had retired to his home state in the south of Brazil. None of the sons wanted to live in the Amazon so the man was staying until the mill could be sold. It employed ten people. He owned one of the half-dozen cars in the town but he cycled every morning down the main street to the sawmill. He sat every evening outside his home, chatting with friends, watching the girls and laughing, while people passing called out to him, 'Good evening, sir.'

The old man had a house guest called Juare, from the south of Brazil, who had come to buy *piassava*, bristles for brooms and brushes, for his brother in Rio de Janeiro. The young man had already bought thirty tons of the coarse palm fibre to be shipped to Manaus and onward by truck to Rio; buying for Cz$25 per kilo in Barcelos and selling in Rio for Cz$90 per kilo.

Juare took me to meet his supplier, Senhor Antonio Morães, a big man with massive bare belly like a Buddha and curly grey hair and moustache.

'He's got the biggest motor in his boat because he's the richest man on the river,' said one of his deckhands, a toothless youth called Banana.

Morães's son was leaving the next morning for a tributary ninety miles up the river to get more *piassava* and he offered me a ride. However, two of his boats were cut adrift during the night by a man said to have beaten his two women with a belt and set fire to the family's possessions during a bout of drinking. Senhor João gave a different explanation: 'Morães exploits people. He's rich. People are jealous. It's the only way to get back at him.'

It took one day to find the stray boats among the islands down the Rio Negro, then another day passed waiting. After lunch on the third day, we set out from Barcelos, towing six empty boats in which *piassava* would be loaded and my own canoe. All my belongings, including fifty litres of gasoline, were strapped under a rainsheet in one of the boats.

Morães sold, on credit, coffee, rice, tobacco, soap, kerosene, flashlight batteries and other staples to families along the rivers, and took in exchange rubber, *piassava*, and *sorva* (for making chewing gum). The business is profitable: a bag of rice costing Cz$40 in Manaus buys 7 kilos of *piassava* up the river, worth Cz$175 when sold.

The boat was steered by Senhor Grandão, whose tranquillity and physical appearance told of his Indian descent. He sat on a rough board over barrels of kerosene, one hand on the wheel, eyes watching the river.

Marido, Morães's twenty-five-year-old son, lay in his hammock all afternoon on the second day, working through a magazine of word puzzles, dozing and occasionally getting up to check the roaring diesel engine and the bilge pump.

His cousin, who was on holiday, talked without ceasing in such foul Portuguese that I barely understood anything he said. Both men were recovering from hepatitis and jaundice, so our food was even more bland than usual. The first night we ate bananas boiled in water and sugar.

It was impossible to lie in a hammock after lunch without sleeping. Grandão was still steering the boat when I woke; his head dropping, then rising with a jerk, his hands turning the wheel to correct our erratic course and his head falling to his chest again.

'Take over,' he said when he saw I was awake, and climbed over the barrels to the small aft deck to sleep until the sun sank behind the forest. We moored for the night to a tree on an island.

Grandão went ashore to cut a sapling as tall as himself, then sat on the deck, holding the sapling steady with his toes, to strip the bark. I held the other end of the pole while he carefully cut a deep notch with a machete and a small knife. He mounted a three-pronged harpoon in the notch, glueing bits of wood in the gaps with a black tree-gum heated over a match and tightly bound the end of the pole with fine twine.

'Ready for fishing,' he said. We set out in my canoe after supper. It was a tranquil night in which forest and river had merged in blackness. Grandão paddled the canoe under an overhanging branch, glancing up with the flashlight as we entered. The canoe moved silently towards the rotting trunk of a half-submerged tree. He held the harpoon in his hand and lowered it slowly and steadily until the three prongs almost touched the surface of the water. He shone the flashlight for an instant then jabbed with the harpoon.

Strike one: a fourteen inch *arakú* with black stripes along the sides. It was a tasty fish but with lots of small forked bones 'Already!' I said when the dead fish fell from the harpoon into the canoe.

'Already,' said Grandão grinning.

The flashlight shone again into the amber water round the rotting tree trunk.

Strike two: a second *arakú*.

Grandão shone the flashlight into the shallows. Light struck the sandy bottom and betrayed a motionless *arakú* which he speared also.

We paddled into a small opening in the bank, ducking beneath black branches.

Three more strikes landed three *tucanarés*.

'Are you tired?' asked Grandão when we'd looked for yards along the bank without seeing another fish.

'A little.'

'Let's go.' We paddled back to the boat with the catch of eight fish. Several of them would be cooked in next day's soup. The other would be rotten by then.

A clear night with flashes of lightning in the distance heralded a wet day. The sky was low and dark, as if someone had put a sheet of lead over the forest. Grandão had been steering the boat since first light, whilst everyone else slept. 'Take over the wheel. I'll make some coffee for us,' he said. I could feel goose pimples rising on legs and arms in the cold wind.

Grandão brought back hot coffees and sat on a barrel while I steered. He had worked as carpenter and painter at the Mission in Barcelos, where he was born, since finishing school there eight years before. The school was on holiday for three months so he was working for Morães as pilot, cook and fisherman.

Heavy rain fell later in the morning, obscuring the forest through grey mist, the water bouncing on the surface of the river. The open boats were swamped and had to be bailed out with a five-gallon drum. I stripped to my underpants and clambered from boat to boat to bail out my own canoe which was close to sinking. After a week of baking sunshine, it felt good to be drenched by torrential warm water.

'The Ilha da Saudade comes soon,' said Grandão in the afternoon, after the rain stopped. We reached the Island of Longing three hours later and moored on the left side near an empty white house and an open-sided *barraco* with raised floor and thatched roof. My three companions would depart in the morning up a nearby river to trade *piassava*. I would continue in my own canoe up the Rio Negro to Santa Isabel. They invited me to continue with them and to go to Santa Isabel later, but I had waited a long time to begin this journey and wanted no delays.

Grandão set a gill net on the other side of the island and caught three *arakú* before twilight.

'Then I don't want piranha,' shouted the cousin, throwing back the small white fish he had just caught.

Marido gutted and cleaned the fish while Grandão split damp wood into slivers and shaved dry tinder for a crackling fire that soon settled into hot cinders ideal for grilling fish. I sat with Grandão beside the fire and asked about the Rio Marauiá, where I had decided to go.

'Good fish. Lots of Indians there,' he said.

'Acculturated or primitive?'

'Not wild.'

'Wild?'

'Those that kill people with arrows as soon as they see them,' he replied, raising his arm as if to fire a bow and arrow.

I asked how to find Santa Isabel on the wide river with so many islands. The small town would be my last stop before ascending the Marauiá river, the tributory I had decided to explore.

'Good and straight, but keep going to the right,' he said.

The boats left before first light next morning. I delayed for one day to organise food and equipment for the journey and to be quiet before starting out alone.

Bright orange light filled the eastern horizon when I woke on the morning of departure. Clear sky overhead and calm air promised a day without rain or wind. An ugly black fish, caught overnight in my gill net, would provide lunch and supper.

Boxes and sacks had to be loaded in the canoe with weight balanced from side to side and from bow to stern, safe from bilge water in the bottom of the canoe and covered with a blue plastic sheet to keep off the sun and spray. When all was ready, I sat on the bank for breakfast of oatmeal porridge with cinnamon and black coffee and eyed the trees on another island across at least half a mile of open water: my canoe was not much longer than a pair of adult dolphins.

Even with low throttle, the canoe surged　　ward when the long propeller shaft hit the water, lifting the bow of the canoe and making my grip tighten on the vibrating rudder rod. I sat stiffly on the left side of the canoe, half-turned towards the trees, watching the surface of the water for snags or the ripples of submerged trees.

It would be a few days before I learned to handle the *peke-peke* easily and to gain confidence that this canoe would not suddenly sink with the motor still running, leaving me without food or shelter in the middle of the forest. And if the motor were oversized for the canoe, at least there would be plenty of power for any turbulent stretches.

Grandão's instruction had been to keep to the right, so after a few miles I steered into a channel between three islands on the right, where two children with their mother watched in front of their home and returned my wave.

This crescent-shaped channel was a mistake. It divided into three dead end fingers after half an hour's journey. A grey dolphin rose and dived as if watching the lost intruder. Black water flowed from the open river beyond the dark tangle of flooded trees but there was no passage for a canoe. It was a bad start. I halted to rest on a small beach and fried a piece of the ugly black fish for lunch.

Late in the afternoon I stopped back at the small house at the mouth of the channel. The husband and his young son came down the bank to shake hands. I offered a cigarette and was invited up to a bench in front of their home. His wife brought sweet black coffee in a vacuum flask and stood in her doorway listening while her husband asked what I was doing and where I was going.

'Santa Isabel is straight from here. Not up the small channels,' said Senhor Carlos da Silva. He was a rubber-tapper, gathering 20 gallons of white sap from about 250 wild trees in the forest each day, enough to make 15 pounds of solid pressed rubber to be sold to passing traders such as Antonio Morães. 'Ninety *cruzados* a kilo. A good price,' he said.

'A lot of walking,' I said.

'But not much work.'

I mentioned the old method of congealing the rubber sap over smoky fires. 'The press is better. It's quicker and that's more time for sleeping,' he said.

Senhor Carlos gave me permission to tie my hammock on the edge of their clearing near the riverbank. By then, it was time to prepare for night: to bathe and wash the T-shirt and shorts serving as day clothes, to put on clean T-shirt and Bermuda shorts for evening, to hang up hammock and take out flashlight, candle lantern and notebook to write my diary, to padlock canoe to tree, cover motor with plastic sheet, and check all luggage in canoe was safe under large rainsheet in case of heavy rain or strong wind.

After supper, Senhor Carlos invited me to eat supper with him. I offered the remainder of my fried fish and some crackers. His wife served fish soup and *farinha* but ate alone inside the two-roomed home while the children sat eating in the doorway, watching their strange visitor. We ate as much as we wanted and afterwards washed our hands with soap in a bowl of water and dried them with a towel and drank glasses of cool water. The wife took all the pots in a huge aluminium basin to the river to wash. We all drank little cups of coffee when she came back, and then we sat on the bench looking over the silvery river. It was almost dark and insects were calling. Mercifully there were of course very few mosquitoes because of the acidity of the Rio Negro's water. Toads were already hopping across the ground around us. A programme of music ended on the radio and a man read out messages to families isolated along the rivers.

A whispering breeze was blowing next morning, rippling the surface of the river. I gave the family a packet of coffee after breakfast, shook hands and set off. The canoe hit rough water half a mile upstream, where the river raced over a sandbar. Waves splashed over the sides as we pitched and dipped in the troughs, rolling from side to side. There was nothing to do but keep as close as possible to the clay bank, avoid going broadside on, and bail out the water washing round my feet. The canoe and I passed through three such rough places within a few hours and when we steered into a large beach on an island later in the morning it was with greatly increased confidence.

Two dogs came running over the sand, barking and wagging their tails, followed by a man who said good morning and shook hands when I stepped ashore. He took a cigarette and invited me to his house for coffee.

'Are you a *garimpeiro*, sir?' he asked.

He said the waves would be too rough upstream and invited me to stay. 'He'll wait,' he called to the family in the next door shelter.

'Now excuse me, sir, I go to work.' He walked off with three small milking churns to collect the white sap of the rubber trees, leaving his wife on the top step of their thatched shelter where she sat until it was time to light a small charcoal burner to prepare lunch. I gave her a kilo of rice.

Four men returned with churns brimful with sap at midday. They poured it into sturdy boxes and mixed in *tucupí*, an acidic by-product of making *farinha* from manioc. This would set the rubber.

All seven adults and two boys in the two shelters washed in the river before we sat on the floor in the neighbour's home to eat plates of grilled fresh fish, grilled dried fish, two types of fish soups, rice, *farinha* and flat tapioca pancakes.

A heap of fish bones lay on the floor beside each person when we had finished eating and washed our hands. People lay in their hammocks to rest. My host, Senhor Raimundo, a short, gaunt man with white stubble chin, was soon snoring. He woke when the heat of the day had passed and white sunlight no longer bleached all colour from the trees and river. He poured coffees and poked the congealed rubber in the box. 'My father came here from Portugal when he was eleven years old and he stayed,' he said. We finished my last cigarettes and he took out a packet of tobacco and papers.

Both families would be leaving soon as the rains started in two or three weeks, he said, to return to their permanent homes on the south bank of the river and would then go to gather Brazil nuts in the forest on the mainland in May. This was their first stay on the island, having rented the rubber trees from the owner for the six-month season.

The two families had lived side by side for six months in the clearing on the river bank. Although obviously aware of everything said or done in their neighbour's homes, they maintained an imaginary garden fence. The mother from next door stood nursing her daughter, waiting to be invited to sit down on the bench overlooking the river. One of the men asked to borrow my Wellington boots to protect himself from anacondas while cutting down a small tree in rough grass. 'Only small snakes are poisonous here,' said Senhor Raimundo.

Anacondas and boa constrictors kill by constriction, but there is a belief among people in the interior that these snakes become poisonous in May. Both snakes have the same name in the Indian Tupi language, and it reminded me of Curupira, the mischievous spirit who lives in the forest. His body is short and hairy and his feet point backwards. Curupira has the power of enchantment; he is able to call children and adults to him in the forest by whistling or stirring up sudden winds. Some reports say he protects trees against unnecessary destruction though he has not been much in view near bulldozers and chainsaws. Everyone agrees that strange noises in the forest are Curupira calling.

'Does he stay here?' I asked.

'I've never seen him. But I've heard him,' said Senhor Raimundo.

The wind stilled when the sun set. The surface of the river was calm again. Bats darted back and forth across the clearing and the women in both households put out flaming kerosene wicks in the doorways to burn all night and keep away the fruit-eating and vampire bats.

A few leaves swayed in the breeze at dawn but the surface of the river was calm, promising a safe passage through the rough water upstream. We spotted a black squirrel monkey in a bush on the bank while we were having coffee and crackers for breakfast. The boys ran for their catapults and the monkey scurried up the tree. Senhor Raimundo and I walked down to the canoe. He gave me two dried fish for the journey and added tobacco and papers when I gave him a gas lighter and a bag of crackers. We shook hands. The men were taking careful aim with the catapults and missing their target when I passed the clearing in my canoe.

A granite boulder appeared on the water's edge near midday, the first evidence of the geological feature known as the Brazilian Shield, whose weathered rock is some of the most ancient in South America. I stopped at an abandoned *barraco* on the riverbank and decided to make camp, after checking that no creatures were coiled or clinging to the rafters. While the rice boiled on the fire, a substantial boat passed, going downstream. Its engine room bell sounded and I expected to be visited by its passengers. Instead, a lone man arrived in a dugout canoe. 'Where's the owner?' he asked.

'I don't know. There's no one here.'

'I sometimes buy fish from the owner.'

I invited him for lunch of rice and grilled dried fish. He declined but took tobacco and rolled a cigarette. 'Where are you going?'

'Santa Isabel and the Rio Marauiá.'

'Marauiá? I've just come from there, bringing an Indian who was fleeing from there.'

'Fleeing?'

'Yes, sir. He kidnapped a woman with a child to be his wife, and three Indians came to kill him and take the woman back.'

'Where are they now?'

'I don't know. The three Indians arrived in Santa Isabel so the couple will have to go much further downstream.'

I nodded.

'Imagine, the Indians still kidnapping their wives,' he said. We chatted about the possibility of rain and prospects for fishing, the price of my motor and its power. 'See you later,' said the man and he paddled away.

Next day, I paused in the small community of Santomé where the mysterious belfry I had seen a year earlier was still falling into the forest. With its rapids and rocks, the river would be more dangerous from here on, but when I left the community the water was like black glass reflecting every leaf and sculpture of tree roots along its banks. For the first hour I passed between small islands and the forest, up through swift waters racing against boulders, and motored on steadily as the open river was brushed with wavelets by a freshening breeze.

The sky darkened as the wind gathered strength, until the canoe was pitching over choppy waves and I knew we had to stop at the first good campsite. An abandoned *barraco* stood on the bank several miles farther upriver. I hung the hammock and plastic rainsheet inside and, while rice cooked on a fire, hurried to bring up the boxes and sacks from the canoe. Water splashed over the side of the canoe. Wind blew white spray from the tops of the waves across the river.

Waiting for rain was always unpleasant; little flies flitted around, not biting, but tickling when they landed. They would vanish when the rains arrived. Rain was already falling on the other side of the river, cooling the air and refreshing the colours of the forest. Thunder reverberated across the sky like kettle drums. I bathed and made a mug of tea. It began drizzling. Plastic sheeting tied in place with cord covered the motor, and another sheet protected the food and equipment on top of the bank. Heavy rain fell suddenly, pouring through holes in the thatched roof, making a pool in the plastic sheet over my hammock. Lightning far away flashed closer and closer until thunder boomed overhead. I sat in the hammock beseiged by the storm, watching bolts of rain splatter the mud covering the ground.

Rain poured so heavily for a couple of hours that the dark afternoon passed into twilight and night without interruption, until I was suddenly aware that darkness was hiding the forest and river after each flash of lightning.

I checked the canoe once more before sleeping. Water poured from the rainsheet when I poked one corner to drain the pool over my head. The thunder passed up the river, sounding like a tin sheet being beaten across the sky. The rain continued all night. I curled up in the hammock, wrapped in a cotton sheet, with hands wrapped round my belly for extra warmth. Sleep was easy, once everything was secure.

The rain continued for two days, confining me to the hammock, practising tunes on a tenor recorder I had brought with me, and reading a book about the Yanomami Indians, whom I hoped to visit on the Rio Marauiá.

Napoleon Chagnon's *Yanomamo, The Fierce People* is a classic book of anthropology, though it has been criticised for overemphasising the tribe's ferocity. Certainly, the book's foreword was direct:

'A high capacity for rage, a quick flash point, and a willingness to use violence to obtain one's ends are considered desirable traits. Much of the behaviour of the [Yanomami] can be described as brutal, cruel, treacherous.'

What sort of contact would I have with them, I wondered? There seemed to be three possibilities; they would make me leave immediately; they would kill me immediately; or they would allow me to visit. The risks were worth taking, for primitive Indians (as I thought of them at the time) are very rare these days, and only survive in isolated places. It was my deliberate decision to carry no gun – how else to demonstrate that you come in peace? This was a calculated risk, but one that did not seem so great. There was probably far more chance of drowning on one of the five waterfalls that I would have to ascend on the Marauiá to reach the Indians than of them murdering me.

Despite a cloudy sky on the third day, I was sure all the water in heaven must have fallen so I reloaded the canoe. The motor started on the first pull and we puttered steadily up the river keeping close to the bank avoiding fallen trees. I had had doubts about using a *peke-peke* – it had seemed an admission of weakness – but these had gone. Paddling the canoe up the turbulent waters would have taken so much energy that I would never have reached Santa Isabel before it was time to return.

The town was as quiet as it had been the year before. I moored on the beach beside a small covered boat where a family lived and asked them to watch the canoe. The 80-mile journey from the Island of Longing to Santa Isabel had provided me with a week of testing and confidence-building. I sat on the verandah of a shop sipping *guaraná*, a soft drink said to be an aphrodisiac, while two girls laid the tables for lunch. This was Dona Maria's restaurant and the best eating place in the town.

'Eat! Eat!' encouraged Dona Maria, seeing me reluctant to sit alone at a table she had spread with plates of stewed turtle, peas in mayonnaise, beans and fried fish.

A teacher, a man called Sargeant, and his wife joined me at the table for lunch, both of them surprised to meet a gringo who could speak Portuguese and curious to find out why he had come and what he was doing. I felt no great urge to speak after the week's solitude, but I knew it was important to identify and explain oneself early when arriving in a small community.

Men eating at another table belonged to 'the aeroplane' – the same one I had seen in São Gabriel flying over the forest, prospecting with electronic detectors for uranium, tin ore, gold and minerals. There is no hotel in Santa Isabel and it is one of the sad ironies of the Amazon that these *garimpeiros* of the air should be accommodated at the Mission whose pupils would be most affected by their discoveries.

Sargeant was an army engineer involved in building an airstrip in cleared forest near the town as part of the Calha Norte project. We met again at supper, after a hot afternoon I had spent dozing, changing the oil in the motor and answering questions from the friendly town policeman. Sargeant's wife asked what I had seen around the town and this prompted her husband to list the wonders of the area. 'Tomorrow, a group of us are going to the Marauiá,' he said. The river was one hour away by speedboat. I asked to go with them. 'Sure, tomorrow morning at eight,' said Sargeant. The trip would be a chance to reconnoitre the mouth of the river to be sure I could find it when I went up on my own in the canoe.

'Where are you sleeping?' asked Sargeant's wife.

'I don't know. There's an empty boat on the beach. I can put my hammock there,' I replied.

'No, no. Sleep at the depot,' said Sargeant.

I accepted the offer gladly but first had to paddle my canoe into the security of the bright lights of a river trader's boat, which no one was likely to rob. The depot was a barn built of concrete with a tin roof that kept the place hot at night, and divided into two rooms; there were supplies and communication equipment at the back and a line of beds and a counter and engines in the front room. A young civil engineer from Belem was the only other occupant. He had a bed at the far end of the room, beside a big fan and a loaded shotgun.

'A last resort. Just for emergencies,' he said when he went to sleep with his girlfriend and left me with it, alone in the depot behind locked steel doors.

Next morning Sargeant's company speedboat swept over the waves in the middle of the channel like a fish fleeing from a predator. I watched carefully, hoping to remember our route between islands and boulders and up through the rapids. Forty minutes above Santa Isabel, Sargeant announced we were almost out of gasoline. The youth who worked with him kept the engine puttering to keep us straight in the current while my fellow passengers, the doctor, the tax collector, the teacher and Sargeant debated what to do. They decided we should continue slowly to the Marauiá river and be prepared to paddle home if necessary.

A bar of white sand blocked the river farther upstream. We turned to the right, crossing a line of foam where the water of the Marauiá flowed into the Rio Negro. A big white boat, a steel barge, a smaller boat and canoes were moored side by side half a mile up the Marauiá.

'It's Dom João Bosco of Santomé,' said Sargeant. 'Let's have a drink with him.' Dom Bosco owned land and rubber trees along the Rio Negro around Santomé and was one of the rich and powerful local men. We pulled alongside the big white boat to be greeted warmly by Dom João's wife, who was flouring fish for lunch.

'Bosco! Bosco!' she called, offering each of us her elbow to shake. Her husband came from the cabin and fetched out a bottle of cane liquor when he saw us. He was upset because someone had stolen his longest gill net from the channel during the night but he cheered up after a drink to tell us he was waiting for the Marauiá to rise so he could take the barge up river to load gravel from one of the beaches. Bosco was a big tubby man with gold chains hanging down his hairy chest. He hadn't shaved for a day or two and he reminded me of Brutus, Popeye's arch enemy. His wife was smaller, with sandy hair greying at the sides, and the pale suntan of a Portuguese lady.

We stayed a couple of hours with them; then, supplied with extra gasoline to get us home, we headed into the mouth of the Marauiá. The swollen river was opaque brown after the recent rains. The rains may also have triggered the profusion of flowers that showed along the liana-covered banks. Orange birds of paradise, red orchids and clusters of purple blossoms seemed dazzlingly bright to eyes accustomed only to greens.

Sargeant's young lad said there was a waterfall not far upstream where the fishing would be good, but after a couple of miles of calm water we came to a neat *barraco* on the right bank, so we stopped to ask the old man living there.

'Are there any fish in this river?' asked Sargeant.

'*Tucanaré*, but not now. Not with the water rushing. In the lake there are some.'

'The lake?'

'Yes, not far from here.'

We moored the speedboat and climbed the bank to greet the man and his grandson. Sargeant, the doctor, the tax collector and the teacher were influential men in the town and our hosts shook hands with each of us. They led us through the forest about a quarter of a mile to the small lake. The teacher took out his fishing line and lure.

'Are there any caymans in the lake?' asked the doctor.

'Oh yes, sir. But only small ones. I think I've killed all the big ones.'

The tax collector suggested bringing the old man's dugout canoe from the river to go fishing in. Faced with the important men of the town, our host could not refuse.

It took twenty minutes to get the canoe through the forest to the lake and then my companions quickly paddled out onto the lake.

'I've never seen such a desire to fish,' I said, while returning to the *barraco* with our host.

'It's aways the same. It's those who come from outside who want to do these things. Those from outside who hold the people down when they try to rise. But they do rise, little by little.'

We sat in the cool shade inside one room of the small *barraco* made of woven palm leaves. The old man wanted to know where I was from and what I was doing and nodded his head as he listened to my answers.

'Do you have a little tobacco to roll a cigarette?' I asked.

'Finished,' he said.

'I'm coming back in a day or two. I'll bring you some from Santa Isabel. What else is finished?'

'Sugar. The sugar's finished.'

'One kilo or two?'

'Oh, one kilo is enough,' he said. His daughter served a single cup of coffee, sweetened with honey, on a tray. She had spent the season with her father while he tapped rubber from 250 to 300 trees along each of five walks in the forest. They would all be leaving on April 25, he said.

'Why April twenty-fifth?' I asked.

He explained that the rains would start and the river rise.

'On the twenty-fifth precisely?'

'I know the river. I've been coming here for seven years. Sometimes, even in May, the river is still dry, almost nothing, just beaches. But, generally, the twenty-fifth of April is the day to leave.' He would return with his daughter and grandson to their home near Santa Isabel.

We heard shouts in the forest after an hour and returned along the path to find the fishermen heaving at the dugout canoe.

'And where are the fish?' we asked.

'Not one. Not one. We nearly caught three *tucanaré* but they got away,' said Sargeant. He suggested buying a couple of fish from a local fisherman on the way back to Santa Isabel, to impress his wife.

12

Rio Marauiá:
Oh Spirit of the Whirlpool!

'[The Indians of Brazil] seem strange – and, to some, inferior – because they express themselves differently; their vision of the world is not the same as ours and while possessing a rich and harmonious concept of life, they lack the narrow blinkers of a scientific, materialistic ideology which assumes the ability to control and understand all things but has in truth barely scratched the surface of life's diversity.'

Robin Hanbury-Tenison, *Worlds Apart.*

THE RIVER FELL AT least a foot in the few days I stayed at Santa Isabel, exposing rocks and forcing the water through ever-narrowing gaps in the channels between the islands upstream of the town. When I left, my canoe floated so low in the water that even when I was standing it was difficult to pick a course between the boulders and the waves where the currents clashed.

Half a mile upstream of the town, I swung the canoe towards a gap on the left side of a line of rocks fifty yards ahead and approached cautiously between boulders below a small cataract. It was too late to turn back when I saw the full force of the water surging through the rocks towards me. The gap itself was only twice the width of the canoe and a cross-current swept across the top of the cataract. I increased speed and gripped the rudder, eyes darting back and forth and my heart pounding. The bow of the canoe reared up when we entered the cataract and the stern was sucked down. I could hear the pitch of the motor fall as the propeller fought against the current.

We seemed to stall against the force of water, held by the racing current, unable to move forward and with no retreat possible. I couldn't move my eyes from the rocks and the water, nor take my hand from the rudder to increase the speed of the motor. Slowly we gained on the water, inching between the rocks, heading for the cross-current, water surging and spilling into the canoe. I pointed the canoe into the cross-current at the top knowing we could easily be swept onto the rocks.

Suddenly the motor changed its note. We were above the cataract and released from its grip. I headed towards the right shore, across choppy water, skirting isolated boulders and fallen trees. The canoe hit submerged rocks several times but survived.

It was noon when I reached the mouth of the Rio Marauiá. João Bosco and his wife had gone downriver, leaving a crew of three Colombians to look after the big boat and barge. They welcomed me aboard with coffee and asked where I was going and what I was doing. They said they'd seen a twelve-foot anaconda in the water that morning and showed me two poisonous spines, one of them four inches long, cut from a stingray they had caught.

'If you catch one of those in your foot, your whole leg swells and you're sick for days,' said one of the men, showing the scar of a hole on his foot. Wrapping the puncture in green tree bark reduces the burning pain by keeping out the air, he said.

A commercial fishing boat arrived just before lunch and the captain came on board.

'You're going up the Marauiá? To the Mission?'

I nodded.

'It's full of Indians there.'

I nodded again.

'If I could enter there, I'd kill them all. Indians are animals, they're not people.'

The men went to place gill nets and fish with lines in the afternoon, leaving one Colombian and myself on the boat. He explained how to preserve fish by smoking, salting and pickling in brine, using a potato to test the salinity of the water. The brine was good for pickling when the potato floated. Later, he told me how he and some friends had left their homes in Bogota with dreams of wealth a year before, and had hitch-hiked, walked and canoed through the forest to reach a mining camp.

'We'd been told the trail to follow, but there were many trails and we lost the way.'

They were lost in the forest for twenty-one days, eating plants and roots and making coffee, the only food they carried. They thought they were going to die but still went on searching for gold.

'We were crazy to look for gold when we didn't even have food. Crazy, crazy.'

They met Indians who told them how to reach a mining camp. 'It was in Brazil but we didn't care whatever the flag. We were twelve days in the camp and then we went to the Mission at São Gabriel.'

Two of the friends went back to Colombia. The others stayed on as carpenters for the Mission and used the Mission's sawmill to cut up trees bought from Indians and sold the boards to boatbuilders.

One of the fish we caught for supper was covered with black scales like plates. 'It's ugly, like the Devil,' said the Colombian. 'How do I cook it?' He chopped it up to make fish soup with spring onions and herbs. The mush of bony flesh tasted awful but the soup was good.

'I never knew the Devil tasted this good,' he said.

After breakfast the next morning the Colombians gave me a fish to cook for lunch when I left them and entered alone up the Marauiá. The river dazzled with the silver reflection of the sun, obscuring the ripples that might have warned of rocks and submerged trees. But soft sunlight made the forest shine and, though the canoe grounded on sandbanks several times, I smiled with delight as I travelled up the river.

After an hour I reached the old man's tidy *barraca*, where the swirling river we had seen on Saturday was now clear water flowing knee-deep over sand. His daughter told me he had gone to Santa Isabel in his canoe to buy the coffee, sugar and tobacco that I was bringing for him.

'He thought you were not coming,' she said. 'He left in the mouth of the night [two or three in the morning].' She made coffee on the charcoal burner while her son sat on my knee punching my chest. I left the supplies and was soon on the river again, dragging the canoe over the shallow sandbanks, looking for the channel.

It was impossible in these conditions to have expectations of reaching any particular destination. The river upstream might be blocked by rocks, sandbars, or fallen trees. I hoped to meet Yanomami Indians but being on the small river in the forest was enjoyable for itself.

Near lunchtime I came to a large sloping boulder on the right bank where three men were unloading boxes from two aluminium canoes. I stopped and met George, a Portuguese from the Azores, who invited me up to a small house in a clearing planted with manioc, sugar cane, bananas and *cupuacu*. George was a wanderer who, at the age of thirty-nine, had reached this place with his slender Brazilian black-haired girlfriend. Now he was building thatched shelters for tourists who would pay $100 per day to stay in the virgin Amazon forest.

'Feel at home,' said the young owner of the house. The men's work of the morning was done and we sat on benches in the cool gloom inside the house drinking coffee, rolling cigarettes and waiting for the women to cook fish, beans and rice for lunch.

'It's difficult,' said the men when they heard where I was going. 'The river's very dry. You can't get up the *cachoeiras* – waterfalls – alone, gringos are crazy. I couldn't get up and I'm a son of this land.'

'The first *cachoeira* is easy, the second very difficult, the third difficult, the fourth hard work and the fifth easy,' said one of the men.

'If you get up the second *cachoeira* you'll get up them all. But you won't,' said another.

I said I would try.

'Aren't you afraid of the forest, the jaguar?'

'No,' I said. 'No fear, but lots of respect.'

'You have to respect the forest and the river,' said George. 'That's what the forest is here for, to teach respect. Those who don't learn respect, they die. After nine years, I still know nothing. But when I came here I knew absoluttely nothing.'

Everyone had their story of being lost in the forest and advice on what to do. 'You must stay calm, make coffee, have a cigarette and think your way out. If you go rushing about, you'll be lost for ever,' said George.

Hammocks were hung between the trees for an after-lunch snooze, while two of the men used wood from the core of a strange black tree to dye parachute cord. The thick lines, baited with five inch hooks, become invisible in the water and are used to catch catfish that can weigh up to 220 pounds. These baited lines hang near the bottom of the river, tied to big balsa wood floats that bob up and down when a fish is caught.

George had a speedboat, and when the sun was low in the sky we went up a mile of deeper water, swerving round rocks and sandbars, then walked up a stream to the site of George's planned tourist *barracas*. There were no buildings yet but saplings, underbush and vines had been cleared. It was cool and quiet.

'We leave the trees. If not, the insects are homeless and more bother. We will use only materials from the forest, in the traditional manner. Nothing imported. There's a month's work here, but how long it will take is a different thing. The people here have a different work mentality. They don't realise they could earn more money.'

The first tourists were due in a few months. Later George would build himself a separate house with electricity, running water and 'everything', he said. He had bought all the land up to the first *cachoeira* and far inland. 'I don't want neighbours,' he explained with a smile.

Upstream, there were many rocks in the river and after nearly a mile we reached clumps of boulders lying right across the river. We motored to a gap on the left side and I jumped onto the rock holding the rope. 'Secure the rope well. The boat's already gone if not,' shouted George above the roar of water. Moments later, he was up to his neck wading to reach another rock. I threw the rope to him and he pulled the aluminium boat through the gap.

'That was not the first *cachoeira*. That was just a splash,' said George when we embarked again.

The first *cachoeira*, which I would have to negotiate alone the next day, was a wall of stone about ten feet high, half a mile upstream. The river poured over a gap in the middle, crashing over the rocks just below the falls with a thundering roar and high waves. We stood at the brink of a gorge on the left side where the sun glistened on the water. I tried to imagine how to get up the falls with a canoe.

Everyone was so convinced I could not get up that by nightfall I was quite depressed. After a bath in the river, and removing a small coral snake that had wriggled ashore and died beside my canoe, I sat thoughtfully on a rock while the last macaws flew to their roosts and the martins darted up and down catching insects in the air. The place was too beautiful to let me turn back. Even if I could not get up the river, I could always spend a week or two walking in the forest and fishing.

I gave George a packet of my best tobacco before leaving next morning. An older man warned me to be careful at the *cachoeiras*. 'Go up on the right side on the first and second, the left side on the third and fourth and the right on the fifth.'

The water had fallen a few inches during the night, exposing more rocks, but the river was calm for the first mile. It would be impossible for me to pull the canoe through the gap where we had hauled George's aluminium boat. I approached the line of rocks as slowly as possible, standing in the canoe to look for a way through, then sat down, increased speed and headed in through a different channel. The bow lifted high and the propeller hit rocks but we kept going and were soon through to the calm water below the first waterfall.

I shut off the motor and steered to the boulders on the right side below the falls and tied the canoe securely to a fallen tree. Baiting a fishing line in the hope of catching lunch was the first job, though I didn't catch a thing. Then I walked over the boulders and tree trunks washed up in last year's flood season to reconnoitre and find the best overland route to the top of the falls. All the time I kept my eyes open for caymans and snakes sunbathing in the morning sun on the rocks.

It took ten round trips to carry all my baggage and equipment, including the motor and propeller shaft, to the calm water above the falls. But pulling the empty canoe between the rocks where the water thrashed and churned would be more difficult. I sat for a rest, watching the water pour over the middle of the waterfall. This would become a raging torrent from bank to bank when the rains started in a few weeks. Descending it in my little canoe would be extremely hazardous. I prepared a ninety-foot length of rope, using double parachute cord with knots every three feet for extra security. One end was tied to the canoe and the other end to a rock above the falls so that if for any reason I lost the rope, the canoe would not be washed away. The canoe was lightweight in the water when completely empty and not difficult to manoeuvre around the rocks to the foot of the waterfall. It was only sixty feet from there over a huge boulder to the top of the waterfall, but it took me three hours to get up it, and it was with delight and relief that I reloaded the canoe and set off again across the strong current. Later I learned that the Indian name for waterfall is 'The Little Beast'.

There was a small cataract around the next corner in the river without an obvious channel. I circled once to get a better look before deciding to go up the left side, to the left of a heap of rocks in midstream where the water flowed in rolling waves over hidden stones. Cross-currents pushed and pulled the canoe from side to side as we moved up the middle with the motor roaring. Suddenly, the keel of the canoe caught and jammed on a rock in the middle. In slow motion, the current turned the bow of the canoe broadside to the waves, tipping the right side into the water. Just as we were about to capsize, the keel came free of the rock, the canoe righted itself, the motor pushed forward and we turned into the waves once more. The propeller banged on the rocks many times before we reached the safety of smooth water above the cataract.

The second waterfall, called 'The Big Beast', was a mile upstream; a wall of rock over which the river cascaded with such force that it curved over the rim before crashing onto the granite boulders below. But the rocks on the right bank were dry and the waterfall was not as high or dangerous as I had expected. I had no doubt I could get up, though it might take a day to carry all the baggage and motor and to drag the canoe round. The sun was already high in the sky so I decided to make lunch and set up camp for the night before tackling the falls.

I pulled into a pool of slack water below enormous boulders about 150 yards from the falls and was surprised to find another canoe already there. Two young dogs came barking and wagging their tails. A man and his daughter appeared. I offered tobacco and we sat and talked about the low level of the river and the coming of the rains. Senhor Alberto said he'd never been further up the river. 'There are Indians,' he said. We walked to the top of the falls where a sign had been nailed to a tree: 'Indigenous Area. Entry to Strangers Forbidden. FUNAI'.

'Do you have *cupuacú*?' I asked when the wife came to watch us moving my baggage to the top of the falls.

'No.'

'What else is lacking?'

'Everything,' she said.

I handed over coffee, rice, maize, tobacco and papers, a little sugar, lemons, soap and a *cupuacú* fruit.

They had arrived a week earlier from their permanent home near Santa Isabel to harvest manioc Alberto's brother had planted, and they were staying in a crude shelter, measuring twelve feet square and open on two sides, which had taken them a day and half to build, with materials from the forest.

We emptied my canoe and left the equipment protected from rain under a large plastic sheet at the top of the falls. We took baths in the river before sitting down on low stools for a lunch.

Alberto didn't use a gill net because he didn't have the money to buy one and didn't know how to make one. I hung up the gill net I was making and he stood watching my fingers and the bobbin darting between the strands. He was quick to learn, and we spent a happy afternoon perfecting the technique and gaining speed, while his daughter and wife lay in their hammocks watching and commenting.

'I'm not going to buy any hooks, only line to make myself a net! I always thought it was difficult, but it's easy.'

Later the wife, whose name I was never told, sat on a rock overlooking the river, splitting canes to weave large, square sieves. In boredom, their daughter began teasing a brooding hen with one of the puppies.

'Don't teach the dog to kill chickens,' said her father, but the fun didn't stop until feathers had been torn and all the hens had fled into the forest.

'That dog's called Brahma Chopp,' said Alberto, which was the name of a popular brand of beer.

'Where's Antarctica?' I said, naming another popular brand.

'He's gone. A snake took him, a little way down river.'

Near sunset we carried my canoe to the top of the falls without difficulty and, after bathing and gathering our washed clothes that had dried on the rocks, we ate supper and listened to music from Manaus on Alberto's radio while a chorus of frogs sang along the river bank.

Alberto almost lost his canoe next morning when a giant catfish, caught on his night fishing line, tried to jump out of the canoe. The fish seemed to be still alive when Alberto started slicing fillets from it and its mouth and gills stopped moving only when the kidneys were cut out.

I was invited to stay for the feast. After an hour we sat down to enjoy a new pot of fish soup.

'For your journey,' said Senhor Alberto when he took out three bunches of plantains from the place where he had hidden them in the nearby trees. 'One day we went fishing and when we came back someone had stolen all the bananas.' On another occasion, the family returned from a visit down river to find that salt, foods and fishing line had been stolen. 'Now, I hide everything in the trees.'

The river was tranquil above The Big Beast, without rocks or sandbars. Thick foilage of bushes and trees reached into the slow-moving water and my little red and blue canoe seemed to steer itself up this artery of the forest with the bright sky overhead. For how many seasons had the river risen and fallen, serving only its own purpose? I stopped once to look at flowers made up of hundreds of scarlet needles like bottle-cleaning brushes, growing on the stems of a bushy tree. They had been blooming by the riverbank long before Renaissance Europeans came to the Amazon. And when I saw a toucan, I wondered for how long toucans had eaten fruits in the trees, unseen and unknown by homo sapiens, content with the toucan view of the world.

The third waterfall, called *Irapaje* (the name of a bird), was an hour upstream. Water plunged with a roar down twenty-five feet through a gap in the centre. I tied up the canoe and walked over the hot boulders to reconnoitre. It took eight round trips to carry the baggage, motor and gasoline to the grey sandy beach above the falls. I worked without haste and rested in the shade to eat a banana before the hard work of bringing the canoe as close into the falls as possible and then hauling it over rocks with the rope, using short logs as rollers.

It was early afternoon before the canoe was fully reloaded and I had made and drunk a bowl of lemonade. I had intended to halt for the day at the first suitable site, but the fourth waterfall, called *Tucuman* (the name of a palm tree), lay round the very next bend. The fall was about thirty feet, down a series of slopes about a hundred and fifty yards from top to bottom. Dragging the canoe on rollers was tiring but not difficult. I stopped abruptly when a big cayman appeared on the rocks fifty feet away. I stepped slowly forward, and suddenly smiled when I realised the outline was a flatish piece of tree root and the shadow of a crack in the rock.

According to what people had said, the Salesian Mission could not be far beyond the fifth waterfall. This was my primary destination on the river and I did not want to arrive very tired in the afternoon, so when I reached the fifth I circled in front of it and then headed for a tumbled-down *barraco* on the high bank opposite. It was the sixth time I had unloaded or loaded the canoe that day but, after taking a bath surrounded by hundreds of pale yellow or lime-green phoebe butterflies on a sandbank in the middle of the river, I returned to my camp refreshed, and hungry for a fried fish supper and a few mugs of tea. Two pairs of blue and gold macaws flew overhead, the sunshine vanished and *cigarras* began their whining calls.

I was too tired to think of what might happen tomorrow and woke only once during the night, when a rafter of the *barraco* collapsed dropping the hammock and myself to the ground in the dark.

The name of the fifth waterfall was *Piraíba*, the big catfish, and I decided to enjoy the rest day and perhaps do some fishing in the afternoon before going further. I did not know what sort of greeting I might receive upriver and was content to lie in my hammock for the morning, sipping coffee, eating porridge and reading more about Chagnon's experiences and the Yanomami, especially about local etiquette and behaviour:

'Giving in to a demand always established a new threshold; the next demand would be for a bigger item or favour, and the anger of the Indians even greater if the demand was not met. I soon learned that I had to become very much like the Yanomamo to be able to get along with them on their terms: sly, aggressive, and intimidating.

'. . . had I failed to demonstrate that I could not be pushed around beyond a certain point, I would have been the subject of far more ridicule, theft and practical jokes than was the actual case,' wrote Chagnon.

I was stripping to take a bath at noon when two canoes appeared on the river above the falls. Both were loaded with bundles of thatching. I counted two men and five youths but it was not until they had passed the waterfall and were paddling towards me that I saw their straight black hair cut in a fringe at the front and their flat, broad faces and knew they were Yanomami from upriver.

'Good day,' I called out politely in Portuguese when they came near. No one answered. One man held a shotgun.

A man and two boys came up the bank and looked around. A second man, wearing only underpants, came up and held out his hand until I shook it. All of them looked at my sacks and boxes of supplies.

'Who are you? What you are doing here?' the older man asked in Portuguese. I replied in Portuguese, and the group then spoke amongst themselves in Yanomami.

I offered tobacco, taking some myself to roll a cigarette. The older man, who was wearing a scruffy pair of long trousers and a dirty shirt, did the same and the man in underpants and the two boys made sausage-like plugs of tobacco to put between their bottom lips and teeth.

The Yanomami stood in a line facing me across the heap of all my belongings. They were watching me and the sacks and boxes carefully.

'Are you taking the thatch down to the Portuguese?' I asked.

The older man nodded. 'Give me rope,' he said, picking up a roll of parachute cord from the top of a box. The others watched to see my reaction.

'No, take this,' I replied, pointing to a short string holding the cooking pot over the fire.

The group spoke amongst themselves in Yanomami. I waited. The other two boys from the canoes arrived and joined the line watching me and eyeing my belongings.

The man in underpants pointed to the sack.

'Coffee, rice, sugar,' I said, glad most of my stuff was wrapped and out of sight.

Attention shifted to the fire. The man in underpants spoke and the younger boys made it up with sticks.

'Why have you come here?' asked the older man.

'I want to learn about the forest.'

'You have a gun?'

'No.'

'You are a *garimpeiro*?'

'No. I am a writer. I have a pen and paper.' They looked at my fountain pen and notebook.

'What is this?' asked one of the boys, lightly touching my recorder with his finger.

I played some notes. Everyone laughed and took turns blowing it while the others watched with big grins. I think we all felt the tension slacken between us.

'Give me this,' demanded the man in the underpants, picking up the steel harpoon with the three barbed prongs.

'What will you do for me?' I asked.

There was silence. 'I have a beautiful arrow. I will give it to you.'

'Good, I want to learn to make and to use,' I said.

'I will teach you.'

One of the boys took a small kitchen knife, then put it down. It was blunt.

The older man fingered the plastic rain sheet. 'Give me this. When you go down.'

'What will you give me?'

'Yes, we will exchange,' said the man in underpants.

'How long will you stay?' asked the older man.

I hesitated to commit myself. 'I'll go before the rains.' They invited me to go down river with them but I refused. I said I wanted to go on up the river.

'Don't go up the river. Wait for our return. If you go up they will take everything. Stay here. We will go together. My uncle has vowed to kill the next white man to come from far away to the Marauiá river. He will steal your canoe and food and throw your body in the river.'

It was impossible to know whether these threats were real or merely a way of manipulating me to make sure they obtained my trade goods on their return.

'We will come back after two or three or four days.'

'What is your name?' asked the man in underpants.

'*Den-ee-son,*' I said slowly. I did not ask their names because, according to Chagnon, it was bad manners among Indians. Bad spirits might hear and would then know where to attack that person.

The man in underpants helped himself to a packet of crackers. I watched but said nothing. 'Excuse me,' he said. I nodded and everyone helped themselves. It was only later that I realised my lack of good manners in not immediately offering meals to all seven Yanomami. 'I am hungry' is almost a form of greeting with them, Chagnon reported. The crackers were eaten in a moment and the man in underpants cleaned out the plastic bag. 'For me,' he said, folding the bag.

'We here, are good people,' said the older man helping himself to more tobacco. 'If someone comes taking gold, then I myself will kill the man. That is my right. But people working on their own business, like Dennison; no, that's different. I don't want to steal. It's better to barter.'

Suddenly, we heard a dull thud from the river. I thought it was a boulder falling over the waterfall. It was a gunshot. Several more shots were fired.

'Let's go to see,' said the man in underpants to me. He and his companions wanted to take my canoe. I said emphatically 'No' but offered to take them upriver to investigate the noise myself.

'I'll stay,' said the older man.

I didn't want to abandon my food and equipment but the canoe was too small for passengers and my gear. Besides the seven Yanomami could take everything by force if they chose, and I had to show trust if I wanted them to trust me.

'OK, but don't mess with anything.' I had no doubt that he would look through all my belongings while we were away. This would at least prove to them that I had spoken the truth about having no gun nor any equipment to prospect for gold or precious stones on their river.

The man in underpants and a youth, both with shotguns, and two boys climbed into my canoe and we motored off towards the small waterfall, which we passed easily.

'Why have you come here?' asked the man in underpants, staring eye to eye with me.

'Visiting,' I said. 'I want to learn about the forest. I hope you will teach me.'

'You wait for us when we come up. We are good people. Up the river, they are bad. They kill white men.' The two boys were grinning with the novelty of motoring up the river.

I wondered how much of their own culture these Yanomami still maintained. They were what Brazilians called *civilizados*, meaning pacified by missionaries. They used steel tools and shotguns, possessed clothing and spoke some Portuguese. Auca Indians in Ecuador would call them 'tamed'. Anthropologists say they have begun the process that ends with the destruction of their culture. But it is patronising to assume that a man who gives up his bow and arrow to hunt with a shotgun has lost his culture. Trade goods have often been the beginning of tribal disintegration, but the causes go deeper than aluminium cooking pots: Indians do not often willingly give up their own values for the barbarism of the 'non-people' – as many tribes call the civilised.

We entered a narrow opening in the forest and stopped thirty feet inside a dried-up channel.

'Do you know how to walk in the forest?'

'Yes,' I replied, though barefoot. We set off through the shallow pools of water up the channel then climbed a rotting tree trunk up into the forest. I kept only a few paces behind the man in underpants, following wherever he stepped to avoid spines, sharp roots and blades of leaves that cut the skin. We kept up a rapid pace for a mile, almost running, between saplings and big trees before we stopped. The boys bellowed loudly twice. I was the only one sweating. The youth with the shotgun had vanished. We ran a little farther and stopped when we reached a faint trail.

'The way to Santa Isabel,' said the man in underpants. 'Wait here.' He ran off, disappearing in the vegetation after only sixty feet. The two boys bellowed again, their calls absorbed by the trees. The place was cool and dark and there were few mosquitoes.

Are they going to leave me here and steal the canoe, I wondered? I waited for any sign and watched the boys sitting together on a log.

Eventually, the man in underpants re-emerged from the trees and we returned the way he had come, meeting the youth with the shotgun along the way. The boys bellowed again and laughed. The man in underpants went off again and we sat and waited. A black and yellow spider stayed motionless on its web in front of me. We sat in silence hearing the boom of distant thunder.

'Pigs!' called one of the boys, leaping from the ground up into a tree. He climbed six feet up the trunk and burst out laughing again.

Rain was starting to fall. We moved on deeper into the forest and met the man in underpants carrying a wild pig on his back with a tumpline made of bark. He dumped the animal on the ground, shouted angrily at us in Yanomami and sat down. The youth and one of the boys went off in silence into the trees. The other boy broke a length of palm frond to keep off the rain. Another man, a stranger, appeared, dumped another on the ground, shook my hand and returned among the trees; they were presumably his shots that we had heard originally. He appeared later with his young wife. She was wearing only shorts when she first emerged, then donned a T-shirt until nightfall when she took it off again.

I was given two shotguns to carry back to the canoe, behind the boy with the palm frond over his head. It was raining hard. Thunder cracked over the tops of the trees and the forest was gloomy like twilight. It took three trips with the canoe low in the water and someone bailing water constantly to ferry a total of five dead animals and all the people back to the waterfall. The animals were butchered on the rocks and everyone had a job to do; hacking the carcasses into big hunks, holding the pigs' legs apart, gathering dry firewood or safeguarding the canoes. They had arrived without food, there was now plenty, and everyone was happy. I had proved my usefulness. I wondered how much of their suspicion had gone.

The sun had set before we all returned to the *barraco*. As expected, all my belongings had been searched. Nothing had been taken except a short length of cord. There were ten Yanomami now and they divided into three family groups inside the shelter, each hanging his hammock like bunk beds near separate fires. The meat was divided between them and, though we were eleven people in a space eight feet by twenty feet, each family had its own heap of firewood and separate conversation.

Being thoroughly chilled by the rain, I asked one of the boys for a mug of hot water. His father nodded and I was soon sitting in my hammock sipping hot tea listening to the oldest man and the man in underpants talking in Yanomami. Their language sounded like a series of soft sighs spoken at the front of the mouth and further muted by the thick plugs of tobacco held between their teeth and bottom lip.

The oldest man was the chief of the community. His mission name was Renato. The man in underpants was Gabriel. Using Western names is a handy custom because they are not real names and therefore do not violate any taboos. However, not everyone in this community uses these. I blundered later when I asked a boy his name, expecting his non-name, and he whispered his Yanomami name and ran away.

Renato and Gabriel were brothers-in-law, an intimate relationship of giving and receiving, closer in fact than that of two brothers, who may compete for wives. Gabriel's son poked sticks on the two fires to boil a stew of pig meat and offal for our supper and to roast the meats covered by green leaves. They asked whether I had parents and a wife and how I had come up the waterfalls alone.

'I thought there was another white man with you, with a gun. Now I know you are alone,' said Renato. 'Does the Portuguese have many things? Tobacco? Hooks?' he asked. He told me their canoes were loaded with bundles of thatch for the Portuguese, below the first waterfall, to use on his tourist huts. They in return would receive trade goods or money to spend in Santa Isabel.

This was the first time the Yanomami had worked for money, gathering bundles of thatch and they were thinking of the trade goods they would earn. Steel knives, steel pots and fish hooks have had a fatal fascination for Indians. They were used by missionaries and slaving parties to lure tribes out of the forest to settlements down the rivers, where they usually died of disease or despair. They are still used today by road-builders and ranchers to pacify tribes. The wondrous tools were often traded far into the interior from tribe to tribe, spreading news of the white man's existence long before the first actual encounters. A shotgun is the most valuable possession a family may own.

'Wait here until we return and you come to our village. Do not go up alone. My uncle will kill you,' said Renato. I promised to stay, though it was still impossible to know whether the threat was real or merely to ensure I did not bypass their village and go farther upriver, thus depriving them of the trade goods Renato now knew I had, after searching the sacks in my absence.

At dusk I took out a lantern. Several people stopped what they were doing to watch.

'What is it?' asked Gabriel. I showed the candle inside that rose on a spring as it burned.

'Give this to me, when you go down.'

'I only have one. I need it.' I said. The candle lantern hung on a string over my hammock and I settled to writing my journal for the day. A boy stood with his arms around my neck watching the shapes being drawn across the paper. He took the pen in his fingers and drew a line on his hand. Someone tooted on the recorder then passed it me to play a tune for them.

Renato asked for tobacco to make a lip plug. 'This is too little. Don't you have more?' he asked.

'I only have a little. I must safeguard it.'

'Give me a bag now and when we come back I will bring another for you,' he said. I fetched a small bag from the sack, giving one of the boys a small amount of tobacco out of it.

'This is not full!' screamed Renato suddenly in my face.

'When you give me back a bag, you can take some out of it,' I said gently, shocked by his outburst.

He calmed immediately, though his sudden anger had been frightening, and he invited me to eat with them. I fetched the spaghetti uneaten from lunchtime and we sat in a group on the floor chewing boiled meat and drinking the rich pork stock until we were full. One of the boys fetched river water to wash our hands and to drink. Later, the young man and wife asked for cooking oil and invited me to eat with them. Conversations quietened into whispers of Yanomami until everyone fell asleep. The flames of fires settled into hot embers.

The fires were still burning when the boys got up at dawn to heat the pork soup for breakfast. I supplied coffee, sugar and tobacco which were welcome treats. One man from each group cut palm fronds to make strong baskets to carry the roast meat; Renato left a roast leg to keep me supplied until they returned.

The two canoes loaded with thatching were already too low in the water to carry four extra people, so Gabriel and three others said they would walk to Santa Isabel and sleep in the forest on the way.

'I wanted to bring another canoe but no one wanted to lend a canoe,' said Renato. He had left his wife without a canoe to get to their garden in the forest.

We all went down to the fourth waterfall. Gabriel and the others disappeared into the forest, carrying a basket of meat. With so many helpers, the canoes were quickly down the waterfall and the Yanomami were on their way, turning back to wave as they paddled away. One of them had asked me to safeguard his shotgun and I held it in my hand as I watched them go.

13

Rio Marauiá:
River of Rocks and Rocks

'The land is not a means to a result but an intimate and fused portion of life – a matter not of objective inspection and analysis but of affectionate regard. The making of weapons is felt as a part of the exciting use of them ... The "animism" of primitive minds is a necessary expression of the immediacy of relation between want, overt activity, that which affords satisfaction and the attained satisfaction itself. Only when things are treated simply as means and are marked off and hold off against remote ends, do they become objects.'

John Dewey, *The Philosophy of Civilization*.

NEXT DAY, AFTER A heavy rain storm, I went fishing below the fifth waterfall, using some pork as bait. A large canoe motored up the river coming straight towards me. They were Brazilians. I had met two of the men in Santa Isabel when I arrived in my canoe the week before. They had said they were visiting their uncle's home and land. The uncle was a short, old man with round spectacles and a cowboy hat. Now they were on the Marauiá river with a guide and his son. I followed them to the *barraco*, not wanting to give them any opportunity to search my belongings. I asked what they were doing. The uncle replied that Renato had told them to wait for him.

I was not pleased to be sharing my camp but we had to get along and they were equally suspicious of me. I went to wait for the Yanomami at the fourth waterfall after lunch the next day. Tall grey clouds with jagged tails were gathering by the time my canoe reached the waterfall. Happily, the Yanomami had already returned and we motored all together to the *barraco* where the Brazilians were waiting. The uncle lay in his hammock watching the Indians with a look on his face as if he didn't want to get his hands dirty. The Indians had been away from their community for several days and were anxious to be home with their families before dark.

We started to reload my canoe and found a big tarantula in my baggage.

'It's dangerous,' said one of the boys, striking it dead with a stick and throwing the body outside.

We travelled in two groups, the two motorised canoes towing the Yanomami craft, with Gabriel and his son, Martins, Samuel and Paulino and his wife Georgina riding with me.

'Who are the Brazilians?' I asked Gabriel when we were well above the fifth waterfall.

'I don't know them,' he replied.

'What are they doing here?'

'I don't know. Prospectors. This we have to resolve tonight in the village.'

'They cannot pass,' said the young man called Martins. No *garimpeiros*. They cannot come and take our gold. FUNAI has told us, if *garimpeiros* come, take their motor. Throw their bodies in the river.'

'What does FUNAI do?' I asked.

'Nothing. We need medicine for colds, for malaria.'

'Don't the Yanomami have their own medicine?'

'Yes,' Gabriel said, nodding vigorously. 'But the *hekura* [spirit] does not accept these sicknesses.'

'They are diseases of the white man,' I said.

The weight of the Yanomami canoe pulled heavily on my rudder and I was glad whenever we had to slow to negotiate jagged rocks lying across the river. Many of the *acai* palm up here were heavy with purple fruit.

After a while, Paulino and Gabriel took a few pinches of a hallucinogenic snuff and perhaps that was why we hit a few rocks soon afterwards, nearly capsizing the canoes.

'Gardens,' Gabriel said when we passed clearings behind a fringe of forest left standing along the right bank. 'The rock. That's where we live. There are lots of children. But you must not give tobacco to the young ones who ask. It will be finished. You must guard it for yourself.'

Thirty people were waiting on the rock, watching the noisy approach of the four canoes. One man held a bow and arrow as tall as himself and watched without moving when we landed. Everyone wore at least some clothing – the women in cotton dresses open at the front, the men in shorts or T-shirts and all still wearing the thin cord around their waists which is the traditional sign of being dressed. The Yanomamis are short people. I stood head and shoulders above most of the adults watching the newcomer. In fact their Western clothes had been worn for the arrival of us white men and in the days afterwards they were gradually discarded.

Gabriel and the others greeted their wives and children then they all walked back to their homes carrying their hammocks, shotguns and cooking pots. The Brazilians and myself were left to unload our belongings on our own.

A long path led across fire-blackened earth and banana trees growing in a clearing around the village. I could hear men singing as I approached the Yanomami shelters, built round an open area of bare, beaten ground.

Two men were singing and dancing in the arena, the last of the day's sun shining on their bodies, which were decorated with scarlet and green feathers on their outstretched arms, their feet stomping on the bare ground, their faces and chests painted with waving red lines.

I lay in a hammock looking at my new surroundings. The house was a thatched shelter facing the arena, with an earth floor measuring about fifteen by twenty-four feet and open on two sides. Seven people lived here and their hammocks hung between the poles supporting the rafters of the roof. Renato and his wife Francisca slept on either side of the campfire at one end; and their sons, Robi, Daniel and José sleeping side by side; daughter Louisa sleeping beside Gilberto, her husband-to-be, near the back, a few feet from her brothers; and myself near the front at an angle from a corner post so that I could see both the family and the village.

There was a woven leaf mat for the baby daughter to play on, a harness like a baby bouncer, a pottery pot containing water and two low stools crudely carved from blocks of wood. The family's other possessions were kept in a sack and some tins behind Francisca's hammock and a few baskets hanging from a rafter contained fish hooks and cartridges. The shotgun, fishing rod, bows and arrows and tube for blowing *ebene* (the local hallucinogenic drug) were stuck in between the rafters and the thatch roof, out of the way of children and the dogs.

Renato stood in front of his house, explaining the arrival of the Brazilians to the community. People heckled angrily, it seemed to me. Apparently he said he'd speak again in the evening. The Brazilians went back to their own fire in an open-sided shed built near the river as a school by the Mission and then abandoned. The missionary fathers had preferred to import its tin roof and white-painted school desks up the five waterfalls rather than use materials the people could have gathered in the forest. Such is the force of progress!

The singing had ended after sunset. Evening fires were blazing in every home by the time several boys had carried my belongings to the village and I had bathed in the river. Renato and his wife Francisca crouched on the ground in front of the fire, stirring chunks of pork boiling in a pot.

Children handed me the tenor recorder and told everyone to be quiet. I improvised tunes up and down the scale, the children watching me wide-eyed or peering up the end of the instrument where the sounds came from, mimicking my fingers or rubbing the polished wood of the instrument. A boy stood laughing behind the hammock, with his arms around my neck and his head resting on mine. His fingers felt the bristles on my chin and the hairs around my nipples. The Indians in the Amazon have almost no body hair and although elders sometimes do not pluck out the whispy grey hairs from their own chins, they regard the hairiness of the white man with fascination and revulsion. When I handed back the recorder for the children to blow, one boy hummed perfectly the nonsense I had just played. Every boy wanted a turn blowing, and afterwards I handed the instrument to two girls standing in silence. Later they came back with other girls to toot on the novelty.

The men ate supper first, sitting on blocks of wood only inches above the ground, with the smoke-blackened cooking pot of boiled pork, gourd bowls of *farinha* and unleavened bread and a dish and spoon in front of each of us. Francisca and the children ate separately. The dogs ate last. Then we settled in our hammocks to hear in the soft sighs of Yanomami what must have been the story of the journey down the river, the waterfalls, the Portuguese, the five pigs, the Brazilians and the other white man with the beautiful canoe and the full sack of trade goods. Francisca chastised her husband, I think, for not bringing home more trade goods from the expedition. Fires in the homes settled. The dogs were quiet. The moon shone brightly in the darkness.

The Brazilians came back after breakfast. Renato arranged two poles on the ground for the men of the households to sit on. Children stood watching behind. The Brazilian Uncle stood to speak and looked at all the faces watching him. 'I have come to help the Yanomami as I have helped many Indian groups. To make your lives better,' he said. He took out photographs and passed them to elders. The first picture showed him with the State Governor during the election the year before. The second showed him with Indians living in timber-built houses with tin roofs and a motor car in the dirt street. The third photograph, carried by all Brazilian husbands to prove they are good family men, showed his wife and children.

Uncle spoke of FUNAI and the missionaries up the river, and everyone had complaints against them. Renato stood up, to emphasise what he said. The priests were no good, he said, because they expected too much work for very low wages. He spoke in Portuguese so that his visitors could understand. 'They have a big plantation which the Yanomami made, earning little. The priests want to keep the Yanomami backwards.' But the way the Yanomami used to live had changed, he said. 'It was long ago. Those people are gone. The Yanomami want to progress, to gain the things the white men have.' People nodded their heads and everyone spoke at once.

Uncle said the State Governor and the Mayor of Santa Isabel wanted to help the people to advance. Other Indians had electric lights; he and his friends had come to help the Yanomami get theirs. They would build a school and make their lives better. He introduced one of the other Brazilians as an officer of the Federal Police. 'If the missionaries oppress you or do something wrong, tell me and I will stop it,' he said and spoke of all the help they were going to give to stop people oppressing the Yanomami.

Then Uncle revealed the real reason for their visit so far from Manaus and up the five waterfalls. He brought out from his pocket a small plastic bag of coloured rocks: topaz, agate, emerald and others, and handed them to the men to inspect.

'We will work together and life here will be better,' he said. The stones were paid for by the kilo, not by the gram, but still had value. A couple of men fetched their own coloured stones from their houses to show.

A boy tugged my arm, summoning me to a house at the other side of the arena. A young man wanted fish hooks and tobacco. We sat together in a hammock talking in Portuguese, and smoking or sucking tobacco. 'What will you take in exchange?' he asked. His friend offered me the young woman lying with him in the next hammock. She was beautiful, with firm, plump breasts and teasing smile and black hair cut in a fringe.

Several times towards the end of my stay, there were invitations for me to take a wife and live with the Yanomami. But when a man marries he is obliged to provide an unmarried sister to the bride's family. I told my hosts my sister was already married and therefore not available. This exchange of women helps bond families and alleviates the shortage of women caused by the preference for male children as hunters and protectors and the consequent killing of female babies at birth. Mothers will not jeopardise a nursing child by competing with a newborn baby of either sex.

'Your canoe is very beautiful. Give me your canoe.'

I shook my head. 'How will I reach my home?'

'You can take mine. When you come back I will make another canoe for you.'

I laughed at his insistence. 'Why do you want to exchange, if you already have a canoe?'

In this way, conversations moved back and forth throughout the days I was able to stay in the village, faltering sometimes when we didn't understand but nodded anyway. Several of the men and women spoke Portuguese and always there was someone in the group to translate from Yanomami to Portuguese if necessary.

The stones had been put away and the Brazilians were singing for their hosts with Uncle playing his guitar when I went back to the group gathered around them.

'What do you think?' asked Gabriel.

'I think you have to deal with them with a lot of caution. They are *garimpeiros* but they want you to do the work,' I said.

'This I have told Renato. I will tell him again.'

We followed the crowd to the distribution of gifts at the Brazilians' camp in the abandoned school. Every man, woman and child in the village held out their hand for a few fish hooks, a piece of soap or some soap powder, steel wool, some shirts, underpants and trousers, lead to refill shotgun cartridges, a money belt, flashlight batteries and the promise to bring sacks of gifts next time. People went home when the bounty ended.

The Brazilians met a bare-breasted girl in the village when they came before lunch to talk to a village man called Domingo. They were genuinely shocked. One of them immediately took off his own shirt to cover her. Wearing clothes is one of the first rules imposed by the civilised before Indians can receive gifts, though the definition of 'clothing' is entirely one-sided. Traditionally, Yanomami, and the men of many other tribes, keep the foreskin of their penis tucked up under the thin cord tied around their waist. The women also wear a hipcord, and Yanomami women crouch with their legs together. They are dressed. Only animals are naked.

In the Western tradition, the Fall occurred on the day Adam and Eve *learned* they were naked and were ashamed. Europeans have variously interpreted Indians' nudity as either pre-Fall innocence or post-Fall sinfulness, but in both cases proof that they are heathens needing improvement.

I took a bath in the river, watched by several small boys, and we ran back to the village in the rain to find men and boys gathered around my hammock waiting to start trading. I had intended the fish hooks, rope, machetes and other items as gifts, but it was more honest to exchange the goods. 'A white man never gives something for free. There is always a price,' I said, when Renato and others were discussing the gifts of the *garimpeiros*. 'Is it better to know the price before you buy or to learn the price afterwards?'

'Will you exchange three arm-lengths?' asked a man inspecting the roll of parachute cord. We measured three double arm-lengths, about six yards. 'I'll bring something,' he said. Several other people claimed three double arm-lengths before he returned from his house with four clusters of green parrot feathers. I was reluctant to accept these decorations, which are worn by the men when they dance and chant to the spirits. My hesitation was understood as dissatisfaction with the feathers. 'Is it too little? We have only feathers.'

I told Gabriel that I did not want to exchange feathers if the men would then have none to wear when they danced, but my meaning was lost between English, Portuguese and Yanomami. In any case, it was naive to think people would not keep their best decorations hidden and sell only their old feathers, faded and dirty with smoke. We set prices by common consent. A machete cost one bow and two arrows. Gabriel's younger brother, Martins, told me to keep one for him and hurried off to make two arrows. Fifteen double arm-lengths of fishing line cost two clusters of feathers. A man began going through all my belongings, watched by a dozen people eager for bargains. 'What is this?' he asked.

'A razor blade, for shaving,' I said.

'I know, I know,' he said, already looking for something else.

Renato got annoyed at the rummaging through my belongings. He thought the men were taking without paying. He stood in the arena when the group went home for lunch and addressed the community. At first he spoke in Portuguese: 'If you want to exchange, then make the exchange. But curiosity – no!' He then told them in Yanomami that I was travelling alone, that I was not with the other white men, that I was a guest in his house.

'I paid!' a man yelled angrily. Renato answered in Yanomami. The other man shouted back. Renato shouted. Other people shouted their comments, goading Renato into a tirade of yelling, pacing in front of the house in the hot sun with his arms waving, turning to me and pointing at the heap of my belongings on the ground. He wiped tears from his eyes. His words were harsh, whatever he was saying. The dangerous tension was only relieved when the Brazilians kicked a football into the arena and played between themselves. Renato turned to the house, sweating and agitated. I offered him tobacco to roll a cigarette.

'You spoke well, thank you,' I said.

Perhaps the warning was necessary. A burly youth came later in the afternoon and after negotiations, took away a mirror, fishing line and hooks, and a kitchen knife. He was careful to confirm that a plastic salt cellar was a gift to him.

'I'll pay for these and this is a gift,' he said before leaving with his shopping.

'You're buying a lot,' someone said as he walked away. He came back with a bow and two arrows. I did not have a great use for several sets of bows and arrows, but my hosts confidently expected me to sell them to my own people.

The Brazilians left after lunch, to search upriver for topaz and diamonds. Renato's eldest son and a senior man, Domingo, went with them. Their plan was to visit the Mission, said to be three days' paddling upstream from the village, though the water in the river was still falling and they might not get through.

The village was quiet for an hour in the afternoon, when people lay in their hammocks. A boy came to me, holding out his hands to display the cat's cradle around his fingers, made with the long loop of string that all the children carried around their necks or over one shoulder.

'This is the jaguar. This is the alligator,' he said, changing the arrangement of strings between his fingers. Other children came to show other arrangements or to toot on the recorder with a giggle and pass it to me for a tune. Many of the children spoke at least some Portuguese and sometimes they translated for others who spoke only Yanomamo.

Two women dumped baskets of manioc on the ground and

Francisca, her sisters-in-law and several other women sat between the hammocks, peeling the tough-skinned roots with sharp knives. Renato painted his face and chest with red *urucu* seeds, tied on black feather armbands and joined men in the shaman's house to take *ebene* as part of a ceremony to help a woman who was sick.

I went to Gabriel's house later to sit with him while he tied tiny green feathers, tipped with scarlet, onto slivers of wood. He put them in his ear lobes when he was done and smiled at his own beauty. All the men had pierced ears and Gabriel, Paulino and several others also liked to wear feather's in tiny holes drilled in the flesh of their chins.

It is the adult males of the Yanomami, and many other tribes in the Amazon, who are the more brightly-decorated sex, using feathers and complete wings, dried seeds, shells, lip plugs, and painting their bodies and faces with complex designs.

Gabriel's younger brother Martins sat beside him on a low stool, binding a six-inch blade made of palm to the shaft of an arrow. He drew red lines on the blade when it was mounted and handed it to me, with another arrow and a bow, in exchange for a machete.

'This will kill pig and *anta*,' he told me. He called his wife to bring their baby son. 'Do you have medicine?'

Many babies and younger children suffered fungus infections on their scalps, necks, behind their ears and under their arms. Infections on the scalp had become open sores and their hair was falling out.

Mothers seemed to have stopped washing the hair of their infected children, apparently for fear of getting it wet. The hair of a few children was therefore filthy and buzzing with tiny flies. I had nothing to treat fungal infections and knew from my own infections that treatment was long and reinfection highly likely. We dabbed on iodine ointment, at least to clean around the sores and to discourage flies. I explained several times that the purple face paint would not cure their babies.

Domingo's wife, a stout woman with a tongue as sharp as an arrow, presented an unwilling son with a deep cut across his knee. It was not yet infected but the wound reopened each time he took a step. A man presented the infected insect bites on his legs to be cleaned. A lemon tree with fruit grew just outside the village: I told each mother to clean bites and small cuts with lemons to prevent infection, but no one listened. Everyone knows that it is *hekura* (demons or spirits) who cause illness. The Yanomami seem to be the only Indians in the Amazon who do not use medicinal plants from the forest, though some groups cultivate magical plants which, for example, can cause miscarriages in enemy villages.

Four men emerged from the shaman's house dancing in a line into the arena. They danced one behind the other, their feet stepping with the rhythm of their chant and their out-stretched arms rising and falling.

'*Hekura*,' said Gabriel. 'They are killing the spirit, sending it away.'

I went for a bath in the river, before the women's bathing time nearer sunset, and crouched on the rock with one man and a line of boys watching me shave. My smooth chin was a new fascination that evening. My fingers stained by the iodine brought a new request.

'Will you exchange? I want it to paint myself,' explained Paulino. The colour was new and the stain durable but I refused, saying it was medicine.

'Only a little. You can buy more in Santa Isabel.'

'And if I meet someone who needs it for a wound?'

'You will not.'

Lots of men asked for iodine body paint so I agreed to leave it with Renato when I left, nominally for medicine but I had no doubt that it would be used for decoration if he thought that a better use.

Men and boys were squatting beside my bags when I returned. They accepted tobacco and inspected fish hooks, nylon fishing line and steel leaders. 'Piranhas can't bite through them,' I said.

No one was interested. Paulino played with the short steel wires in his fingers. 'Can you wear them round the neck?' He hooked two together and put on his new necklace.

'And these?' asked a boy holding small brass swivels, used to avoid tangling fishing lines. They were taken as earrings and I gave many as gifts to the women, along with plastic combs, cotton and the very few needles I had.

'Next time, bring clothes for the women,' said Francisca.

Gabriel sat with us for supper and afterwards talked in Yanomamo with Renato. I lay in my hammock with children, writing my diary, until the two men came to tell me their plan.

'Tomorrow, let's go in your canoe with the motor and collect reeds to make arrows,' suggested Gabriel.

I readily agreed to go, but did not want other families angry with me for giving help only to Renato and his family. 'Who will pay for the gasoline?'

'I will make an arrow for you,' said Gabriel.

'Tell people that I will take anyone to collect reeds or bananas or to go fishing far from here in my canoe for the same price; one arrow.'

Renato nodded. 'I've said each person can exchange what they want.'

Gabriel added, 'I've told that someone who doesn't have anything must make something; with feathers, whatever. Something small, no? We will leave very early, six or seven, and go up the river.'

Renato spoke quietly. 'The people here, from here to Paulino's house, are good. The others? No. Wild. They have said to me, "Let's kill the white man and take his canoe and everything he has." But don't worry. You are in my house. They won't do anything. They want to kill me but it is only words. They don't know that if they kill a man who comes from far, no one else will come, no one to exchange machetes, line, hooks, clothes for them.'

I asked Renato about the *hekura*. 'They come from the spirit village below the earth,' he told me. 'The rivers, the lakes, those are their routes, their place and city. Over there is their church, and there is their radio and there is their place to make *farinha*.'

Chagnon explains that these spirits have gardens but no neighbourhood to hunt game, 'so they send their spirits up to earth to capture the souls of living children and eat them. There is a constant struggle between the evil spirits of (those) shamans and the evil spirits of shamans on this layer, earth.'

The layer above the earth is inhabited by the souls of the dead. 'They have gardens, make witchcraft, hunt, eat, and in general do what living man does. Everything that exists on earth has a counterpart or *hedu*, a sort of mirror image, although the activities of the two groups of objects and beings are independent of each other.' The stars and planets in the sky are attached to the underneath of this layer.

Our layer, the earth, 'Is a vast jungle, sprinkled with innumerable Yanomami villages . . . Even foreigners are thought to live in a type of house that resembles the Yanomami dwelling; after all, foreigners derived from the Yanomami by a process of degeneration.'

Mist was rising from the river when we motored upstream next morning to collect reeds. The sluggish water was brown and the forest on both sides looked gloomy, as if not yet awake. When the sun rose, the water appeared green, or clear, and we could see the gravel and sands and stones at the bottom. Martins sat in the bow, a shotgun in his lap, pointing to the dangerous rocks and the channels between the gravel beds and sandbars. He and Gabriel and his son were watching for ducks and other game birds; for macaws valuable for their long tail feathers; for *agouti*, *capybary* and *peccary* that might be drinking at the water's edge; for *acai*, *pupunha* and other palms with ripe fruit; for the hives of honey-making bees; for signs of intruders on their lands, such as rubber-tappers or other Indians; and for the ripples and splashes of *tucanare*, *pacu* and other fish.

We met Gabriel's elder son and another boy already fishing in their dugout canoe two miles upstream and towed them alongside us for three miles to a cataract of boulders where big fish were said to be plentiful.

'The river is dry, dry,' said Gabriel above the cataract, just before we hit a rock with such force that I was sure the canoe had cracked. Gabriel's younger son bailed out the water around our ankles while we zig-zagged through the rocks. Gabriel pointed to the left bank and Martins raised his gun. I could see only two parrots on a branch. Gabriel and his son stuck their fingers in their ears. Martins took aim, fired as we passed and a slender black bird toppled onto the bank. We stopped and picked it up.

Half a mile upstream, we pulled into the left bank and tied up. This was the site of a previous village, long ago, said Gabriel. Now the place was thick with bushes and the tall reeds. It is from the five-foot shoot carrying the grass-like seeds of this reed that the Yanomami make the shafts of their arrows. Martins and Gabriel worked separately cutting down thirty-foot reeds to gather shafts for themselves but both were disappointed to collect only six shafts between them. We found a *pupunha* palm with unripe fruit, then walked inland until we found another *pupunha* with riper fruit.

The trunk of the *pupunha* palm is covered in short, hard spines so Gabriel tied a barb on a long reed stem with which to pull down the bunches of fruit. Then he made a small hoop with strong vine to wear around his feet, climbed a neighbouring tree, pulling himself up with his arms and gripping the trunk with his feet held by the hoop, and stood in a fork in the tree while he reached with the long barbed stem across to the *pupunha* palm. Hard, green fruits bounced on our heads when Gabriel tried to pull loose the heaviest bunch, but after a few attempts the bunch fell free, to be caught on the barbed stem. A second bunch fell to the ground. Gabriel slid down the tree and stood laughing beside the fruits.

We carried them back to the canoe while Gabriel chopped down the other *pupunha* with the axe. The wood valued for making bows and clubs is the outer inch of the trunk. It is dense and black, strong and flexible, holding the tree up and bending in the wind. The whitish pulpy wood inside the trunk is discarded. Gabriel and Martins split a section of the black trunk lengthways into pieces and shaped these crudely with their machetes into six bows taller than themselves and a club for Renato. He had asked for this specially and may have been backing up his promise to defend his guest.

There was a beach on the other side of the river with sand hot enough in the midday sun to burn my feet as we strolled along the riverbank. Martins suddenly jumped into a bush. A cicada flew out. Gabriel chased it across the beach and jumped and captured it in his hands as he fell on the sand. He got up laughing and pulled off the insect's wings and legs, and held the fat-bellied creature in his hand. We found five more, to be used as fish bait, on the leaves in the bushes along the beach. I never spotted any until Martins pointed them out to me when he couldn't reach. Their wings were so fine, so perfectly patterned and coloured as the leaves that, even in the hand and inspected closely, it was impossible to be sure their wings were not in fact leaves. We walked to the end of the beach and when we turned back to the canoe Gabriel's son put his hand in mine to walk together.

Gabriel paddled the canoe to keep us straight as we drifted quietly down the river, and Martins fished with a long bamboo rod, flicking the cicada bait across the water as if fly fishing. The line snagged many times on bushes but no *pacu* nibbled the tasty bait, so we stopped on a beach to dig up worms from a mud puddle and caught a few *pacu* with them, and a sardine. The sardine then served as bait for a black piranha, the size of an oval dinner plate. Later, we saw another swimming beside the canoe. Gabriel went into the forest to gather bark of the *virola* tree to make the hallucinogenic snuff called *ebene*. The rest of us sat in the hot sun on the beach with butterflies landing on our arms to drink our sweat and the tiny black *pium* flies biting us.

We started for home feeling hungry and tired but happy. The canoe was so loaded with *pupunhas* and bananas, bundles of bows, rolls of *ebene* bark, plant roots, a duck, a few fish and three passengers that I could not see where we were going. Martins and Gabriel laughed when I told them this, but they mostly watched the river banks for ducks and peccaries and only sometimes gave hand signals.

Motoring downstream through the stretches of rocks was more dangerous than going up – we were travelling three times faster, unable to see the currents and obstacles on the other side, unable to alter course without getting broadside and, of course, unable to stop. We chose our course quickly, then travelled blind, steering as I felt the waves and eddies play the canoe until we emerged at the bottom and bailed out the water that had accumulated round our bare feet. I thought of the five waterfalls downstream and wondered if they would be passable when the rains started and the river began to rise.

Martins directed my course over a gravel bank by flapping his hand like a stranded fish. We ran aground.

'Martins, you can't do this,' I shouted in Portuguese, waving my hand in the air as he had done. 'You have to give direct signals. Go here, or go here.' The words needed no translation.

'I said to go,' he told me, flapping his hand again. He was a shyer man than Gabriel, his fast-talking, laughing, clowning brother. But when I took a photograph of the spoils of our day's expedition when we reached home, it was Martins who fell down theatrically as if killed by the 'shot'. Everyone laughed and inspected what we had brought. One of Gabriel's male relatives plucked two black and white speckled feathers from the duck and put them in his ears.

Renato came to sit beside my hammock when it was dark. I offered tobacco and we rolled cigarettes. He was well pleased with the outing.

'What does the Mission do?' I asked.

'Nothing!' He told me he had studied at the Mission school in Santa Isabel.

'The Yanomami life is changing a lot,' I said.

He nodded. 'Yes, the life is changing. It is not as it was before.'

'Is it better?' I asked.

'Oh yes. In the time of my father, people did not have matches. They made their fire by twirling a fire stick. They did not have matches, pots of metal, cloth hammocks, clothes. They did not have manioc, only bananas.'

Renato told me how the Yanomami obtained the secret of fire. Only the cayman and his wife had fire and ate cooked meat. The cayman kept the fire in his mouth and refused to share it. All attempts to make him open his mouth failed, until one day a Yanomami made him laugh. Then a hummingbird flew down and snatched the fire. Since then all Yanomami have had fire.

14

Rio Marauiá: 'A Ton of Shotguns!'

'There is absolutely no point at all in discussing whether magical and religious phenomena are *true*. We know nothing about truth, we have not a single clue; since Palaeolithic times our consciousness of the universe has widened, we know more facts, we have discovered how some small parts of the mechanism work, but there is no reason to suppose that we are any nearer than the Magdelian cave artists to understanding the nature of the universe, which remains a complete, and if dwelt upon, terrifying mystery.'

E. Hyams, *Soil and Civilisation.*

'THE FIRST DAY of winter,' remarked Renato when thunder boomed over the forest. 'It will rain very, very much.' People lingered in their hammocks or crouched beside the fires before beginning the day's jobs. Gabriel came for coffee (a luxury my visit provided) and to borrow my straw hat before leaving with his wife and one son to harvest manioc in their garden. Francisca went with other women to toast tapioca into small hand grains a bit like popcorn, leaving Renato and myself at home.

Renato scraped the *ebene* bark Gabriel had brought from the forest and dried the material on a plate over the fire. He worked carefully, sitting on a stool on the floor, pounding and mixing ash with the roasted seeds and using a feather to brush the grey powder into two containers. This is the hallucinogenic snuff the Yanomami use in order to see the spirits.

'Dennison, come here.' He gave me some for later. 'This is for you. But don't show it to other Yanomami. No. Only for you and your family. Don't show to others. If they see, they will kill you.'

I was writing my diary when Renato's uncle came to ask what I was doing and to see what else my sacks and box contained. This was the old man with the wispy grey beard who reputedly wanted to kill me.

Renato was also curious, after all the visitors to his home, and searched through every container, showing the men who watched, measuring fish line for them, holding up the folding scissors, and saying 'I know, I know,' when I told him what they were. He only grunted boredly when he found the disposable gas lighters and my camera but everyone in the village was fascinated when he produced the photographs of the Yanomami in Chagnon's book.

The book was taken by many children to show their mothers. They quickly identified the tribe in it that was described as the people 'with poison' – curare, the muscle relaxant made from two types of lianas. The blackish-brown drug kills by paralysing the chest muscles so that the victim asphyxiates. Its name means 'he to whom it comes must fall'; a particular advantage when hunting animals, such as monkeys, which fall from their perches as the poison takes effect. It is a silent killer. I was told that the Yanomami 'with poison' used to visit the village, but their visits ceased suddenly when a party stole the daughter of a Brazilian and killed the father by cutting his throat and sticking an arrow in his head between his eyes, just above his nose. Brazilian soldiers came, and one Yanomami and one soldier were killed. The others fled to their village in Venezuela and had not come back since.

Taking photographs was not easy because the people believed it would capture a portion of their soul, called *noreshi*. This was especially dangerous to a child, who would die if the *noreshi* were not put back into its body.

Sometimes people just wanted something in exchange for being photographed, as I had exchanged hooks for feathers. This was fair, but I refused to pay directly because I did not want them to exhibit themselves just to obtain fish hooks or nylon line. I preferred giving tobacco to friends who, as friends, allowed me to photograph them later.

Renato's uncle thumbed through every page of Chagnon's book, chuckling with recognition at the Yanomami and what they were doing. 'Where do they live?' he asked a companion who asked me in Portuguese.

'They are many and are strong and big,' said Renato. 'They live in the forest.'

'The Yanomami have many wars, this book says,' I told them.

'Yes, many wars.' He told me his own group had narrowly escaped fighting recently when the man from the village upriver kidnapped a woman and child and came to his village. 'They have family here. They wanted help. I said, yes, help them, but if they do, we will have a war with the other village. So we didn't help them, but we didn't stop them passing through our village.'

Francisca brought a basin of the toasted tapioca popcorn, set it on the floor, and nursed her baby daughter. Renato said he was hungry. 'Go fishing!' she shouted. She left the baby with the daughters. All morning they had played with miniature hammocks tied between the posts of the house. They didn't have a doll, so they had dressed a large banana with a cloth and rocked the hammock back and forth or cradled the banana in their arms.

Renato took down a basket and showed me a long necklace of small coloured beads. 'It comes from up the river. It is worth a lot of money. A ton of shotguns!' He lay dozing in his hammock beside the fire until a strong wind arrived, gusting through the palm trees and sending leaves and dust swirling through the homes. Then he rushed outside shouting at the wind and shaking his fist.

Gilberto returned at noon, soaked with the rain, smiling and proud, carrying many fish threaded on a vine. He hung them on a rafter near the fire, hung up the shotgun and his fishing line and hooks, took the tobacco I offered and lay down in his hammock at the back of the house. Gilberto rarely spoke in front of Renato or Gabriel, perhaps because he was an outsider. He was not yet married to Renato's ten-year-old daughter Louisa, but behaved as the son-in-law and was treated as such. How people behaved with each other was almost as important as their blood relationships. It would be considered incestuous for an adopted girl to marry the man she had treated as 'brother'. Gilberto was said to be thirty years old, but people used numbers to give broad impressions of time, not exact chronological periods. In their own language, the Yanomami have only three numbers: one, two and more-than-two.

A man serves his prospective parents-in-law by hunting and fishing, working in the garden and helping with house building. Only when the man has proved himself a good provider, after one or three years, can he take his new wife to his own village. Gilberto was waiting to take Louisa home when she was 'formed'; after her first period. This would be marked by her confinement behind a screen at home for a week.

Unlike many tribes in the Amazon, the Yanomami have no initiation rites for men. A boy becomes a man when he can hunt and fish to feed a family, displays the courage and ferocity to attack enemies and defend his family and, above all, when the older men and his mother treat him as an adult.

One of Domingo's teenage sons set out that morning to visit the other village upriver. 'Not far,' he assured me. A three-day journey. He asked to swap my machete for his, perhaps because he had stolen his from someone in the other village who might recognise it. He took a sack of *farinha*, hammock, and his bow and arrow, and paddled away in a dugout canoe.

After lunch we helped Gabriel and his wife grind the manioc roots they had harvested that morning. A small gas motor driving a grinder has replaced the traditional method of grinding manioc by hand on boards studded with rows of tiny stones. Afterwards, the manioc was put into a trough of water and left to soak to wash out the prussic acid it naturally contains and allow the tapioca flour to settle.

Francisca scooped by hand the yellowish *farinha* into a *tipití*. This is a narrow tube about six feet long, woven with basket fibres and closed at one end. It is hung from a rafter and stretched with a pole acting as a lever through a ring at the bottom. The tube constricts as it lengthens, forcing out water from the *farinha* which can then be toasted dry in a broad pan over a fire.

Renato's uncle sat all afternoon on the floor of his house with the length of black palm wood that had been brought by Gabriel between his toes. The old man held a pig's lower jaw in one hand, running it up and down the club, using the razor-sharp teeth to smooth it. Perhaps Renato sensed a confrontation coming. He had said last night, 'At the moment, everyone is excited because you are here. But it will pass and it will be calm again.'

I put a pan of water on the fire late in the afternoon to make a cup of tea and I explained what I was doing to the men, women and children who came to watch. We tore open a teabag for everyone to inspect. It was passed from hand to hand by the men, while their wives looked over their shoulders.

'Is it snuff?' someone asked in Portuguese.

'It's a type of leaf,' I said, to be translated into Yanomami.

Many of the adults sipped the tea, with powdered milk added, but no one liked it. The habit of afternoon tea was not adopted. Children sat in a row facing my hammock and shared a mug of tea between them. The ink in my fountain pen, the writing in my notebook, the candleholder and the recorder were unending novelties during my brief stay, and children often lay with me in the hammock, rubbing the hairs on my arms, legs and chin, and fingering through my hair, looking for lice. This communal grooming is an important and necessary display of caring, and I shared it with the children.

One boy never came close. He was unable to speak and kept away from other children. But he watched what was happening, roamed where he wanted throughout the village, returning to his home for meals, and smiled sometimes if he thought no one was watching.

That night an argument in Yanomami erupted throughout the village in the twilight before supper. 'What are they saying?' I asked the youth watching the writing in my diary.

'Nothing,' he said, though people were shouting at each other, shaking arms in the air, slapping their hands and, as tempers rose, advancing into the central arena.

I learned that the argument had begun over the distribution of *pupunhas* brought back from our outing the day before, and spread with accusations both that Renato and Gabriel were keeping the benefits of my visit for themselves and that some people had not paid for what they had taken. I kept quiet, like most of the people in the village, waiting for the combatants to exhaust their rage.

It was unpleasant to watch men fiercely threatening each other because of a few palm fruits, but I was a stranger here, with no experience of living without privacy, where a man and wife must go into the forest to make love, or living in a place without food stored for tomorrow.

Rage within the Yanomami pours into frequent and quickly-passing arguments, derisive laughter, threats and fights. A child in a tantrum hits his father in the face, a mother flings a stick from the fire at her son. Or, more seriously, formal chest-pounding duels take place, side-slapping duels and club fights between individuals or villages. A contestant in a chest-pounding duel strikes his opponent as hard as possible with his fist hoping to knock him on the ground. Four blows may be struck before the opponent has a chance to hit back. Club fighters hit each other on the head until blood is drawn. Renato's uncle's new club warned of his fierceness, though the club stayed at the back of the house.

Darkness came down during the argument in the arena. One of the boys tooted on the recorder, suggesting to me at least that the squabble was over. The shouting stopped. People ate their suppers. On another night two youths argued in half-mocking song across the arena after one of them had returned home deliberately late, in order to show off the quantity of fish and birds he had hunted that day.

Renato and I went into the forest next morning, following the barks and yelps of the three excited dogs. 'They're hunting,' explained Renato when he called me from the tedious work of chopping manioc stems to uniform lengths and tying them in bundles with long lengths of tree bark. We heard the dogs barking further inside the forest and followed for some distance. We turned back when, according to Renato, the dogs gave up their chase.

Renato told me that every person was allied to an animal in the forest. The animal's soul, called *noreshi*, was complementary to the *noreshi* in the man, woman or child. 'When the animal dies, the person dies; and when the person dies, the animal dies also. If a hunter kills the animal, the person becomes sick and dies. If the animal is hit in the arms or legs, nothing happens. In the middle, the person becomes sick.'

Men therefore avoid hunting their own *noreshi* animal species, such as all monkeys, to avoid accidentally killing the *noreshi* animal of a family member. According to Chagnon, men inherit the species of *noreshi* animal from their fathers, women from their mothers. 'The *noreshi* animal of woman always travels on the ground below the animal of the husband. *Noreshi* animals duplicate the behaviour of the person to whom they correspond. When [a man] goes hunting, so does his *noreshi* animal. When he is sick, so is his *noreshi* animal. If he takes a journey of two days, the animal likewise travels an equal distance.'

'What happens if you meet your particular *noreshi* animal?' I asked Renato.

'You die,' he replied.

We returned to the garden to resume work with Francisca and another couple, digging with machetes and pulling up manioc roots from among the creepers, grasses and small dead branches tangled over the ground between half-burnt logs.

The untidiness of these clearings in the forest, compared to the straight rows and tidy, weed-free appearance of well-kept European gardens, hides many advantages. There are only enough nutrients in the soil to grow manioc for a few years. Seeds and roots remain in the soil, despite the fire that clears the ground after the trees have been felled, and abandoned gardens are quickly reclaimed by the forest. Therefore it is not worth spending time and labour clearing land that will be soon abandoned. Weeds, branches and the half-burnt trunks of trees provide ground-cover protecting the soil against the beating of heavy rain and water erosion, and against the heat of the sun.

Pium flies buzzed around our faces and legs as we worked clearing
the ground, cutting in half the eight-foot stems of the manioc plants
to use for replanting, digging up the tuberous roots and slowly filling
another big basket with them to take back to the village. Manioc was
introduced to the Yanomami in Brazil and Venezuela by missionaries to supplement their staple of bananas, but I was surprised no
one had yet made a tool to loosen the soil around the manioc roots.
Instead we relied on digging with a machete, which was very
inefficient.

Francisca and the other mother stopped work during the morning
to nurse their babies. Otherwise the older daughters looked after the
children, carrying them on their hips, and helping the boys build a
shelter of large leaves when it rained for an hour and the rest of us
got soaked.

We worked until a third basket was filled, then carried these
extremely heavy loads and the bundles of manioc stems back to the
canoe and, with the five adults, five children and three dogs,
paddled and drifted home, half a mile down the river. My minor
share of the work that morning was well received by Renato and the
people in the village, who were pleased that I was working for the
food I was eating.

There was no lunch that day until Gilberto arrived with fish. By
then, our stomachs were rumbling. The fish was boiled and served
with *farinha* and when Renato's middle son arrived with more fish it
was given away. Exchanges of food are an important bond between
families in the village, guaranteeing food for everyone when fishing
and hunting are poor, especially during the rainy season, or when
people are sick. It also provides each individual with a greater
variety of food. Francisca received a leg of a peccary shot during the
morning and skinned by a husband and wife on the rock at the river.

A young man came with a bow and two arrows each adorned with
a little scarlet feather. 'Mirror, line and hooks,' he said.

'Finished,' I said.

'No, I have taken already.'

I nodded: *thank you.*

'Good. Until later,' he said and went away.

A bare-breasted mother brought her baby after lunch to have
iodine painted over spots of fungal infection. I explained it would
not cure the fungus but would help keep away other infections. The
mother nodded, though I believe mostly in satisfaction and pleasure
at seeing her child receive the purple paint.

Afterwards, we sat on the perimeter rail of the house with girls and boys and several mothers, passing the recorder up and down the line for everyone to have a toot and a laugh. It was a surprise to me that despite their dexterity no one learned to play a single note properly. The village was filled with the songs of welcome to *hekuras* being chanted by the men taking *ebene* in the shaman's house. The father of a sick child arrived intoxicated with *ebene* with green mucus dribbling down his chin, face painted red, green parrot feathers tied on his arms. He took one of the arrows I had traded and danced with it in the arena. Later, he brought the arrow back, having repaired the blade that had been loose. Renato wore scarlet macaw tail feathers tucked in black armbands made of the scalp of currasows (the largest jungle fowl) and danced in the arena, stamping his feet, turning with arms outstretched, green mucus from both nostrils dribbling down his chest.

Men and women wore less clothing now, as they became used to my presence and their sense of disruption and invasion diminished. Women left off the T-shirts or shirts that were uncomfortably tight and a nuisance when breast feeding their babies. Men took off their trousers and shirts and bathed in the river. Their clothes were all shabby and their only service was to discourage flies and to keep people warm when it rained.

Martins sat with me later. 'When will you come again?' he asked.

'I don't know. It's a long way.'

'Oh, but you will come?'

'It's difficult, but if I do, I know what to bring.'

'Yes – machetes, knives, hooks, fishing line, rope, coffee, sugar, toys for the children, tobacco. Maybe the next time you will come with a companion who also has things to exchange.' His wife Maria, who was the sister of Gilberto, came with their fourth baby cradled in a sling. The other three children, including a six-year-old daughter, had all died.

I asked Martins about the *hekura* and he said he did not know the songs but liked to take *ebene* just to be intoxicated. Gabriel complained angrily in Yanomami to Renato on several nights when his brother took *ebene* and sang loudly. 'He should not sing. It is no respect,' Gabriel complained.

The chanting stopped; already the sky was darkening and fires were being rekindled to cook supper. Martins and I went to the river to bath before nightfall, for I was still reluctant to go into the water after dark. Then I lay in my hammock until Renato called me to eat with Gilberto and himself and he set out the low stools, bowls and spoons. Francisca and her daughters ate beside the fire.

Renato came afterwards, when I had lit the candle lantern and lay in my hammock. He took tobacco with me, swinging gently, the soft light of the candle shining on his face in the darkness.

'When will you leave?' he asked.

'One or two more weeks,' I said disappointed that he seemed to want me to leave as soon as all the machetes, line, hooks and other trade goods were finished. I was giving as much food from my sack as I was eating, was working in the garden and had promised the gift of a valuable rain sheet to Renato when I left. Perhaps I was being oversensitive. It was a strain being alert all the time to the expectations, behaviour and reactions of people who changed so swiftly from tenderness to hostility.

'You have been to Manaus, Belém. What did you think?' I asked Renato.

'I liked them. I would like to live there,' he replied. 'I met a man who told me to sell the canoe, everything and go with all the family to Manaus. He had a house for me and work painting. I wanted to go but I lost his address in the Rio Negro.'

'Why do you want to go to the city?'

'It is a better life for the children. People are educated there. Here, no.'

'In the city, life would change very much,' I said.

'In the city, the Yanomami life would end. It is not worth anything there. In the city I smoke cigarettes. I don't use a tobacco plug.'

'And the others? Domingo and his wife?'

'Domingo wants to go. Sometimes he threatens to go. He threatens he will leave the family and go to the city. I have already said the same. I will go. I will leave, destroy the garden and that will be the end of everything. No white man will come to exchange goods. The village will be finished.

'Once there was an argument against me. I packed everything up and said I would leave. Then one came: "No, Renato, do not leave," he said, so I have stayed.'

'And Gabriel and Martins, do they want to leave?' I asked.

'I don't know. If I leave, Gabriel would leave too.'

'If you want to leave, why do you stay?'

'It's difficult. I need work for each person in the family. I could have work there but it would not be enough to feed the family,' said Renato.

I shook my head. 'It is difficult for me to understand why you want to leave Yanomami life. I understood you wanted the metal tools, the hammocks and fish hooks to continue with the Yanomami life, only better, not to leave. There is no Yanomami life in the city. It is finished.'

'Yes, it is finished. We here do not want to live as our parents lived, as Yanomami lived before. That has passed. They all died.'

'And the people in the other village, near the Mission up the river?'

'They have a radio, machetes, knives, pots, clothes. No motor. They want to continue the life.'

'Why are they different to you here?' I asked.

'They are ignorant; donkeys. They don't know how to think. If someone goes there who they don't know, they kill the person; in the night, with a club.'

It was only later that I realised how much of what Renato said about leaving was make-believe. That evening, lying in the hammock in the dark, it was difficult to understand why he wanted to abandon his village only to become a despised *Indio* in the slums of towns and cities where he would earn barely enough to pay for the food and housing that were free to him in the forest. Men like Gabriel and Martins had no idea that in the city they would need money to obtain the trade goods they obtained from me by barter.

It is a paradox that Indian tribes must be considerably changed by contact with civilisation before they can resist its seductions. For more than four centuries there has been initial delight and fascination in the white man and his wondrous tools. But the high death-toll from diseases and the enslavement of whole villages led to armed resistance. Military defeat by the white man has usually been followed by the collapse of Indian self-esteem, by disillusionment, passive acceptance and wholesale imitation of the conquerors. Tribes have disintegrated. Like caged animals, mothers have stopped having children. People have waited to die.

The tragedy is often viewed as the inevitable result of a mechanical process: 'It's civilisation. It can't be stopped. We can't put them in a museum.' But the Indians themselves have frequently confounded this theory. They wonder how to civilise the white man, who is usually regarded as clumsy, rude, greedy, a poor hunter and a liar, and in dealing with him, tribes have attempted to act much as if taking the nourishing meat from a peccary and discarding the indigestible skin. Contemporary missionaries complain that their converts accept Christian schooling, medical help and trade goods but do not give up tribal rituals or adhere to the morals of the Bible. In the 18th century, Jesuits sent Indian boys to be educated in Portugal and were dismayed when they preferred tribal life to civilisation. Above all, Indians are fickle, Europeans have complained. 'By giving them one fish hook I can convert them all, and with another I could unconvert them again,' reported Nobrega, a famous Jesuit in the Amazon in the 16th century.

The Kayapo, in the southeast Amazon, are adapting themselves to the white man's society without joining it. They sell timber and gold from their land, own an areoplane, have a telephone and travel to Brazilia and abroad lobbying to defend Indian rights. Their chief Raomi has travelled to New York, Washington, London and Paris to defend his people from the white man's development projects. They have suffered and survived a period of decline; they do not live as their fathers lived. But a missionary told me of her colleague taking five Kayapo for lunch to a smart restaurant in the city. 'They were shirtless and all had their headdresses on and their lip-disks in and their pipes. They were proud of being Indians and they were showing off to these people (Brazilians) that they're Indians. Ten years ago they would not have done that.'

I asked Renato more about his desire to leave the Yanomami life. He told me how, in the mid-1960s, his father was the first Yanomami in his band to meet a white man:

'He lived in a village far up the Marauiá. One day he left the village and travelled for a month through the forest, down beside the river, almost to its mouth. Below the first waterfall he met an old white man. My father didn't speak Portuguese and the Brazilian didn't speak our language but the Brazilian gave him a machete and a knife and a bag of *farinha*. Then my father returned up the river through the forest to his village. The people saw what he had brought. Three weeks later, a party of men set out again for the mouth of the Marauiá. From there, they were taken to the Mission in Santa Isabel. The fathers gave them big bundles of machetes, knives and pots, and brought the men back to the Marauiá.'

Renato and Domingo went away to the Mission in Santa Isabel for six years in exchange for gifts of metal tools. They had come back to the Marauiá but continually threatened to leave if there was fighting or a power struggle.

'And the third generation? Will your son leave?' I asked.

'Perhaps.' Renato sucked his tobacco, unconcerned.

Life in the village settled into its slow routine of assigned duties, talk, dance and play; waking at dawn when the mist lay over the tops of the trees; sharing a big bowl of tapioca porridge; the older boys leaving to fish and hunt; the men lying in their hammocks playing with the smallest children, while mothers and daughters carried the pots to wash in the river. Gabriel took his shotgun when he left the village wearing my straw hat. 'My children are hungry,' he had said the night before. Paulino fetched poles and palm fronds from the forest to extend his house and other men repaired patches of their roofs and walls now that the rains had arrived.

Renato's uncle put on trousers and came with exquisite turquoise and purple feather ear plugs as gifts for me and sat laughing over the pictures, in Chagnon's book of the Yanomami on the Orinoco, with a fat sausage of brown tobacco protruding from his bottom lip. No one came to exchange trade goods or to look excitedly through the white man's belongings. I lay in my hammock watching women greeting one another in a house on the other side of the arena before toasting *farinha*.

The arena and the thatched shelters in the circle seemed to be the hub of a vast wheel. From this place streams and paths radiated through the forest, to the edge of the world, that was the rim of the wheel. We were living in the centre, connected to the world by the spokes.

In contrast, each civilised city or town in the Amazon is a stockade in the wilderness. Church, school, hospital and shops are the local representatives of civilised values, surrounded by untamed forest which one day, people tell you, will be developed and conquered.

Renato, Francisca and I went to work in a clearing outside the village. It was easy chopping up the long stems we had fetched from the other garden two days earlier. Renato dug shallow holes while Francisca gathered firewood from the branches and logs scattered across the fire-blackened earth. Renato showed me how to insert manioc sticks into the soil. Despite the biting flies, it was pleasant work planting manioc but, with a wry smile, I soon caught myself wondering how to do the same work more efficiently and quicker.

Black thunder clouds filled the sky over the forest in the east when we stopped after a couple of hours for a snack of dry tapioca and a banana. Heavy rain fell for several hours, pouring from the thatch roofs of the houses, washing over the bare arena, streaming behind the ridges dug to keep the water from entering the homes. Men and boys came back from fishing and hunting and wiped off their guns before rolling new tobacco sausages and lying in their hammocks. We ate lunch, then lay cocooned in our hammocks, with people conversing in Yanomami, until the rain slackened to drizzle and the hunters and fishermen left the village again.

Renato stripped to his underpants and tied his precious strings of beads round his biceps and sat on a stool for his youngest son, José, to blow *ebene* up both nostrils. Saliva drooled from his mouth and green-stained mucus from his nose. Then he began chanting to the *hekura* and dancing in the arena in the drizzle, his arms waving as if he were struggling with a demon.

Children climbed into the hammock with me, a few adults came to take tobacco from my pouch and to sit tooting on the recorder and looking at the pictures of the Yanomami. The trade goods were finished, the curiosity of my belongings was ended. People asked about my parents and my house instead, and thought it odd I should be away for several months. 'Are you not afraid to arrive all alone among people you don't know?'

'Sometimes,' I replied, interested how their questions differed from the Brazilians': 'Are you not afraid of the forest?'

'And if some fierce Indians kill you suddenly?'

'What could I do? I have no gun.'

I went for a bath late in the afternoon, and by then the river had changed. The sluggish flow in which we had bathed and played for a week, throwing the children into the water with laughter and loud splashes, avoiding thousands of black tadpoles wriggling at the waterline along the rock, was transformed by the rains into a swirling muddy torrent carrying branches and rafts of leaves and debris, washed from gullies that had been dry for weeks. My hope of staying in the village for another week or two or of getting to the village and Mission up the river was ended. I looked at the height of the river against the rock and at the force of the water pushing down the channel and wondered how violent the passage would already be over the five waterfalls, and for how long they would be passable at all in my red and blue canoe. I would have to leave very soon if I was to have any chance of getting down the river safely.

Near sunset, the youths who had been fishing and hunting since dawn returned to their homes with the fish and any animals or birds they had caught. The women fetched home great baskets of wood on their backs and rekindled the fires to cook supper. The two pet parrots in Domingo's home were put in their cage for the night with a lot of squawking. The men washed themselves and played with their children or tied new hooks on their fishing lines or cleaned their shotguns. Renato sat each evening before supper and marked off the day on a calendar. He was the only person to possess such a document and I was not surprised when he told me his father knew neither weeks nor months.

The uncle came from next door and paused beside my hammock in the afternoon on the next day. I didn't understand what he said he wanted so he mimed for 'the pages' but the book was out on loan. He took tobacco and sat watching for a few moments before motioning for me to get up and go with him. He led me to the shaman's house where eight men were sitting taking *ebene*. I had so far avoided these afternoon gatherings, watching from outside, not wanting to intrude.

The uncle put his stool near the front and Gabriel pointed to a place for me to join the semi-circle of men. Short wooden tubes and plates of the grey *ebene* powder lay in front of them on the ground. I squatted on a stool beside Samuel who was sitting with his legs apart, head bent forward, green mucus hanging from his nose almost to the floor. He looked up, nodding slowly. Thick lines of black paint, made from wood ash, were drawn on his face, little orange earrings and single parrot feathers stuck out from his ears. The men sat stupefied on the stools in a semi-circle, spitting saliva onto the floor or wiping mucus from their nostrils. A man was chanting slowly, crouching on a pole on the ground at the front of the house, his body swaying from side to side, the movement exaggerated by the zig-zagging red lines of *urucu* seeds painted on his bare body and the rise and fall of fresh green parrot feathers sticking in his ears.

The shaman, in unadorned underpants, sat at the front of his house near the uncle. He carefully pushed the open end of one tube into the powder, tapped lightly on the side and, when he was satisfied, handed the open end to the uncle. The shaman put the narrow end up one nostril and closed the other with his thumb. The uncle lay aside his sausage of tobacco, put the tube to his mouth, puffed out his cheeks and blew with a long sigh and a final hard blast. The shaman's head jerked back with the pain, he coughed hoarsely and slapped the back of his own neck. Saliva drippled from his open mouth, his eyes watered and he crouched immobile for several moments before reaching forward to refill the tube with powder.

He looked up suddenly after taking another dose, staring at us with a smile and wide eyes. One arm stretched out and it shook, then both arms were outstretched and shaking; his hands were turning in the air, his body swaying, his head rotating, his wide eyes still staring. He shouted 'Weesh-sh!' and jumped up, as if alarmed by something approaching through the forest, and prepared to defend the village, his arms out, knees bent, feet apart, the muscles of his legs taut, his chest swaying from side to side and the words from his mouth no longer song nor chant but sudden cries. 'Daa. Zoom!' His whole body was jumping, lurching from side to side, leaping from one leg to the other, his feet pounding the earth. He rushed into the arena, turning round and round, staring at the sky, pointing with his arms to the earth and now to the sky and crying aloud, 'Waah!'

Then he calmed and walked back into the house, but smiling, with his eyes still wild. He sat on the ground face to face with Renato's uncle, stretching his legs on either side of the old man, who by now had also taken *ebene*. He spoke a few words and the old man chuckled. They patted each other on the back, pulling themselves together, wrapping their arms around each other until they were chest to chest and cheek to cheek with their chins on each other's shoulders. Locked in this embrace, they rocked from side to side until they fell over, sat up and hugged each other again in a display of reassurance and friendship.

The shaman took another double dose of *ebene*, his mouth smiling, his eyes gazing over the men, his face turning away suddenly as if he heard a call behind him. 'Wa-uh-hu-huh!' He shouted and crouched, falling on the earth on his back, with his legs and arms in the air. He went out to chant and dance around the arena like a strange, betwitched puppet.

Most of the men in the house took the powder and smarted and coughed with each puff. Samuel offered a loaded tube to me. I shook my head. 'I don't know how to sing,' I said.

'He appears,' he replied, wiping away the long green mucus hanging from his nose and stood up to leave.

I went later with Gabriel, Martins and Paulino and lots of children along the path to the river to try to mount my motor on Renato's canoe so that we could make an excursion to gather *açaí* and other palm fruits down the river. But everyone's advice, efforts and laughter did not bring success and we returned disappointed to the village for a supper of boiled smoked chunks of peccary and *farinha* and a couple of bananas from the stem ripening in the rafters over our heads. It was the first night during my stay that both Francisca and her daughter ate with the men. I noticed when we crouched to eat that Gabriel no longer wore a yellow rubber dinosaur pencil eraser that he had taken to wear as a pendant.

'I saw it in a dream. It brought a [common] cold, so I took it off,' he said.

I had decided before coming to the Marauiá to stop if I caught a cold and not to proceed until well again. Few Indians have resistance to the virus and snuffly colds can last for months. It was unlikely, but perhaps remotely possible, that my gift could have given Gabriel a cold. Later, he put both hands solemnly on my shoulders and stared into my eyes. 'My friend, are you making me ill?' he asked. 'I have dreamed of you.'

'How are you ill?'

'I have pains in my stomach.'

'My friend, I can give you pain in your throat or in your nose as a cold, but I cannot give you pain in your stomach,' I said slowly, facing him eye to eye.

He nodded but he may not have been convinced.

On the next afternoon in the shaman's house Renato took two blasts of *ebene* powder in each nostril. He spat out a mouthful of saliva, and began chanting, still sitting on his low stool, with head slowly moving from side to side, beads and feathers tied on his biceps and his hands stroking his arms and legs. His body swayed from side to side as his chanting grew stronger, until he stepped out into the arena, bare feet striking the ground as the rhythm of his chant rose and fell, slowed and quickened. 'Daaah!' he shouted, waving arms. 'Hoor-hoor-hoor! Wooh-wooh-hi!' he called, rushing round the arena, chanting and dancing, throwing up his arms, pacing, turning, stepping back, moving forward, singing, arms waving, his feet quickening and slowing and quickening. 'Soooh!' he cried, stomping and waving, turning and thrusting in his private vision of the *hekura*. It stopped abruptly. Renato returned to the stool, sat down and gazed around.

Moments later he was in the arena again, one arm raised, standing with legs bent and feet firmly on the ground, as if ready to receive a blow or throw a spear. 'Heeesh! Heeesh!' he cried, then stopped again to take more *ebene* before dancing and chanting round and round and round the arena until his chest was covered in smears of mucus and green saliva.

Men came to the house decorated with beads or black curassow bands and red feathers on their arms and single green feathers in their ears. Some, like Gabriel, had painted red their faces and chests. Some wore underpants and others took these off and sat dressed with their foreskins tucked up under their hipcord. They put aside their sausages of tobacco and filled tubes with powder from small containers they brought with them. Gabriel took two blasts and went outside, walking in the sunshine in the arena before beginning a song of welcome to the *hekura*, walking five or six paces, pausing with arms stretched, chest swaying, a foot patting the earth; walking forward, chanting on each step, pivoting at the waist, bent forward, head twisting from side to side; running forward, pausing; stepping forward, stopping; crying aloud 'Mooeeni! Mooeeni! Mooeeni! Mooeeni!', fists held to his face, jumping round and round, feet stomping the earth.

The men inside the house talked in Yanomami or sat in silence. Samuel vomited a few times, others sat with mucus smeared on their chests. Boys lay in the hammocks at the back of the house watching, sometimes being called to blow *ebene* for their fathers. The sun shone brightly over the village, though thunder rumbled in the grey sky over the forest to the east. Gilberto came home with a good catch of fish and lay these on the tripod over the fire to cook, and rested in his hammock before looking in the pots for something to eat and then joining us in the *ebene* session.

Gabriel sat down beside me and after a long silence said approvingly, 'It's strong, very very strong.'

I realised now that my tact in avoiding these sessions had been a mistake; the men were pleased I was with them. There was a man who one day had run at me wagging his finger, screaming at me when I wanted to take a photograph of the fire burning across his garden. Now he offered a tube of *ebene* to me and when I accepted, people nodded and smiled and the boys looked out from their hammocks to watch. Renato was worried not to give me an overdose so the man put just a little powder in the end of the tube, tapped it with his fingers and handed the narrow end to put up my nostril and I closed the other nostril with a finger.

The impact of the powder was not as violent as I had expected. I coughed, patted the back of my neck, my eyes watered and I sneezed violently half a dozen times. 'Good, wait,' said someone after the second blast. We waited but no visions came; it was like taking a couple of strong drinks on an empty stomach. By then it was late in the afternoon, the sun was low and the shadow of whoever was dancing stretched far across the arena.

'Tomorrow a full dose,' someone said.

The man tapped his container. 'This is stronger. With this you see beautiful things.' He saw my money belt, that I always wore, and asked what it was.

'Documents and money. Papers of my land to come here,' I answered. 'I had to show when I came.'

He nodded. 'In Santa Isabel?'

'Manaus. I have to show again when I go back.'

'And if you don't have?'

'A big problem,' I said.

'They will kill you?'

'No, but a big problem.'

'I know. They will kill you,' he said.

The river rose six inches more during the afternoon, flooding the flat area on the boulder where people had cleaned fish and skinned and butchered animals. The water had risen three feet in five days. The flood would cover all the obstacles the canoe had hit coming up the river and, I imagined, transform the five waterfalls and numerous little rapids into thundering collisions of swirling waters in which it would be impossible to control the canoe. I had been careful so far, and lucky, but I knew that you could travel safely for weeks or months until one mistake, a small accident, a little miscalculation or a moment's foolishness could capsize the canoe.

We heard a motor on the river during supper that night and knew the Brazilians had returned from their journey upriver in search of topaz and diamonds. Renato's eldest son Robi and Domingo came back to their homes. Robi spoke rapidly in Yanomami to Renato before Brazilian Uncle arrived.

No one made a sound in the house when Brazilian Uncle sat on a low stool to talk softly in Portuguese with Renato. I lay in my hammock listening: They had brought 120 pounds of stones. They must return to Manaus immediately to wash the stones in acid, to see what they had collected and to sell them. Then the Brazilians would come back, bringing a gasoline generator for lights, a motor for the canoe and build a school to help their Indian friends. Renato was not taken in and insisted that he and Domingo go with the Brazilians to Manaus. Uncle agreed and went back to the Brazilian camp near the river.

Renato came to me as soon as he'd gone and said he would go to Manaus the next day.

'Then I must leave also,' I said sadly.

Gabriel and another man came and we sat round the light of my small candle lantern. Boys stood or sat around us, listening in silence as we talked. One of them kept his arms round my neck and his cheek pressed to mine. Another absent-mindedly stroked the hairs on my legs. Robi, who had been up the river with the Brazilians, brought out some rocks he said he had kept for himself.

'Diamonds,' declared Renato, though it was wishful thinking.

Gabriel said tomorrow they must show everything they had taken.

'I have something to give you, to help.' I handed Renato a small magnifying glass, a gift from friends at home.

Gabriel repeated his warning about the Brazilians. Renato pulled down the lower lid of one eye. 'I have my eyes open.'

'Remember they do not give presents,' I said. 'They did not come for free. They came to take something. You must be on your guard all the time.'

'It's true. It's our land, our rocks!' said Gabriel vehemently.

'We will go together to Manaus, Dennison, and talk there about what happens,' said Renato. He asked about the cost and make of my outboard motor.

'First, you should find out the value of the stones, then decide what to buy,' I suggested.

'I know. They will give just a motor, or other things, and take the money for themselves. I know.'

They were suspicious and excited, calling out a list of everything they wanted Renato to bring home: fish hooks, parachute cord, tobacco, coffee, fishing line, plastic sheeting, sewing needles, cotton, soap and sugar.

'We have to look after ourselves,' said the other men and everyone agreed.

'I have my eyes open,' said Renato.

All was transformed on the river when we started downstream early in the morning. Renato and Domingo sat in the larger canoe with the Brazilians and I travelled alone in my canoe.

The water moved so rapidly down the middle of the river that we reached the channels where the river divided between the islands within half an hour. The river was flowing again through the larger channel on the left but I decided to follow the main flow round the longer route I had used on the way up. Only the tops of a few of the rocks that had peppered the river on the ascent were visible above the swirling water.

I saw the Brazilian canoe pass below the island and enter another channel behind forest on the right. I thought I observed where they went but I soon found myself approaching thrashing water spilling over rocks all across the river. I stood up quickly to have a look, chose an opening on the right where the surface of the water was fast but calm and a moment later it was too late for a second chance. The current took the canoe, sucking us in, taking us through a gap where water crashed and spilled over black rocks, dropping us into a commotion of waves and seething currents where the canoe pitched and rolled and bobbed, totally out of control.

The Brazilians circled their canoe just below the cataract watching my passage and then turned down the river when I reached a calmer stretch and started bailing. The second cataract was far fiercer than the first. The waves were never more than a foot high but this only disguised their danger. The water was moving with such speed and force that a canoe would capsize or be dashed to pieces if it hit a hidden rock. I followed exactly where the Brazilians descended, turning sharply to the left across the waves, feeling the water pushing sideways, turning to the right, avoiding boiling eddies and whirlpool currents, making an S-bend between hidden rocks until both canoes rushed out into the calm water below.

Downstream, the sky to the east was the colour of lead and heavy with rain. I stopped the motor to pull a plastic sheet over what luggage I now carried, letting the canoe drift in the stream. I could see the storm approaching over the forest, darkening the sky, the wind shaking branches and leaves. The Brazilians pulled into the right bank and I did the same farther down, tying the canoe to the branch of a fallen tree and pulling the plastic sheet over my head against the raindrops bouncing on the water, raising a spray that covered the grey river.

After ten minutes the rain clouds passed over. We reached the fourth waterfall after lunch. The river had been transformed by the rains; rushing water covered the smooth rocks on both sides and the main channel was a torrent cascading over rocks, crashing through the gap, swirling and boiling. Renato told us that one of the villagers had drowned here, taken by the spirit.

'You couldn't descend the river alone through this water,'

commented one of the Brazilians. Certainly, I would have kept tight to the bank. We unloaded both canoes and carried the baggage, motors, spare gasoline and sacks of rocks to the bottom of the fall. My canoe seemed light and it quickly shot down the waterfall. The Brazilians' canoe was longer and heavier and deeper in the water. Five of us turned it stern-first and, holding it on a long rope, pulled the bulky vessel out into the fast stream. We waded knee-deep into the channel of rushing water, with two people on either side manoeuvring the canoe through a gap. I let go of the canoe as it moved forward and was left standing in knee-deep water gushing over the slanting boulder. I could not move. If I moved, I would be swept into the ferment of water crashing through the rocks below. I could not call out, only wait for one of the men to see the terror on my face. Then they made a human chain into the water and pulled me ashore.

When we arrived at the second falls, the grandfather with his daughter and grandson had departed. Water now plunged over almost the whole width of rock across the river, cascading into roaring white foam below. Domingo, not one to carry anything more than an empty cooking pot, went off to make a fire while we unloaded both canoes and rolled the larger canoe and carried mine across rocks down into calmer water. I took my luggage farther down, beyond another turbulent channel, reloading the canoe from a rock that had been high above the water when I came up. Renato helped carry baggage and was cheerful. I was glad we were travelling together, though I noticed his behaviour had changed. Renato's leadership and dignity were gone; replaced by a sub-servience to the Brazilians.

'We'll be in Santa Isabel tonight,' said Uncle with a chuckle. 'Arriving in the dark.'

I was silent but did not believe we could reach Santa Isabel so quickly. Also I was fearful of trying to navigate in the dark.

It seemed mad to be rushing down a river when we were all tired and it was already late in the afternoon. Poor light disguised waves over rocks and ripples where obstacles where hidden in the brown water but, now they had the stones, the Brazilians were in a rush to get back to the city. We drank mugs of warm palm fruit tasting like milky cocoa, smoked a couple of cigarettes and were swept downstream again in our canoes.

Daylight was fading, and river and forest were merging in the twilight as we approached the mouth of the Marauiá. All of a sudden the canoe was rolling and pitching, with waves splashing over the sides. I was sure we were going to sink. Renato lurched backwards to raise the canoe at the front as we hit the waves and narrowly missed tree branches sticking above the water. The turmoil lasted less than a minute, then we were spat out of the Marauiá river into the calmer water of the Rio Negro. The three Colombians, still waiting on the big boat just beyond the mouth of the river, waved for us to visit them. I pointed to Renato and shrugged my shoulders, and they gave a thumbs-up sign as we passed.

The sky opened from the split of light between the banks of the Marauiá into a vastness of the Rio Negro which reached to the horizon. The sky was a dull grey board with a smear of cream far up the river where the sun had set. Grey clouds, long and flat like caymans, hung over our heads. We motored across the expanse of black water, feeling breaths of humid warm air rising from the river, watching the colours fade, hastening to get as far downstream as possible before nightfall, and going aground only once, on a sandbank in the middle of the river. We aimed for the silhouette of two distant trees until they vanished in the darkness. Then we travelled in a black void with Renato in the bow holding a flashlight that shone a few feet in front of us.

There was neither light nor time on the river. We journeyed until we came, miraculously, to the bank. Renato signalled to stop and we waited for the Brazilians to arrive. It was so dark we could not see our own feet as we groped our way up a sloping rock to reach the house of the Brazilians' guide. A kerosene lamp burned on the table inside the door. We hung up our hammocks, passing the end ropes round the frame of the wattle and daub walls, while the guide's wife made coffee on a charcoal fire and a daughter sliced a sweet pineapple. We ate and slept; relieved to have lived through our madness with the river.

I left by myself after coffee next morning to go down to Santa Isabel. Few boats travel to Manaus from so far up the Rio Negro so we knew we would meet again on any boat going downstream.

Dona Maria's cooking was the highlight of the two days I passed in Santa Isabel while waiting for her son's boat to depart for Manaus. I gorged on diced vegetables in mayonnaise, casseroled black beans and turtle meat, and busied myself finding a buyer for the canoe, motor and equipment. Prices were higher up the rivers than in Manaus but there are no banks and few people could afford to buy a motor and canoe. I finally sold everything to the civil engineer from Belém who lived in the Army depot, dropping the price a little because he said he wanted the canoe for himself. He resold the canoe immediately to someone else for a profit, reminding me that I had returned to civilised ways.

The Yanomami arrived with Brazilian Uncle and his two companions shortly before the boat left for Manaus loaded with rubber, *sorva*, *piassava* and a dozen passengers in hammocks over the stacks of Coke bottles. It was a five-day journey to Manaus and I was glad Dona Maria had come with us and was supervising the cooking. Renato and Domingo, both now looking scruffy in long trousers and shirts, talked with the Brazilians in huddles and came to tell me in hushed voices their ideas and schemes to avoid being cheated. 'I have my eye open,' said Renato as we motored down the Rio Negro towards Manuas, the city of a million people.

15

Manaus: Aftermath

'We are declared aliens in the domain of nature. Nature sustains us, but we are not of her kind. With the progressive advancement of man's estate, nature has lost her quasi-human and superhuman status. Nature has become the raw material of civilisation: the point where man applies his scientific techniques. Now that we have arrived at a working concordat with nature, we can leave it to nature poets and nostalgic mystics to pretend there can be any re-establishment of the old intimacy.'

J. Katz, *The Will to Civilise.*

TEN DAYS PASSED in Manaus before I saw the Yanomamis again, despite many telephone messages to the neighbour of one of the Brazilians, with whom Renato and Domingo were staying in an area called Compensa II.

'It's a dangerous place. Be sure to get out before the sun sets,' said a journalist friend before I went to visit them.

No person on the bus into Compensa II knew the street, but it was not difficult to find the double-storey house built of rough boards and tin roof.

Renato and Domingo looked tired and bored. The son of the Brazilian's guide, who had also come to the city to get a share of the riches, was sullen.

'How are the stones?' I asked Renato. He replied with a thumbs down.

'Why?'

'They are not worth. The stones are only stones,' he said slowly, as if someone had broken his dream, which they had. Now, he and Domingo wanted only to leave the city and get home. 'We are completely unoccupied here.' They talked of walking home through the forest.

'Where's Brazilian Uncle?'

'Gone. He's come two times since we arrived. He came two days ago but he did not return my stone. He has stolen it. We went to his house but he was not there. His son says he knows nothing. The *garimpeiro* lied to us, all lies. He knows nothing.'

Domingo only nodded his head.

The stones were not topaz, apparently, nor agate, only little coloured stones worth nothing. It seemed possible, though unlikely, that Brazilian Uncle was saying the stones were worthless and waiting for the Yanomamis to go home before claiming their true value. I suggested getting an independent expert to check them.

Meanwhile, Renato and Domingo and the guide's son were without money to get home and without the gifts they had listed with such glee in the village. Now they were dependent on the two young Brazilians for food, accommodation and spending money. One of the Brazilians arrived in the house. He was tense, tired and with a tough look in his eyes that I had not seen before. He told me that he and his friend had financed that trip up the Marauiá by borrowing money on the advice of Brazilian Uncle. 'He has not given one centavo. Nothing,' he said. This pair too, therefore, were extremely disappointed with the results of the journey that should have made them rich.

I promised to talk to a man who could get the stones professionally appraised and to return after two days. I stopped to telephone a friend on my way to catch the bus out of the area.

'How's it going?' she asked.

'As I speak, the shopkeeper across the road is beating a man over the head with a length of wood. Blood's pouring from the man's head. He's fallen down. The shopkeeper's going back to his store.'

I returned to Compensa II as promised two days later with my friend Ernesto who operated a tourist lodge in the forest. He explained that his brother-in-law knew a geologist working for the Federal Government who could test the stones independently before they went to a dealer. Renato and Domingo nodded their heads and said that is what they wanted.

The Brazilians said a friend had already tested the stones. However, everyone agreed to have a sample tested again.

We went to a bar in the street for a beer. Fernando, one of the Brazilians, took me aside to warn that he and Domingo had carried home Renato drunk two nights earlier. Domingo put his arm round my shoulder and said they wanted to go home as soon as possible. 'There's so much noise and fighting here. We miss our women and families.'

Fernando wanted to take a sample of the stones to the nearly state-run School of Mining when we left the bar. Renato invited me to go with them. We agreed before entering to say the stones came from another river to avoid an invasion of prospectors if the stones were valuable.

We left samples, but when we came out Fernando suddenly announced he had already sold the rest of the stones because he was tired of carrying them from merchant to merchant in the city. 'I sold them. They were of no value. No one wanted them. The merchant said he bought stones by the ton but I implored him. That is the only reason he bought them. He paid Cz$25 for each kilo.' (This was twenty cents per kilo compared to Uncle's estimate of US $360.) 'They had no value and we needed money to buy gasoline.'

Renato seethed with rage. Domingo kept silent and glanced at Renato.

'How do you know they had no value without an analysis?' I asked.

'The merchant only bought them because I implored him. He put the sack in one corner. If we want, he'll give back the stones,' said Fernando.

Fernando, Renato and Domingo did not show up next morning to go back to the Federal geologist though I waited two and a half hours reading a book in the street. Renato told me, at the house in Compensa after lunch, that the Brazilians had gone to work leaving them without money. We agreed to go to the geologist the next day.

The Yanomami were leaning out of the window into the street when I returned at nine o'clock on Wednesday. They waved their arms for me to stay outside. Renato came running and told me to wait down the street. The two of them arrived twenty minutes later inside a taxi. Both men were resolute and happier than for days. I did not ask what had happened nor where we were going. The meeting with the Federal geologist was forgotten as the taxi hurried through the traffic to the landing where the boats left to go up the Rio Negro. The regular ferry would depart the next day. The captain wanted cash for the fares and would not allow them to work their passages, so I agreed to pay both tickets to Barcelos. I could not afford the fares to Santa Isabel on a cargo boat because I was poor again, but it would be easy for them to hitch a free ride on a boat from Barcelos as I had done.

The reason for my renewed poverty was that I had returned to Manaus to be told by Ernesto that his house had been robbed. He had been safeguarding my passport, airline ticket and $2000. I was sure he had taken the cash to pay his debts but there was nothing I could do. I was left now with only the money from selling the canoe and motor. Ernesto eventually repaid $1495 but for weeks I had little money and was unable to travel further.

Renato and Domingo left their plastic shopping bags of clothes and hammocks on the boat and we took a bus to the centre of Manaus. I was aware, more than ever before, of the crush of people and the rush of traffic. My companions looked around them with apprehension, waiting until the street was completely clear of cars before daring to run across. I have to admit that they did look comical in their ill-fitting trousers, walking with their heads down, stepping aside for everyone in the street.

'Our hearts are dying,' said Renato. He pointed out that the Brazilians were already at home with their wives and families. He and Domingo were in an unfamiliar place and they wanted to go home. 'Will you come with us?' he asked me.

We went to the Hotel Iguacu for lunch. It was early but we were hungry and I wanted to avoid the staring and mocking questions that greeted the forest people in Manaus. 'Do you still kill people? Are there still Indians who don't wear clothes?' We devoured the large servings and Renato and Domingo followed my lead, using a knife and fork. I explained how to use a toilet.

I suggested going out to the five-star hotel on the edge of the city after lunch to enjoy the quiet and trees. We met an acquaintance of mine, Helcio, at the bus stop. He wanted to buy an Indian hammock made of cotton which Renato could buy from the other Yanomami village.

'How much?'

Renato didn't know. 'Cz$1,500,' he said.

'Cheap,' said my acquaintance.

'That's in the village. Then there's the problem of getting it here,' I said.

Renato nodded quickly.

'You don't live in Santa Isabel? Well, I'll give you my telephone number and telephone me when it's ready and I'll make arrangements,' said Helcio. He whispered on the bus that he wanted to give the Indians a shirt.

'If you give a shirt, you must give to both.'

The Hotel Tropical stands amid lawns and trees on the banks of the Rio Negro on the outskirts of Manaus. The bus arrived at the end of the road in front of the gates just as a rain shower ended. 'What a beautiful place. We could build a village here,' exclaimed Renato. Domingo nodded and giggled. I left a photocopy of my stolen passport with the armed security guard at the gate, who merely nodded when I said my companions didn't have documents.

We wandered through the grounds with Renato and Domingo telling me the names of trees, when they would fruit or what they could be used for. The hotel is famous for its small zoo.

'Have you ever been this close to a jaguar before?' I asked when we stood a couple of feet from the creature in the cage. Domingo giggled again, and pretended to loose an arrow.

The rain started again and we sheltered with the gardeners. One was a woman from the Rio Branco (a tributary of the Negro). 'I've been in the city nine years. But I'm not used to it yet,' she said. Another woman nodded. 'You get paid on Friday and there's no money left by Sunday, except for food.' All the women said they wanted to return to their homes in the interior but that their husbands wanted to stay. 'Everything is difficult here. If you don't have money, there's nothing. You have to buy fish and it's expensive. There's no one to give you a fish today or invite you for lunch,' she said. It was good for Renato and Domingo to hear this because they regarded the city as overflowing with so many desirable things – available free, just like the forest.

We took the bus and walked to reach Helcio's smart house and sat at the side of his small swimming pool. Helcio was waiting to give swimming lessons to the young daughter of a shoe company director who had recently moved to Manaus from São Paulo.

'I'd like to go to your village very much. If I arrive, can I stay?' asked Helcio.

Renato thought for a minute and, perhaps remembering that we were guests, said yes. Domingo kept silent.

The Paulista father and daughter arrived and Helcio began the lesson with floats in the pool. We sat with the father, who asked Renato and Domingo where they were from and about food and religion. He said his wife was a spiritualist with the spirit of a famous Indian inside her. He said he wanted to help the Indians. He said his neighbour was the regional director of FUNAI and that he would ask him for help.

'These two need passages up the river,' I said.

'Forget the money for passages. And I'll try to get them a motor. What size of motor would be best?' He promised to telephone my hotel the next morning. Renato signalled to me that we should leave. Perhaps he was bored, or perhaps he sensed the man was only speaking to hear himself.

We bought flat tapioca bread on the way back to the boat. Renato and Domingo chewed with excitement at the prospect of receiving a motor, and shrugged off my warnings against false hopes.

We never heard from the Paulista; his promise had been only 'in the moment', like many Brazilian promises. 'He conked out,' I told Renato the next afternoon.

'He lied!' Renato exclaimed in another furious outburst. 'My father never killed anyone. But now the hour has arrived. We will kill the next people to arrive at the village. Only you may come, you are our only friend here,' he said, embracing me with both arms. 'Only you have never lied.'

'Let's go and eat, you'll get no food on the boat tonight,' I suggested. Helcio came with us to a table on the terrace outside a bar and we ordered plates of chicken and fish, and a couple of beers.

'Show me the stones,' said Helcio.

Renato waved his head from side to side and smiled meaning 'no'.

'You have some here. Show them to me.'

Domingo was silent. Renato looked at me. 'It's best not to show them to anyone,' I said. Renato nodded.

Helcio asked again after another glass of beer and, after insisting for ten minutes, the bag was on the table and Helcio was inspecting Renato's own stones.

'This is a diamond?' he asked. Renato shrugged his shoulders but I saw the idea take hold.

I took the stone and rubbed it against the glass of the beer bottle. 'It is not a diamond! Look! It makes no scratch,' I exclaimed, fed up with all the talk of riches that so easily turned the heads of my companions.

'It is best not to show the stones,' said Renato.

'What is the Yanomami word for white man?' I asked when we had eaten.

'*Oow-oow*,' said Domingo.

I laughed. 'That's good. In my language people say ow! ow! when something hurts.'

They talked of seeing Senhor Juan, head of FUNAI in Barcelos. They talked of killing the next white man to visit them. They talked of being home and of holding a feast.

When they were silent, I turned to Renato. 'I want to advise you one thing, Renato. Never, never, never show these stones to anyone. If people ask, say there is only sand in the river. No gold, no stones. If you show them, people will get ideas and all the world will arrive and they will fight with you and kill you.'

'I know, I know. We will be silent.'

The main engine was already running when we returned in the dark to the boat. I paid the two fares to the captain and obtained a receipt but could give my friends only Cz$600 for spending money. Food would be provided on the boat.

The time had come to say goodbye. Tears welled up in Renato's eyes. We embraced and he pressed his head to my shoulder and kissed me on the cheek. Tears trickled down his cheeks. Domingo and I hugged tightly and shook hands. 'When will you come again? You will come one day,' he said softly.

'I don't know. It's very far from my land.'

'I know, but you will come.'

'It's difficult,' I repeated.

'Yes, yes, but when will you come to see us?'

'I promise I will come one day, maybe after two years.' A promise was made.

'We will wait for you in the village,' said Domingo.

The Yanomami waved from the top deck as Helcio and I walked away in the dark towards the lights of Manaus.

Will they still be in their village when I return? Change is now coming so fast even in remote areas that no place remains untouched. The white man comes with promises but it is doubtful that the Yanomami will receive what they need from him, which is a guarantee of their land.

They may receive some medical help to combat the white man's diseases, better security to prevent *garimpeiros* entering their river. But, in the long run, as every other tribe has discovered, there is a fundamental conflict with the white man.

For Brazilians, as for North Americans and Europeans, the land is a means to an end: it is resource to be used – wood, land, minerals, medicines and tourism. The present environmental movement, the struggle to preserve the Amazon forest and all it contains, also springs from this view of the world. Tropical forest is a precious *resource* that must be preserved.

It is a world-view that puts us *outside* the land, allowing us to deal objectively with nature; to study it and, above all, to explain it.

To the Indians, to be no longer *of* the land is to cease to exist. Certainly they need the produce from the forest for food and shelter to survive. More than that, however, they *are* the forest; their cultures do not make sense without the forest. The tall trees are the pillars of their universe, their stories are an explanation of the forest world.

A Kiowa Indian has elegantly stated their position:

'You say that I *use* the forest, and I reply, yes it is true, but it is not the first truth. The first truth is that I *love* the land; I see that it is beautiful; I delight in it, I am alive in it.'

The white man has always recognised the Indians' oneness with their environment but this belief has produced the two opposing sentiments in the Amazon today:

If the forest must be transformed to be useful, then the Indians who are part of the forest must give way.

Or, alternatively, if the forest is precious (primarily today because it is rare) then the Indians must be safeguarded because they too are rare.

The latter attitude may be the more humane and generous, but both ideas – conquest or preservation – spring from the same approach to the land. Namely, that it is *for* something; that the forest has a purpose; that it is a raw material for industry, for science or for tourism. This in no way diminishes the importance of conservation, but it points towards conservation's wiser future.

Whether the forest exists tomorrow will not be decided by the Indian view of the land, but by the same mind-set that threatens it. Yet I still remember asking Chincinho Viana, the 'Indian of the city' as he called himself, to explain to me about the forest. His reply is as true as it is simple:

'The forest doesn't have an explanation, it only exists.'

Glossary

Açaí (ass-eye-ee) palm tree bearing hard purple berries which are crushed with sugar and water to make a popular drink, rich in vitamin A and fats. There is a saying in the state of Pará near the mouth of the Amazon, 'Arrive in Pará, stop; drink açaí stay for ever.' The palm bears fruit during the dry season and more heavily in the rainy season.

Ayahuasca (eye-a-hua-ska) hallucinogenic drug made by boiling a forest vine in water and used by tribal Indians and river people in healing sessions, to see their enemies and to get high. The active ingredient is an alkaloid called harmine. The vine produces the chemical to defend itself from being eaten by smaller mammals. Also known as *yage, caapi, natema* or *pinde*. Scientific name is *Banisteriopsis caapi Spruce*.

Balsa combination of boat pushing a barge. Mainly used on rivers between roadlinks throughout the Amazon to carry trucks, construction materials, grocery supplies, gasoline, rubber and other natural materials. No passenger accommodation.

Barraco (ba-ha-ko) a primitive shelter usually thatched with palm fronds or large leaves, erected with poles lashed together with vines.

Caipirinha (kie-peer-een-ya) a popular drink in Brazil made from cachaça (cane liquor), crushed lemon, sugar and ice.

Cachaça (ka-sha-sa) the most popular Brazilian liquor, made by distilling unfermented sugar-cane juice.

Cachoeira (cash-way-ra) waterfall, cataract or rapids on a river; the appearance of the obstacle on a river changes greatly from dry to flood season.

Caboclo (ka-bo-klo) Brazilian name for person of mixed Negro, Indian or European race and living along a river in the interior. Often used as a derogatory term by townspeople meaning country bumkin. *Mestizo* is the equivalent Spanish word for a

222

person of mixed race, *ribereño* for a person living along the river.

CANDIRE (can-dear-ee) tiny, almost transparent catfish which is attracted by urine. It enters to eat a host's body through any orifice and, once inside, is held in place by barbs along its back.

CAPYBARY Rodent (*Hydrochoerus capybara*) over four feet long often seen along rivers and lakes.

CHICHA (chi-cha) corn beer made from fermented sprouts. A very popular drink in the Andes. An Indian may spill a little on the ground before drinking to offer to *Pacha Mama* (Mother Earth).

CHULLO colourful woven hat with earflaps worn by men and babies in the Andes.

EBENÉ (*Virola theidora*) hallucinogenic snuff made by Yanomami Indians from the reddish bark resin of several Virola trees.

FARINHA manioc flour. Made by grating, washing and drying the manioc tuber (also known as cassava). It is added to beans and rice to give texture and taken with drinks such as *açaí*. It looks like coarse sawdust and has little flavour.

FAROFA *farinha* toasted in butter and appearing and tasting like fine breadcrumbs. Often served with fried turtle liver.

FUNAI National Indian Foundation, under the Ministry of the Interior in Brazil. Replaced the Indian Protection Service which became infamous for bombing and infecting Indians with diseases.

GARIMPEIRO (ga-rim-pear-oh) mineral prospector, usually working alone or in small groups for gold or diamonds.

GUARANA (goo-wa-ra-naa) large, woody climbing plant (*Paullinia cupana H.B.K.*). The seeds are roasted and pounded and the powder drunk with water or as a syrup or as a carbonated soft drink. Said to be a health tonic and an aphrodisiac.

HEKURA (heh-kura) supernatural beings both good and evil.

MANIOC a tall plant grown for its starchy root (*Manihot esculenta*). Used to make *farinha, yuca, masato, farofa, tapioca*.

MASATO beer made from manioc, traditionally made by chewing and fermenting with women's saliva after boiling.

MESTIZO Spanish name for person of mixed black, Indian or white race.

NORESHI part of a person's soul; also an animal living in the forest that corresponds to that soul, like a shadow.

PALMITA heart of palm. Soft, fibrous core at the top few feet of certain palm trees is shredded for salads and soup, killing the palm tree. Delicate flavour – barely tastable.

PEKE-PEKE Peruvian name for canoe powered by a motor mounted on the square transom with a long propeller shaft reaching diagonally into the water – pivoted, allowing propeller to be raised easily to avoid obstacles. Called *rebeta* in Brazil.

PIASSAVA palm (*Leopoldinia piassaba Wallace*) growing along some tributaries of the Rio Negro. Produces a thick mane of fibres from its fronds to the ground which are gathered and exported for making brooms and brushes.

PIRANHA (*Serrasalmus sp*) sixteen species in the Amazon, only four are aggressive to the point of being dangerous. They are found in tributaries and lakes not the main river. Easily caught with a piece of meat on a small hook and delicious to eat, though bony.

PIRARACÚ (peer-ra-ra-ku) largest freshwater fish in the world, up to ten feet and 330 pounds. Cares for young for the first four months by secreting a milky fluid from pores in its head. It has gills and lungs and breathes air about every three minutes.

PIUM a tiny black fly with a massive bite. (*Simuliidae* family) They congregate in sunlit places, such as riverbanks and garden clearings in the forest and can be carriers of onchocenciasis (river blindness).

PUPUNHA (poo-poo-n-ya) palm with spine-covered trunk (*Guilielma sp*). The fruit is shaped like a spinning top with orange flesh and is boiled before being eaten. Called peach palm in English, and *pijuayo* in Peru, it tastes like a roast chestnut or dry sweet potato. 'To eat a pupunha' in Brazil is to work hard for a small reward.

SHAMAN witchdoctor – healer, sorcerer.

SORVA tree gum used as the base for making chewing gum.

TAMBAQUÍ (tam-ba-kee) one of the largest fruit and seed eating fish in the Amazon (*Colossama macropomum*) growing up to three feet and sixty-six pounds. Usually caught in nets but can be caught, it is said, by hooking a fruit on a line bobbing in the water as if falling from a tree. The fish is an important disperser of seeds in flooded forest.

YANOMAMI tribe living in the area of the Brazilian-Venezuelan border and one of the last in the Amazon to have contact with civilisation. Their name means 'the folk' or 'human being'. Also called Yanomamo or Yanoma and sometimes Waika, a derogatory term not used by the Yanomami themselves.

YUCA boiled pieces of sweet manioc (non-poisonous). Eaten in the Peruvian Amazon instead of *farinha*.

URUCU (oo-roo-koo) (*Bixa orellana*) planted and cultivated throughout the Amazon for its scarlet oily seed, used by Brazilians to colour food and by Indians to paint their bodies. Also called annatto.

Reading List

The Vanishing Forest: The Human Consequences of Deforestation. A Report for the Independent Commission on International Humanitarian issues. Zed Books, London, 1986.

Altman, Irwin & Chemers, Martin, Culture & Environment, Cambridge University Press, Cambridge, 1984.

Anglemyer, Mary & Seagraves, Eleanor, A Search for Environmental Ethics, Smithsonian Institute, Washington DC, 1980

Averbury, John Lublock, The Origin of Civilisation and the Primitive Condition of Man: Mental and Social Conditions of the Savage, Longman, Green, 1912.

Bates, H. W., The Naturalist on the River Amazon, 2 vols, John Murray, London, 1863, 1873, reprint 1962.

Bates, Marston, The Land and Wildlife in South America, Life Nature Library, New York, 1964.

Berry, Wendell, Home Economics: Fourteen Essays, North Point Press, 850 Talbot Ave, Berkeley, San Francisco, California 94706, 1987.

Bezerra, Arare, Marrocos e de Paula, Ana Maria T., Lendas e Mitos da Amazonia, DEMEC Pará, Belém, Brasil, 1985.

Biese, Alfred, The Development of the Feeling for Nature in the Middle Ages and Modern Times, Burt Franklin, New York, 1905.

Branford, Sue & Glock, Oriel, The Last Frontier: Fighting Over Land in the Amazon, Zed Books, London, 1985.

Brown, John, Two Against the Amazon, Hodder & Stoughton, London, 1952.

Caufield, Catherine, In the Rainforest, Picador, London, 1985.

Clark, Kenneth, Animals and Men, William Morrow & Co., New York, 1977.

Cohen, John Michael, Journeys Down the Amazon, C. Knight, London, 1975.

Collier, Richard H., The River that God Forgot, Collins, London, 1968.

Cutright, Paul Russell, The Great Naturalists Explore South America, Macmillan & Co., New York, 1940.

Darwin, Charles, The Origin of Species, Collier Books, New York, 1962.

Denslow, Julie Sloan & Paddoch, Christine, editors, People of the Tropical Rain Forest, University of California Press, Smithsonian Institution, Berkeley, Calif., 1988.

Denton, Michael, Evolution: Theory in Crisis, Burnett, London, 1985.

Dewey, John, The Philosophy of Civilisation, Capricorn Books, New York, 1963.

Dickinson, John, Brazil, Longman, 1982.

Dorst, Jean, Before Nature Dies, Houghton, Boston, Mass., 1970.

Dubos, Rene, A God Within, Scribners, New York, 1972.

Dubos, Rene, Beast or Angel? Scribners, New York, 1984.

Duerr, Hans Peter, Dreamtime: Concerning the Boundary between Wilderness and Civilisation, Basil Blackwell, Oxford, 1985.

Edmundson, Rev. Dr George, editor, Journal of the Travels and Labours of Father Samuel Fritz in the River of the Amazons between 1686 and 1723, Hakluyt Society, London, 1922, 2nd series 1.

Elisabetsky, Elaine & Sertzer, Rachel, Caboclo Concepts of Disease, Diagnosis & Therapy: Implications for Ethnopharmacology & Health Systems in Amazonia, unpublished.

Evernden, Neil, The Natural Alien, Humankind and Environment, University of Toronto Press, Toronto, 1986.

Fawcett, Col. P. H., Exploration Fawcett, Hutchinson, London, 1953.

Forsyth, Adrian & Miyata, Ken, Tropical Nature: Life and Death in the Rain Forests of Central and South America, Charles Scribner's Sons, New York.

Fountain, Paul, The Great Mountains and Forests of South America, Longman, Green, London, 1904.

Fowles, John, The Tree, Little, Brown & Co., Boston, 1979.

Furst, P. T. editor, Flesh of the Gods, Praeger, New York, 1972.

Goodland, Robert J. & Irwin, Howard S., Amazon Jungle – Green Hell to Red Desert?, Elsevier, Amsterdam, 1975.

Goodman, E. J., The Explorers of South America, Macmillan, New York, 1972.

Goulding, Michael, The Fishes and the Forest: Explorations in Amazonian Natural History, University of California Press, Berkeley, Calif., 1980.

Hanbury-Tenison, Robin, Worlds Apart: An Explorer's Life, Granada, London, 1984.

Hanson, Earl Parker, South from the Spanish Main: South America Seen Through the Eyes of its Discoverers, Delacorte Press, New York, 1967.

Harrison, John, Up the Creek: An Amazon Adventure, Bradt Publications, Chalfont St Peters, Bucks, 1986.

Haskins, Caryl P., The Amazon, the Life History of the Mighty River, Doubleday Doran, New York, 1943.

Hemming, John, The Conquest of the Incas, Penguin Books, Harmondsworth, 1983.

Hemming, John, editor, Change in the Amazon Basin: Vol 1 Man's Impact on Forests & Rivers; Vol 2 The Frontier After a Decade of Colonization, Manchester University Press, Manchester, 1985.

Herndon, Lieut. William Lewis & Gibbon, Lieut. Lardner, Exploration of the Valley of the Amazon Made Under Directions of the Navy Department, Robert Armstrong, Washington DC, 1853.

Hyams, Edward, Soil and Civilization, Harper & Row, New York, 1976.

Kandell, Jonathan, Passage Through El Dorado, Avon Books, New York, 1984.

Katz, John, The Will to Civilize, Secker & Warburg, London, 1938.

Kelly, Brian & London, Mark, Amazon, HarBracej, San Diego, 1983.

Kiemen, Mathias Charles, The Indian Policy of Portugal in the Amazon Region 1614–1693, Athlone Press, London, 1952.

Krutch, Joseph Wood, The Modern Temper: A Study and a Confession, Harcourt, Brace, New York, 1931.

Lamb, F. Bruce, Wizard of the Upper Amazon: The Story of Manuel Cordova-Rios, Houghton Mifflin Books, Boston, 1975.

Lange, Algot, The Lower Amazon, G. P. Putnam's Sons, New York, 1914.

Lernoux, Penny, Cry of the People, Penguin Books, Harmondsworth, 1982.

Levi-Strauss, Claude, Tristes Tropiques, Criterion Books, New York, 1961.

Lopez, Barry, Arctic Dreams: Imagination and Desire in a

Northern Landscape, Charles Scribner's Sons, New York, 1986.

Markham, Sir Clements R. editor & translator, Expeditions into the Valley of the Amazons 1539–1540, B. Franklin, Hakluyt Society, London, 1859, reprinted 1964.

Martius, Karl Friedrich Philipp von & Spix, Johann Baptist von, Travels in Brazil in the Years 1817–1824.

Materlinck, Maurice, What is Civilization?, Books for Libraries Press, Freeport, New York, 1926.

Maxwell, Nicole, Witch Doctor's Apprentice, Collier Books, New York, 1975.

Medina, Jose Toribio, The Discovery of the Amazon, American Geographical Society special publ. 7, New York, 1934.

Meggers, Betty J., Amazonia: Man and Culture in a Counterfeit Paradise, Aldine, Chicago, 1971.

Montefiore, Hugh, Man and Nature, Collins, London, 1975.

Moog, Vianna, Bandeirantes and Pioneers, George Braziller, New York, 1964.

Morrison, Tony & Brown, Ann, & Rose, Anne, Lizzie, A Victorian Lady's Amazon Adventure, British Broadcasting Corporation, London, 1985.

Mors, Walter B. & Rizzini, Carlos T., Useful Plants of Brazil, Holden-Day Inc., San Francisco, 1966.

Nobel Symposium, The Feeling for Nature and the Landscape of Man, 45th Nobel Symposium, 1978, Rundqvists Boktryckeri, Goteborg, 1978.

Noice, Harold H., Back of Beyond, George Harrap, London, 1940.

Orton, James, The Andes and the Amazon: Across the Continent of South America, Harper Brothers, New York, 1857.

Pendle, George, A History of Latin America, Pelican Books, New York, 1983, last revised 1976.

Phelps, Gilbert, The Green Horizons, Simon & Schuster, New York, 1964.

Portway, Christopher, Journey Along the Spine of the Andes, Oxford Illustrated Press, Oxford, 1984.

Price, Willard, The Amazing Amazon, William Heinemann, London, 1952.

Quammen, David, Natural Acts: A Sidelong View of Science and Nature, Laurel Paperback, Dell Publishing Co. Inc., New York, 1985.

Reuss, Percy Albert, The Amazon Trail, Batchworth Press, London, 1954.

Roberts, J. M., The Triumph of the West, British Broadcasting Corporation, London, 1985.

Rondon, Col. Candido Mariano da Silva, Lectures, Greenwood Press, New York, 1916.

Roosevelt, Theodore, Through the Brazilian Wilderness, Scribner, New York, 1914.

Schreider, Helen and Frank, Exploring the Amazon, The National Geographical Society, Washington DC, 1970.

Schweitzer, Albert, The Philosophy of Civilization, Macmillan, New York, 1949.

St Clair, David, The Mighty Mighty Amazon, Souvenir Press, London, 1968.

Sterling, Tom, The Amazon, World's Wild Places series, Time-Life Int., New York, 1974.

Sternberg, Hilgard O'Reilly, The Amazon River of Brazil, Steiner, Weisbaden, 1975.

Stoll, David, Fishers of Men or Founders of Empire?: The Wycliffe Bible Translators in Latin America, Zed Press, London, 1982.

Stone, Roger D., Dreams of Amazonia, Elizabeth Sifton Books, Viking Penguin, New York, 1985.

Thacker, Christopher, The Wilderness Pleases: The Origins of Romanticism, Croom Helm, London, 1983.

Ure, John, Trespassers on the Amazon, Constable, London 1986.

Wachtel, Nathan, The Vision of the Vanquished, Barnes & Noble, New York, 1977.

Wagley, Charles, Amazon Town, A Study of Man in the Tropics, Oxford University Press, New York, 1976.

Wagley, Charles editor, Man in the Amazon, Florida University, Gainesville, 1973.

Wallace, Alfred Russel, Travels on the Amazon and Rio Negro, Ward, Lock & Co., London, 2nd edition 1889.

Wallace, Alfred Russel, My Life, Chapman and Hall, London, 1905.

Wallace, Alfred Russel, Natural Selection and Tropical Nature, Macmillan & Co, London, 1891.

Wallace, Alfred Russel, The World of Life: A Manifestation of Creative Power, Directive Mind and Ultimate Purpose, Chapman and Hall, London, 1910.

Winters, Robert Kirby, The Forest & Man, Vantage Press, New York, 1974.

Worster, Donald, Nature's Economy: A History of Ecological Ideas, Cambridge University Press, Cambridge, 1985.

Wright, Ronald, Cut Stones & Crossroads, Viking Press, New York, 1984.

FICTION

Conrad, Joseph, Short Story Masterpieces: An Outpost of Publisher, Dell Publ. New York, 1954.

Hudson, W. H., Green Mansions, Bantham Pathfinder Editions, 1965.

Matthieson, Peter, At Play in the Fields of the Lord, Random House, New York, 1965.

Rivera, Jose Eustacio, The Vortex (quoted in Passage Through El Dorado), Jonathan Kandell.

Souza, Marcio, Mad Maria, Avon Books, New York, 1985.

Souza, Marcio, The Emperor of the Amazon, Avon Books, New York, 1977.

Wilder, Thornton, The Bridge of San Luis Rey, Avon Books, New York, 1976.

GUIDEBOOKS, DICTIONARIES & MAPS

The South American Explorer's Club Quarterly, South American Traveller's Club, Casilla 3714, Lima 100, Peru, and 2239E Colfax Avenue, Denver, Colorado, 80206.

Aliandro, Hygino, Dicionario Portugues - Ingles, The Portuguese – English Dictionary. Ao Livro Tecnico S/A, Rio de Janeiro 1985.

Bradt, Hilary & George, Backpacking and Trekking in Peru & Bolivia, Backpacking Guide Series, Bradt Enterprises, 1980.

Brooks, John, editor, The South American Handbook, Trade & Travel Publications Ltd., The Mendip Press, Bath, published annually.

Hatt, John, The Tropical Traveller, Pan, London, 1985.

Meisch, Lynn, A Traveller's Guide to El Dorado & the Inca Empire: Colombia, Ecuador, Peru, Bolivia, Penguin Books, New York, 1977.

Mello, Anisio, Vocabulario Etimolgico Tupi do Folclore Amazonico, Suframa, Manaus, Brasil, 1983.

South America on a Shoestring, Lonely Planets, Australia, annual.

Werner, David, Where There Is No Doctor: A Village Health Care

Handbook, The Hesperian Foundation, P.O. Box 1692, Palo Alto, Calif., 94302, April 1985, 10th printing.

MAPS

Healey, Kevin, South America, North Section, no. 151, scale 1:5,000,000, Bradt Publications, Chalfont St Peters, Bucks, England, 1982. Also ITM, Box 2290, Vancouver, Canada.

Mapa Vial del Peru, scale 1:2,200,000, Lima 2000, Joaquin Bernal 271, Lince, Lima 14, Peru. 1987.

South America, North West, no. 153, scale 1:4,000,000, International Travel Maps, Box 2290, Vancouver, Canada. 1986–87. Also Bradt Publications.

Topographic maps of Peru, scale 1:100,000. El Instituto Geografico Militar, Avenida Aramburu 1198, Lima, Peru, 1976.

SOUTH AMERICAN INDIANS

The Politics of Genocide Against the Indians of Brazil, Latin American Research Unit, Toronto, 1975.

Bergman, Roland W., Amazon Economics: The Simplicity of Shipibo Indian Wealth, Syracuse University, 1980.

Bodard, Lucien, Green Hell: Massacre of the Brazilian Indians, Outerbridge & Dienstfrey, New York, 1972.

Broennimann, Peter, Auca on the Cononaco, Birkhauser, Basel, Switzerland, 1981.

Brooks, E., & Fuerst, R., & Hemming, J. H., & Huxley, F., Tribes of the Amazon Basin in Brazil 1972, C. Knight, London, 1973.

Carmichael, Elizabeth, Hidden People of the Amazon, British Museum Publications, London, 1985.

Chagnon, N. A., Yanomamo: The Fierce People, Holt, Rinehart & Winston, New York, 1st Publ. 1968, 2nd ed. 1977.

Driver, David Miller, The Indian in Brazilian Literature, Hispanic Studies in the United States, 1942, reprint 1972, University Microfilms, Ann Arbor.

Gebhart-Sayer, Angelika, The Geometric Designs of the Shipibo-Conibo in Ritual Context, UCLA Latin American Center, Los Angeles, Calif. 90024, 1984.

Hanbury-Tenison, Robin, A Question of Survival for the Indians of Brazil, Charles Scribner's Sons, New York.

Heath, E. G. & Chiara, Vilma, Brazilian Indian Archery, Simon Archery Foundation, Manchester, 1977.

Hemming, John, Red Gold: The Conquest of the Brazilian Indians, Macmillan, London, 1978.

Hemming, John, Amazon Frontier, Macmillan, London, 1987.

Hopper, Janice H., editor, Indians of Brazil in the Twentieth Century, Institute for Cross-Cultural Research, Washington DC., 1967.

Lizot, Jacques, Tales of the Yanomami: Daily Life in the Venezuelan Forest, Cambridge University Press, New York & Cambridge, England, 1985.

Roe, Peter G., The Cosmic Zygote, Rutgers University Press, New Brunswick, New Jersey, 1982.

Severin, Timothy, The Horizon Book of Vanishing People, American Heritage Publ. Co., New York, 1973.

Smole, William J., The Yanoama Indians: A Cultural Geography, University of Texas Press, Austin, Texas, 1976.

Equipment Lists

Different equipment was required for the various journeys in differing regions. Comprehensive lists are given because good travelling needs detailed planning.

Equipment used on all journeys:

1   hammock (except on walk to Amazon source) tied up with 2 × 2 metre ropes
1   cotton sheet, used as a light blanket
1   inexpensive towel (good ones get stolen on the boats)
1   toothbrush, toothpaste
1   plastic comb
1   shaving kit
1   bar of laundry soap (unscented may not attract as many insects)
1   sewing kit
1   money belt
2   prs long cotton trousers, for forest walks and evenings in the city
1   pr Bermuda shorts
2   prs underpants
1   pr socks (also used to wrap camera)
1   pr bathing shorts, worn as shorts and for swimming
1   long-sleeved shirt
1   short-sleeved shirt
1   T-shirt
1   pr 'thongs', also called flip-flops, the most practical footwear
1   pr 'tennis' shoes
1   Wellington boots, ¼ inch thick rubber (except on walk to Amazon source and up Rio Negro first time)
1   35mm Olympus camera with 50mm lens f1.8 and UV filter
1   135mm Olympus telephoto lens with UV filter
1   washable lens cleaning cloth

1   plastic freezer box for all camera gear to hold a quantity of Kodak 400ASA slide film, sealed in pairs or trios in plastic bags and sealed in outer plastic bags

1   fountain pen and bottle black permanent ink (blue washes out and doesn't photocopy well)

1   hardbound notebook (bought locally)

1   map South America

1   flashlight and 2 spare bulbs

1   roll toilet paper

1   plastic bowl and mug

1   spoon, knife and fork

1   machete

1   sunhat

4   bottles of insect repellent

1   tube antiseptic cream

1   small bottle iodine

2   doses to cure malaria

quantity of sticking plasters

quantity of tea bags

couple of books to read

Journey to Source of the Amazon (supplies bought in Cuzco):

1   pr thick corduroy trousers

1   pr thick socks

1   thick sweater

1   heavy woollen jacket

1   pr finger gloves

1   thick woollen poncho

1   woven woollen hat

1   sleeping bag (borrowed)

1   pr suede hiking shoes

1   woven shoulder bag (to carry camera and coca)

3   metres plastic sheeting

2   metres plastic sheeting cut into a poncho

1   small billy can (for cooking soup)

1   map Cailloma area

38   balloons (gifts for children)

80   boiled sweets (gifts and a comfort for a dry throat at high altitude)

250 grams of coca leaves and a little ash (gift and pleasant for a burst of energy)

1   tin powdered milk
2   packets powdered soup
1   kilo cheese
20 flat breads

Journey up the Rio Maraiuá:
1   4½ metre canoe built in Manaus with square transom (5 metres would have been better)
1   5.3 horsepower Suzuki motor bought in Manaus
1   *rebeta* (long propeller shaft)
1   spare propeller and spare nuts
1   paddle (gift from canoebuilder)
1   set of spanners, vice-grips and hammer
3   gasoline containers (2 × 20 litres, 1 × 12 litres)
4   litres of motor oil
1   fuel funnel
1   spring-loaded candle lantern (bought in North America)
12 7-hour candles for candle lantern
2   boxes waterproof matches (lighters don't work well on wet days)
2   gas lighters
1   kettle
1   non-stick frying pan
1   small billy can
quantity of rubber tyre inner tubing (to start fires)

Trade goods for Indians:
100 medium and large fish hooks
30   steel leaders for fishing line
300 metres fishing line
4   machetes
30   plastic combs
3   mirrors
130 metres parachute cord (indispensable!)

Other gift ideas:
plastic beads to make necklaces
50 gram bags of tobacco
Food: (it is impossible to give quantities because so much was given away)
     porridge oats

powdered milk
ground coffee
packet soups
sugar
rice
salt
ground Parmesan cheese
cooking oil
tins tomato paste
crackers
jam
lemons
herbs and spices
tea bags

Index